BREAD BAKING RECIPE BOOK

*100+ Easy, Homemade Bread Recipes—
From No-Knead Classics to Artisan-Style
Loaves Anyone Can Make*

by

Olivia Hart

**Copyright 2025 Olivia Hart.
All rights reserved.**

No part of this book may be reproduced in any form or by any electronic or mechanical means including information storage and retrieval systems, without permission in writing from the author. The only exception is by a reviewer, who may quote short excerpts in a review.

Although the author and publisher have made every effort to ensure that the information in this book was correct at press time, the author and publisher do not assume and hereby disclaim any liability to any party for any loss, damage, or disruption caused by errors or omissions, whether such errors or omissions result from negligence, accident, or any other cause.

This publication is designed to provide accurate and authoritative information with regard to the subject matter covered. It is sold with the understanding that the publisher is not engaged in rendering professional services. If legal advice or other expert assistance is required, the services of a competent professional should be sought.

The fact that an organization or website is referred to in this work as a citation and/or a potential source of further information does not mean that the author or the publisher endorses the information the organization or website may provide or recommendations it may make.

Please remember that Internet websites listed in this work may have changed or disappeared between when this work was written and when it is read.

Bread Baking Recipe Book : 100+ Easy, Homemade Bread Recipes—From No-Knead Classics to Artisan-Style Loaves Anyone Can Make

TABLE OF CONTENTS

Introduction _____ 7

Chapter 1: Getting Started No-Knead and Beginner Breads
_____ 11

Chapter 2: Flavorful Yeast Breads for Every Occasion __ 51

Chapter 3: Whole Grain and Healthy Bread Creations___ 91

Chapter 4: Sourdough Mastery and Signature Loaves __ 135

Chapter 5: International Bread Traditions_____ 179

Chapter 6: Sweet and Enriched Bread Recipes_____ 225

Chapter 7: Specialty and Fun Homemade Bakes _____ 269

Conclusion _____ 314

Appendix_____ 318

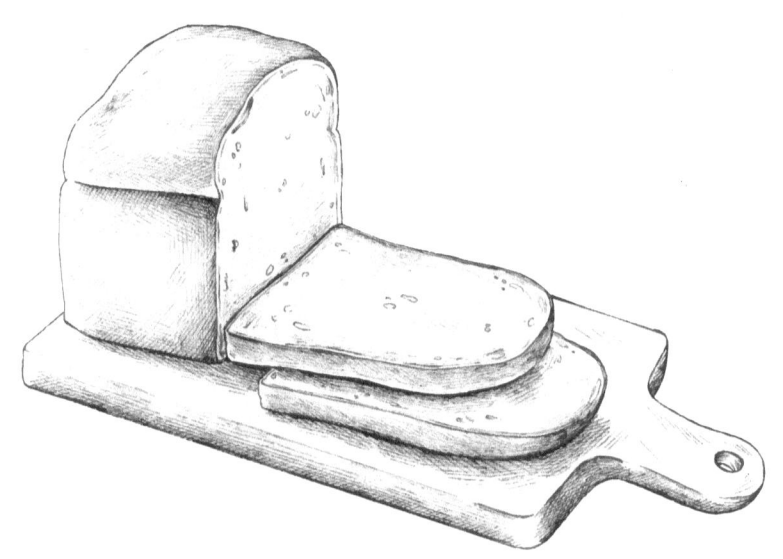

INTRODUCTION

Baking bread at home is a timeless craft that brings both comfort and creativity to the kitchen. There is something deeply satisfying about pulling a warm, golden loaf from the oven—the aroma alone can brighten any day. Whether you are just beginning your bread-baking journey or looking to expand your skills, this book is designed to inspire and guide you every step of the way. Bread baking isn't just about following a recipe; it's about understanding the process, embracing patience, and enjoying the simple magic of transforming basic ingredients into something truly delicious.

The goal of this book is straightforward: to be your go-to resource for baking a wide variety of breads that suit all skill levels and tastes. You'll find more than 100 recipes here, ranging from no-knead breads perfect for beginners to artisan-style loaves that impress even seasoned bakers. The approach throughout is approachable and practical, with tips and techniques that help you feel confident in the kitchen without needing fancy equipment or specialty ingredients. The idea is to make fresh bread accessible and enjoyable, allowing you to create bakery-quality loaves right in your own home.

For many, the thought of baking bread can seem intimidating. There's a common belief that it requires hours of kneading, precise measurements, and complicated timings. While some bread styles do call for advanced techniques, this book breaks down the process into manageable steps. Many recipes use simple methods like no-knead techniques or quick-rise doughs to minimize stress and maximize success. You'll learn how to work with ingredients like yeast, flour, water, and salt, and discover how small adjustments can result in big differences in texture and flavor.

One of the most rewarding aspects of bread baking is how flexible and creative it can be. Although there are fundamental principles to master, once you grasp those basics, you're free to experiment with different grains, herbs, and add-ins. This book encourages that spirit of exploration with a wide range of options—from classic white and whole wheat loaves to flavorful, herb-infused bread and even sweet and enriched varieties. Each recipe highlights different techniques, so you can pick and choose what suits your mood and skill level.

Bread also holds a special place in cultures all over the world, and its diversity is truly remarkable. This collection showcases international bread traditions, offering recipes that bring authentic tastes and textures to your table. Whether you're making a rustic Italian ciabatta, a soft Indian naan, or a crusty French baguette, you'll gain insight into how different regions approach this staple with their own flair. Exploring these breads not only expands your baking repertoire but also connects you to the stories and histories behind each loaf.

Beyond technique and flavor, baking bread encourages mindfulness and connection. The gentle rhythm of mixing, kneading, and waiting invites you into a slower, more deliberate experience. It's a chance to unplug from busy routines and create something nourishing with your own hands. Sharing that bread with family and friends enhances that joy, turning simple meals into memorable moments. This book is crafted with that spirit in mind—to invite you into the rewarding world of homemade bread, where each loaf brings warmth and satisfaction.

You won't need specialized tools to succeed here. While a baking stone or Dutch oven can elevate certain breads, many recipes require just a mixing bowl, a baking sheet, and basic kitchen supplies. This accessibility means you can start right away, with ingredients and equipment you likely already have on hand. As you grow more confident, feel free to explore new methods and tools, but rest assured that great bread begins with simple steps.

Each recipe in this book is written with clarity and attention to detail, emphasizing not only what to do but why it matters. Understanding the role of each ingredient and the science behind rising and baking helps you troubleshoot and tailor your baking to match your preferences. Throughout the pages, helpful tips and tricks are sprinkled in to guide you around common pitfalls, making the process smoother and more enjoyable.

Whether you want to bake a classic white sandwich loaf, experiment with whole grains, or try your hand at sourdough, this guide has you covered. The chapters progress in a way that builds confidence, from easiest to more advanced breads, making it easy to develop skills at a comfortable pace. Rewards come quickly, too—many recipes are designed to produce satisfying results without long, drawn-out preparation times. You'll be amazed at how quickly fresh homemade bread can become a regular part of your cooking routine.

Furthermore, this book champions the idea that bread baking is an evolving journey. Every loaf you make will teach you something new, and learning through practice is one of the joys of this craft. Mistakes and experiments are part of the process, and over time, you'll develop your own instincts and favorite recipes. The goal is to demystify bread baking so it becomes a fun, approachable adventure rather than a daunting task.

In short, the "Bread Baking Recipe Book" invites you to roll up your sleeves and embrace the art of bread making with enthusiasm and ease. From simple everyday loaves to exciting specialty breads, there's a recipe here for every occasion and every baker. As you turn these pages, you'll find inspiration to feed your curiosity and nourish your family with fresh, homemade delights.

Chapter 1
GETTING STARTED NO-KNEAD AND BEGINNER BREADS

Baking bread at home doesn't have to be intimidating, especially when you start with no-knead and beginner-friendly recipes designed to build confidence and deliver delicious results with minimal fuss. This chapter invites you into the world of simple, approachable breads that require little equipment or experience—perfect for those eager to enjoy fresh, homemade loaves without complicated techniques. From the classic no-knead white bread that boasts a crisp crust and tender crumb to easy sandwich loaves and quick-rise dinner rolls, each recipe is crafted with straightforward ingredients and clear steps. These foundational breads introduce essential baking principles while letting you savor the satisfying aroma of fresh bread filling your kitchen, making it easier than ever to develop your skills before moving on to more advanced creations later in the book.

CLASSIC NO-KNEAD WHITE BREAD

No-knead bread has revolutionized the way home bakers approach bread making, especially those new to the craft. The classic no-knead white bread stands as a shining example of how simple ingredients and time can yield extraordinary flavors and textures without complicated techniques. This bread captures the essence of traditional white loaf bread, yet it requires minimal effort, making it perfect for beginners who want to enjoy fresh, homemade bread without the intimidation of kneading or constant monitoring.

At its core, the recipe relies on just flour, water, yeast, and salt—basic pantry staples familiar to nearly every home cook. The magic comes from a long, slow fermentation process that allows the dough to develop flavor depth and a chewy, open crumb, often associated with artisanal bread. You don't have to be an expert to create bread that has an inviting golden crust and a soft yet satisfying interior. This loaf is both forgiving and flexible, providing an ideal starting point for anyone eager to get comfortable with bread baking.

One of the best things about the classic no-knead white bread is how hands-off it is. After mixing the ingredients into a shaggy dough, all you need to do is let it rest, covered, for about 12 to 18 hours at room temperature. This long rise not only activates the yeast slowly but also breaks down the flour's starches, which contributes to the bread's signature lightness and subtle sweetness. There's no need for kneading or elaborate folding techniques; the waiting game does all the work here.

The dough tends to be quite wet compared to traditional bread dough, and this high hydration creates a more open crumb with larger holes inside the loaf. Don't let the stickiness put you off—it's meant to be that way. When it's time to shape the dough, simply turn it out onto a well-floured surface and fold it gently into a round ball. The sticky texture feels unusual if you're used to stiffer doughs, but embracing this is part of the experience and contributes to the bread's artisan vibe.

One essential step in baking this bread is using a heavy, lidded Dutch oven or similar covered pot. Preheating the pot in the oven before adding your dough creates a steamy environment that's crucial for producing a crisp, crackling crust. The lid traps steam released from the dough during the initial baking phase, allowing the crust to expand before it hardens. After 20 minutes or so, removing the lid lets the crust brown perfectly, adding that much-loved caramelized flavor and crunchy texture. If you don't have a Dutch oven, you can use other heavy pots or even place a baking tray with water in the oven to create steam, but the Dutch oven method is by far the easiest and most reliable.

While the list of ingredients is short, the quality of each contributes to the final loaf. Use unbleached all-purpose flour for the best texture and flavor. You'll find that the flour's protein content helps the dough hold its shape despite its looseness. The yeast measurement is modest—just enough to ensure a slow rise, encouraging the flavor to develop fully. Salt not only seasons the bread but also strengthens the gluten network, providing structure during baking.

Timing is a flexible factor with this bread. You can adjust the resting period depending on your schedule. The dough is forgiving and can often sit a bit longer without negative effects, provided it's kept at a consistent room temperature. With this flexibility, you can prepare the dough the night before and bake your fresh loaf the next day, or vice versa.

Once baked, the loaf has a rustic, handcrafted appearance. The crust boasts a deep golden tone with slight blistering, and the crumb is moist with uneven air pockets that give it character and a wonderful chew. This bread is a perfect companion to anything from simple butter and jam to hearty soups and stews. Because it's neutral and versatile, it suits sandwiches, toast, or even being dipped into olive oil and balsamic vinegar for a special treat.

The rewards of making the classic no-knead white bread extend beyond just the loaf itself. Baking this bread fosters confidence and provides a solid foundation for exploring more complex recipes later. It offers a satisfying sense of accomplishment, proving that baking good bread doesn't have to be complicated or time-consuming. Plus, it fills your kitchen with the enticing aroma of freshly baked bread—a pleasure that can't be beat.

In practice, the biggest adjustment is learning to trust the process. It's tempting to rush, to knead, or to poke at the dough, but restraint is key here. Patience lets the yeast do its work naturally. Over time, this quiet fermentation encourages the appreciation of bread-making as both science and art, even in its simplest form.

In summary, the classic no-knead white bread offers a beautiful entry point into homemade bread baking. It combines minimal ingredients, straightforward steps, and flexible timing to make a loaf that's approachable for beginners but satisfying for bread lovers at any level. It empowers home cooks to produce consistent, delicious results with a minimum of hands-on effort, making fresh bread an achievable everyday pleasure.

No-Knead Whole Wheat Bread

Making no-knead whole wheat bread is a fantastic way for beginner bakers to enjoy the hearty flavor and nutrition of whole grains without the extra effort kneading usually demands. This approach relies on a long, slow fermentation that develops gluten naturally, giving the bread a wonderful texture and depth of taste while keeping the process hands-off and accessible. By combining simple pantry staples with minimal active time, you can achieve a rustic, wholesome loaf that's perfect for sandwiches, toast, or just enjoying fresh with butter. It's an empowering recipe that demonstrates how patience and quality ingredients can yield impressive results, setting a solid foundation for further bread baking adventures.

Ingredient Everyday Loaf is a wonderfully straightforward no-knead whole wheat bread recipe that fits seamlessly into the rhythm of everyday baking. This loaf strikes a perfect balance between hearty whole wheat nutrition and the ease that no-knead methods promise, making it an ideal choice for beginners. With just a handful of pantry staples and minimal hands-on time, you can produce a wholesome, rustic loaf that tastes homemade but doesn't demand hours of work.

At its core, this loaf relies on simple, reliable ingredients—whole wheat flour, water, yeast, salt, and a touch of sweetener like honey or molasses to enhance flavor and feed the yeast. Because whole wheat flour absorbs more water than white flour, this recipe typically uses a higher hydration level, which helps maintain a soft crumb despite the bran's natural tendency to toughen bread. In practical terms, your dough will feel wetter and stickier than a classic white bread dough, but don't let that scare you away; it results in a wonderfully moist loaf with a slightly nutty flavor.

Choosing the right flour plays a crucial role here. Using freshly milled or high-quality whole wheat flour will ramp up the flavor and texture. If you prefer a lighter crumb without sacrificing the health benefits, you can try blending half whole wheat with half all-purpose flour. This variation isn't just about taste—it makes the dough easier to work with and yields a loaf that's less dense, which beginners often find encouraging.

Yeast, in this no-knead everyday loaf, acts as the engine behind the rise, though the slow fermentation period does most of the magic. A small amount of active dry or instant yeast mixed into the dough kickstarts the process, but the real leavening happens during the long resting period, often several hours or even overnight. This extended fermentation allows the yeast to gently aerate the dough, developing both texture and flavor while requiring almost no effort on the baker's part. One of the joys of this method is that you can essentially "set it and forget it" before coming back later to enjoy fresh bread.

Water temperature is another ingredient aspect often overlooked. For the best results, use water that's warm but not hot—roughly between 75°F and 85°F. This temperature range encourages yeast activity without risking killing the living organisms crucial for rising. Ambient room temperature will also influence fermentation time, so don't worry if your dough takes a little longer or shorter to rise. The slow fermentation period provides a wide window of flexibility, perfect for busy schedules.

Salt is more than just seasoning; it plays a functional role by strengthening gluten strands and controlling yeast growth to prevent overproofing. Measuring salt accurately ensures your loaf won't turn out bland or overly salty. If you're experimenting with sea salt flakes or kosher salt, be mindful of volume versus weight differences—too much can throw off both flavor and fermentation.

To add complexity to the flavor and extra moisture, some everyday loaf recipes include a bit of fat, like olive oil or melted butter. Though not essential, a tablespoon or two can smooth out the crumb and extend the bread's freshness by slowing down staling. This addition is entirely optional but recommended if you prefer a softer texture in your whole wheat loaves.

Sweeteners such as honey or molasses aren't just for taste; they also help feed the yeast in the early stages. A small amount subtly accents the nutty flavor of the whole wheat and lends the crust a touch of caramelization, resulting in a beautifully golden exterior that's both appetizing and inviting. Sugar alternatives like maple syrup work well too, offering a slightly different but equally pleasant note.

One of the greatest advantages of the Ingredient Everyday Loaf is its forgiving nature. Thanks to the no-knead method, you don't have to worry about perfect kneading technique or precise shaping. Once you've combined your ingredients into a shaggy dough, you simply cover and let it rest. The gluten develops naturally over time, with minimal intervention. This makes it an excellent starting point for those new to bread baking who might feel intimidated by more hands-on techniques.

During the resting period, storing the dough at room temperature or in the refrigerator affects both timing and flavor. Cold fermentation slows yeast activity, which enhances depth of flavor as acids and sugars develop. You can prepare the dough in the evening, refrigerate it overnight, and bake fresh bread the next morning—perfect for fitting bread baking around a busy lifestyle without rushing.

Another tip for success is to use a covered baking vessel, like a Dutch oven or a heavy, lidded pot. This environmental mimicry—essentially creating a mini-steam chamber—helps the loaf develop a powerful rise and an irresistibly crunchy crust. Preheating the pot while your dough finishes rising primes it to flourish as soon as it goes in the oven, transforming a home kitchen into a mini artisan bakery.

As far as variations go, the Ingredient Everyday Loaf welcomes creativity without complicating the process. You might mix in seeds such as flax, sunflower, or even chopped nuts for added texture and nutrition. Just fold them in gently after the initial mixing stage. Adding raisins or dried cranberries also works well if you enjoy a hint of sweetness that naturally complements whole wheat's robust flavor. These kinds of mix-ins elevate a simple loaf to something special without adding any fuss.

Baking times can vary depending on your oven and the size of the loaf, but expect about 30 to 40 minutes in a hot oven—typically around 450°F. The bread is done when it develops a deep golden-brown crust and sounds hollow when tapped on the bottom. Allow it to cool completely on a rack before slicing to let the crumb finish setting up, ensuring each slice holds together beautifully.

What makes the Ingredient Everyday Loaf particularly rewarding is how it reinforces confidence while delivering consistent results. Many home bakers who begin with more complex recipes find themselves returning to this style of bread when life gets hectic or when they want fresh bread without the stress. It embodies the essence of beginner-friendly baking: simple ingredients, straightforward method, and a truly satisfying outcome.

Beyond the technical details, baking this loaf offers a little slice of daily comfort. The aroma filling your kitchen as the bread bakes hints at warmth, nourishment, and tradition. Sharing freshly baked bread, even a humble one like this, brings a feeling of accomplishment and connection to something timeless. It's a reminder that good things don't have to be complicated—sometimes the familiar, easy recipes become the most treasured.

In conclusion, the Ingredient Everyday Loaf is a cornerstone recipe within the no-knead whole wheat bread category. It's a versatile base that teaches foundational baking principles while producing a genuinely delicious and wholesome loaf. Whether it's your first time baking bread or part of your weekly routine, this recipe invites you to enjoy the process without pressure, proving that great bread starts simply with good ingredients, a bit of patience, and a little love.

SIMPLE SANDWICH BREAD

Now that you've got a grasp on the basics of no-knead breads, let's turn our attention to one of the most versatile, approachable, and downright comforting loaves you can bake at home: simple sandwich bread. This is the kind of bread that transforms lunch, breakfast, or even dinner, adapting effortlessly to whatever fillings or toppings you choose. What makes this bread so special isn't just its soft texture or mild flavor, but how beginner-friendly the process is—allowing home bakers to achieve bakery-worthy results without complicated techniques.

Simple sandwich bread is designed to be reliable. Its straightforward ingredients—flour, water, yeast, salt, and sometimes a little sugar or fat—come together with minimal fuss. Unlike artisan loaves that require precise shaping or long fermentation times, this bread is meant to impress with its ease and consistency. For a home cook eager to provide fresh sandwiches or just enjoy a soft, pillowy loaf, this recipe fits perfectly into your baking routine.

One of the biggest challenges when starting out with bread is learning how to balance time and effort without sacrificing quality. Simple sandwich bread excels because it strikes that balance beautifully. The dough is usually mixed by hand or with a spoon, avoiding the intimidating kneading step. Instead, it relies on hydration and yeast activity to develop gluten naturally during short resting periods. This means less chance of over- or under-working the dough, giving beginners a more forgiving experience.

In terms of texture, nothing beats the soft crumb and tender crust of sandwich bread. The crumb has enough structure to hold fillings without crumbling apart yet remains airy and light. The crust is thin and golden brown, adding just enough bite without toughening. This combination makes it ideal not only for classic peanut butter and jelly or deli meats but also for toast or grilled sandwiches. The bread's neutral flavor pairs wonderfully with both savory and sweet enhancements.

Getting this loaf right also teaches a lot about yeast behavior. Since sandwich bread leans on commercial yeast for leavening, it's a great way to familiarize yourself with proofing times and dough readiness cues. You'll start to recognize how the dough expands, how it feels when it's ready for baking, and what signs indicate over-proofing. Mastering these basics here lays a solid foundation to experiment confidently with other bread types later on.

When it comes to ingredients, the beauty is in the simplicity. All-purpose flour typically does the trick, although bread flour can give a slightly chewier bite if you prefer that. A pinch of sugar helps wake up the yeast and can promote browning of the crust, while a little oil or butter adds richness and softness to the crumb. Salt might seem minor, but it's essential for flavor balance and controlling yeast activity, so don't skip it.

Mixing the dough often feels like a meditative process. Most recipes call for combining dry ingredients first, then gradually stirring in warm water along with any fat. You want the mixture to come together into a smooth, slightly sticky dough. It shouldn't be too wet or too dry—you'll learn a lot by how the dough behaves in your hands as you mix. Resting the dough under a clean towel or plastic wrap encourages gluten development and fermentation, turning a shaggy ball into something elastic and bouncy.

Proofing time varies depending on the ambient temperature in your kitchen. In warmer spots, you may find your dough doubles in about an hour. Cooler environments might require a bit more patience, possibly up to two hours. The key is to watch for a noticeable puffiness and gentle spring-back when lightly pressed. This stage develops flavor and ensures the bread will have a tender, open crumb once baked.

After the first rise, shaping is simple and forgiving. You don't need complex folding or tension-building methods here. Gently deflate the dough, then shape it roughly into a rectangle that fits your loaf pan. This pans out as an evenly shaped, neat loaf that bakes into the familiar sandwich bread silhouette. Cover it again for a shorter second rise, letting the dough regain strength and puff up just enough to fill the pan fully during baking.

Baking transforms the dough in magical ways. The oven's heat intensifies yeast activity at first, causing the loaf to surge upward—a moment bakers call oven spring—before the crust sets. The result is a golden loaf with a tender interior and a crust that crisps just a touch, perfect for slicing. For best results, aim for a baking temperature around 350 to 375 degrees Fahrenheit, which gently cooks through the bread without over-browning the crust.

Once baked, cooling is crucial. As tempting as it is to slice right away, allowing the loaf to cool completely stabilizes the crumb and prevents a gummy texture. Have patience here—waiting an hour or so can make all the difference in slicing cleanly and enjoying the bread's full flavor and texture.

Simple sandwich bread serves as more than just a recipe; it's a gateway to endless creative possibilities in your kitchen. Because the base is mild and soft, you can customize it by adding herbs, seeds, or even small amounts of grated cheese during mixing if you want to experiment without straying too far from the basics. This adaptability encourages you to tailor the loaf to your tastes, helping build confidence as a home baker.

Besides its versatility in meals, baking your own sandwich bread carries a sense of accomplishment and freshness unmatched by store-bought loaves. Knowing each ingredient and having the power to adjust them—reducing preservatives, controlling salt, or opting for organic flour—makes this bread not just delicious but wholesome. Sharing it with family or friends amplifies the joy of baking, turning simple sandwiches into memorable bites.

In summary, simple sandwich bread is an essential recipe for anyone just getting started in bread baking. It's approachable, satisfying, and practical. With a few basic ingredients and some patience, you can create a loaf that elevates everyday meals and introduces you to the wonderful world of homemade breads. This bread not only tastes amazing but also lays down important baking foundations that will support your growth and experimentation in all the flavorful breads ahead.

Remember, like all baking adventures, this loaf benefits from a few tries and gentle adjustments to fit your kitchen environment and preferences. Don't worry if your first loaf isn't perfect—each bake teaches you more about how dough behaves, and that knowledge will transform your bread baking from simple to spectacular.

So go ahead and make that first loaf of simple sandwich bread. It may be the start of something delicious and deeply rewarding. You've got this!

Quick Rise Dinner Rolls

If you're diving into bread baking but pressed for time, quick rise dinner rolls are a fantastic way to enjoy the experience without hours of waiting. These rolls combine the comforting charm of traditional yeast bread with a faster fermentation process, meaning you can pull warm, fluffy rolls from the oven in just a couple of hours. They're perfect for weeknight dinners, impromptu gatherings, or any occasion when fresh bread would elevate the meal but time feels tight.

One of the great things about quick rise dinner rolls is that they maintain that soft, pillowy texture and rich flavor you expect from yeast breads, without demanding patience or complicated steps. Unlike traditional no-knead recipes that ferment overnight or require multiple rises, these rolls use rapid-acting yeast and often warmer liquid temperatures to speed things up. You'll still get that satisfying spring in the crumb and a lightly golden crust, making them a delightful accompaniment for everything from rustic soups to roasted chicken.

When you start making quick rise dinner rolls, proper technique helps ensure success even with the accelerated timeline. It's important to keep the dough warm and draft-free during rising so the yeast can do its job efficiently. A cozy spot in your kitchen—near a warm stove or inside an off oven—works wonders. Even with less time, you'll want to allow enough rise so that the rolls develop a light, airy crumb. Rushing this part too much risks dense or doughy bread, which nobody wants.

For ingredients, these rolls rely on simple pantry staples: flour, yeast, sugar, salt, fat (often butter), and water or milk. The fat enriches the dough, lending richness and tenderness, while sugar feeds the yeast and adds a touch of sweetness that's subtle but satisfying. You can also customize these basics by adding herbs, garlic, or cheese if you want a little extra flair without complicating the process. But the beauty lies in the straightforwardness: you can bake these rolls confidently with just a handful of ingredients and basic kitchen tools.

Another tip for quick rise dinner rolls is to choose the right flour. Bread flour provides stronger gluten development, giving the rolls a springy texture and sturdier structure. However, all-purpose flour works just fine for most home bakers, especially when you're focusing on speed and simplicity. A mix of both can also work if you want to experiment with softness and chewiness until you find the ideal balance that suits your taste.

Once your dough has risen and proofed, shaping the rolls is a chance to get creative while keeping things practical. You can roll the dough into small balls for classic round rolls or shape them into ovals or knots for variety. Making them uniform in size ensures they bake evenly, but rustic, slightly irregular shapes also add charm and promise a more informal, homey touch at the table. Whether you're lining them up in a baking dish or spacing them apart on a cookie sheet, the shaping step is simple and satisfying.

Before baking, brushing the tops of quick rise dinner rolls with an egg wash or melted butter adds a beautiful gloss and a richer flavor. An egg wash often results in a shiny, golden exterior, perfect for rolls destined for a holiday meal or special occasion. Butter, on the other hand, keeps things softer and adds a subtle, rich aroma. Either way, this final touch elevates the look and taste with minimal effort.

Baking temperature plays a crucial role in getting that perfect crust and soft interior. Quick rise dinner rolls typically bake at a moderately hot oven, around 375 to 400 degrees Fahrenheit. This temperature allows the rolls to rise further in the first few minutes (known as oven spring) while forming an appealing golden crust. Keep an eye on them; they're done when the tops feel firm to the touch and faintly golden. Overbaking can dry them out, so pulling them as soon as they're done helps retain moisture inside.

Cooling the rolls briefly on a wire rack helps prevent sogginess that can result from steam trapped underneath. Even a few minutes to rest after baking enhances their texture and flavor. These rolls are best enjoyed warm but can be stored with a loose cover to maintain freshness for up to a couple of days. If you make them in advance, reheating gently in a low oven or microwave wrapped in a damp towel brings back that just-baked softness.

Besides their deliciousness, one of the most rewarding things about quick rise dinner rolls is how approachable they are for beginners. You don't need fancy equipment or advanced techniques to succeed. The process mostly involves mixing ingredients, letting the yeast activate, shaping dough, and baking. Each step offers small skills that build confidence for tackling more challenging breads later on. Plus, there's something undeniably joyful about pulling those golden rolls from your own oven, knowing you made them from scratch.

Quick rise rolls are not only versatile but also forgiving, which is exactly what a beginner baker needs. Dough that's slightly over or under risen can still produce delicious results, and the fast turnaround means you can try again soon if the first attempt isn't perfect. Experimenting with different flours, adding seeds or herbs, or varying shapes becomes an easy way to put your own mark on these classic dinner rolls.

If you want to stretch this recipe a little further, try adding a little honey or malt syrup for a deeper, more complex sweetness. Some bakers like incorporating a small amount of yogurt or sour cream in the dough to tenderize the crumb and add subtle tang. Incorporating whole wheat flour up to 25 percent can boost nutrition while retaining softness. These tweaks allow you to customize quick rise rolls without adding unnecessary steps or time.

Even beyond the dinner table, quick rise dinner rolls lend themselves well to sandwiches, sliders, or as soft dinner buns. Their size and texture make them adaptable enough to pair with breakfast jams, hearty soups, or simple butter and jam. Making a batch means you always have fresh bread on hand for cozy moments and family meals, enhancing flavors with homemade comfort.

In summary, quick rise dinner rolls are a perfect gateway into bread baking for beginners. They offer the rewarding experience of yeast breads without demanding extensive time or specialized skills. With easy ingredients, straightforward steps, and a delicious result, these rolls can become a regular feature of your kitchen routine. As you gain confidence, they'll also serve as a foundation to explore richer, more elaborate baking projects while still delivering fresh bread with minimal fuss.

RUSTIC SKILLET BREAD

There's something wonderfully satisfying about pulling a golden, crusty loaf fresh from a skillet. Rustic skillet bread is one of those simple yet impressive recipes that fits perfectly into the no-knead bread category. It requires minimal hands-on time, but delivers maximum flavor and texture. This kind of bread gives you the result of artisanal baking without the fuss or need for special equipment like a Dutch oven.

At its core, rustic skillet bread relies on the magic of a simple dough that's allowed to ferment slowly, developing taste and strength naturally. Its beauty lies in the way it bakes evenly in a heavy skillet—often cast iron—to form a crunchy crust while the inside remains tender and chewy. Cooking in a skillet trapped the steam around the bread beautifully, leading to that characteristic crunchy exterior and an inviting aroma that fills your kitchen.

One major perk of skillet bread compared to many traditional loaves is its quick baking time. Because the skillet holds and radiates heat efficiently, the bread bakes relatively quickly, making it a perfect choice for home bakers craving fresh bread without waiting around all day. Plus, the process is forgiving, so small imperfections won't affect the final loaf much, which is encouraging for beginners.

The ingredients are simple—a combination of flour, water, salt, and yeast—though you can easily experiment with various flours or add herbs, olives, or nuts for extra complexity. Keeping the recipe straightforward is useful when you're just getting comfortable with bread baking, letting you focus on mastering texture and technique before advancing to more complicated formulas.

When mixing the dough, it's important to foster a soft, sticky consistency. You don't need to knead vigorously here; in fact, part of the charm of no-knead methods is that fermentation does the work for you. Once mixed, the dough gets set aside to rise slowly and develop flavor over several hours or overnight. This hands-off rise allows gluten to form naturally without extra effort, so patience is key.

Once the dough has nearly doubled in size, shaping it for the skillet becomes straightforward. You'll gently fold it onto itself before placing it seam-side down in the preheated skillet. This shaping step isn't intentional shaping into perfect rounds or batards but more about rounding the dough just enough so it can bake evenly. It welcomes some rustic imperfection, which gives the bread its signature look and character.

Preheating the skillet is one of the most crucial parts of this recipe. A scorching hot pan assures a great crust forms immediately upon contact. Usually, cast iron works best because it retains heat so well, but other heavy-bottomed skillets can work too. You'll want to heat it in the oven before transferring the dough, so the loaf hits a hot surface that jumpstarts the crust development.

As the bread bakes, you might hear satisfying crackles from the crust forming—one of the most rewarding baking sounds. During baking, steam trapped inside the skillet environment keeps the interior moist, which helps the crumb stay soft but well-structured. Some bakers like to cover the skillet during the first part of baking to mimic a steam environment, then remove the cover to brown the crust deeply toward the end.

The finished rustic skillet loaf displays a slightly blistered, golden-brown crust with a tender, open crumb inside. This texture contrast is what makes it such a standout bread. It's perfect sliced alongside soups, served with butter and jam at breakfast, or used for sandwiches where the crunch plays off the fillings beautifully. Because it's a versatile bread, it fits many occasions and meals seamlessly.

Don't be afraid to personalize your rustic skillet bread. Adding cracked herbs like rosemary or thyme to the dough, tossing in some roasted garlic, or even swirled olive oil can elevate the flavor. Keep mix-ins light to maintain the bread's airy structure and remember to distribute those add-ins evenly to avoid dense spots in the crumb.

When you're ready to store leftovers, it's best kept wrapped loosely in a clean kitchen towel or placed inside a paper bag. Unlike very soft sandwich bread that sogs quickly, rustic bread's crust holds up well for a day or two at room temperature, allowing you to enjoy it freshly baked even the next day. To refresh it a bit, a quick warm-up in the oven can revive the crust's crunch.

Making rustic skillet bread is not just about the end result—it's about appreciating the baking process and learning how simple ingredients combined with time and heat create something truly satisfying. For beginner bakers, it's an accessible project that builds confidence and introduces essential bread baking skills without overwhelming complexity.

In addition, this method taps into the rustic, handmade feel of bread-making, showing how easy it can be to enjoy artisan-quality bread at home. No fancy tools, no long tedious kneading—just patience, a good skillet, and some basic pantry staples. It's an excellent stepping stone toward more advanced techniques and recipes found later in this collection.

By tackling rustic skillet bread first, you'll start to understand dough hydration, fermentation, and heat's role in crust formation—all foundational concepts that apply broadly in the world of bread. As you gain familiarity, you can then comfortably explore enrichments, different flours, or more traditional oven-baked loaves.

In short, rustic skillet bread is a perfect no-knead, beginner-friendly bread that brings warmth and comfort to your kitchen. It invites experimentation and rewards patience, making it an ideal starting point for anyone wanting to bake fresh, homemade bread with ease and delicious results.

No-Knead Baguette

Moving beyond the basics of no-knead bread, the no-knead baguette offers a wonderful introduction to shaping and crust development without introducing complicated techniques. This bread is perfect for anyone who loves the iconic French baguette but wants to avoid the traditional labor-intensive process. The magic lies in the slow fermentation that develops flavor and texture, giving you a baguette that's crusty on the outside with a light and airy crumb on the inside—all without heavy kneading or hours of hands-on work.

At its core, the no-knead baguette uses just a handful of simple ingredients: flour, water, yeast, and salt. The simplicity of the ingredient list is part of what makes this bread so accessible for beginners. But don't let that fool you into thinking it's basic or bland. Thanks to the long ferment time—usually 12 to 18 hours—your dough will develop complex, rich flavors that mimic those found in traditional artisan baguettes. Patience here is key, and the wait pays off beautifully.

One of the greatest advantages of the no-knead method is its convenience. You mix everything in one bowl, stir to combine, cover it, and leave it on the counter. No need for flour-covered countertops or muscle-powered kneading sessions. The dough will feel sticky and loose after mixing—that's exactly how it should be. Over time, the gluten develops naturally, giving the dough strength and elasticity without any manual kneading. This means even beginners can achieve a professional-quality baguette with minimal effort.

When it comes time to shape your baguette, this step feels almost meditative and smartly hands-on. Unlike more forgiving sandwich loaves, shaping a baguette has a slightly different rhythm and intention. The goal is to stretch the dough gently into a long, slender shape, which encourages that signature elegant form and helps create the baguette's trademark crust during baking. Since the dough is delicate due to its high hydration, handling it with light, careful movements ensures it keeps its structure without deflating the precious air pockets inside.

Flour choices and hydration levels play a noticeable role in how the baguette turns out. The no-knead baguette typically calls for bread flour, which has a higher protein content that supports gluten structure. However, beginners might find it interesting to experiment with all-purpose flour for a slightly softer texture. Hydration—the proportion of water to flour—is higher than in many standard loaves, usually around 75 to 80 percent. That results in moister dough and a crisper, more blistered crust once baked. Water is a simple ingredient, but its temperature and quality can subtly influence final results, so use filtered or clean tap water at room temperature whenever possible for consistent results.

Proofing the baguette is another critical phase where your bread can develop its distinctive character. After the initial long rise, the dough is divided and shaped, then allowed to proof roughly 45 minutes to an hour. This step lets the gluten relax and the yeast continue its work of fermentation. During this time, the dough will gently puff up, indicating readiness for the oven. Overproofing can lead to a flat loaf, while underproofing might result in a denser crumb, so keeping an eye on your dough without rushing is essential.

One technique that makes the no-knead baguette shine is the use of steam in the oven. Professional bakers swear by this method because steam encourages a glossy, crisp crust by delaying the hardening of the surface early in baking. At home, you can create steam by placing a shallow pan of hot water on the oven floor or carefully spritzing water into the oven walls right after loading the dough. The steam expands during the initial few minutes, giving the baguette a beautiful crackled crust characteristic of authentic French loaves.

Oven temperature and baking time also impact your finished baguette. A hot oven—generally between 450°F and 475°F—is vital for producing that crisp, blistered exterior quickly, sealing in moisture. Baking on a preheated baking stone or steel if you have one helps provide an intense bottom heat that encourages proper oven spring, the dramatic rise during the first few minutes when yeast activity is still going strong. Baking times usually hover around 20 to 25 minutes, but it's smart to watch for deep golden hues and a hollow sound when tapping the crust, a reliable indication your bread is fully baked.

The beauty of the no-knead baguette extends beyond flavor and texture. It also nurtures confidence in beginner bakers. This bread encourages you to trust the process, to work gently with dough, and to pay attention to timing and subtle visual cues rather than stressing over complicated steps. It's a wonderful gateway to more advanced bread baking without overwhelming any home cook new to yeast or artisan techniques.

It's also important to keep expectations balanced. While the no-knead baguette is gloriously crusty, it won't replicate the thin, wafer-like crust of a bakery baguette exactly. That's mainly due to equipment and time differences in commercial baking. But many home bakers find this style not only approachable but deeply satisfying and delightfully rustic. Plus, the flexibility of timing—you can mix the dough the night before, shape and bake the next day—fits well into busy lifestyles.

Serving your baguette fresh from the oven is a genuine highlight. The crust crackles under the knife as you slice, revealing a soft interior with delightful air pockets. It pairs beautifully with soups, cheeses, or simply a drizzle of good olive oil and a sprinkle of sea salt. Plus, this recipe scales easily, so you can double or halve the dough depending on how much bread you want to make.

Incorporating no-knead baguettes into your kitchen routine paves the way for experimenting with different flours, hydration levels, and even add-ins like herbs or olives as you gain confidence. But at its heart, this recipe sticks to fundamentals, emphasizing patience, respect for fermentation, and bold flavors arising naturally from a minimalist approach.

As you practice and refine your technique over time, you'll find this no-knead baguette recipe evolving into one of your favorites. Its simplicity is deceptive—this bread teaches you lessons about yeast activity, dough hydration, and oven dynamics that will serve you well as you tackle more complex breads later on. For now, enjoy the process and celebrate every fragrant, crispy, tender loaf you pull from the oven.

FOOLPROOF FLATBREADS

Flatbreads are one of the most approachable and satisfying types of bread for beginners. Their shape and texture may be simple, but the flavor and versatility they bring to the table are anything but basic. Whether you're looking for a quick snack, a side for dinner, or a base for toppings, flatbreads offer a no-fuss option that can be whipped up with minimal ingredients and effort. This is why they earn their spot as a starter recipe for anyone just beginning their bread baking journey.

Unlike some loaf breads that require shaping, proofing, and scoring, flatbreads often skip several intimidating steps. You don't need a special mixer or fancy ovens to get these right. Just a bowl, some basic pantry staples—flour, water, yeast, salt—and a skillet or oven will do the trick. Because the dough is usually wetter and softer, there's less concern about over-kneading or under-proofing, both common headaches for new bakers. That forgiving nature means you can focus more on developing confidence and skill with your hands and instincts.

One of the beauties of foolproof flatbreads is their great flexibility. Start with a simple dough and then adjust hydration or add herbs, garlic, or seeds. You can cook them on the stovetop in a hot skillet or bake them in the oven, depending on what you have and how much time you want to spend. The end result is a tender, chewy bread that has enough structure to hold toppings or be wrapped around fillings, but stays soft and flavorful. Their mild flavor also makes them excellent carriers for dips, spreads, and even grilled veggies or meats.

When mixing your dough, it's important to keep things loose and relaxed. Resist the urge to add too much flour, especially if you're used to working with stiff doughs. These wet doughs will feel sticky at first, but that's exactly what creates the delicate crumb once cooked. Avoid overworking the dough, as flatbreads need less gluten development to maintain their characteristic tenderness. A few minutes of gentle stirring or folding will be enough to bring everything together.

Having a reliable recipe for flatbreads is a home baker's secret weapon, particularly when time is tight, or you want bread fresh from the pan in under an hour. These breads don't require long rises, and many of them can be ready to cook after just one short rest. That means you don't have to plan hours ahead or work around multiple proofing stages. It's an ideal way to build enthusiasm and momentum early in your baking adventures, reliably delivering rewarding results.

One practical tip to get the best texture is to keep your skillet or griddle hot before adding the dough. Flatbreads develop little golden blistered spots from direct contact with high heat, giving them authentic flavor and that inviting look. Make sure your cooking surface is dry and lightly oiled, or use a cast iron pan for even heat distribution. Flip the flatbread once bubbles form and the underside is nicely browned. This quick cooking method locks in moisture while building a slightly crisp exterior that contrasts beautifully with the soft interior.

Don't be afraid to experiment with shaping and thickness. Some prefer their flatbreads thin and cracker-like, perfect for dipping into hummus or salsa. Others like a thicker, pillowy version to tear and share or stuff with ingredients like gyro meats or grilled shrimp. This versatility allows you to customize your baking depending on your meal plans or mood. The simplicity of flatbreads also makes them a wonderful canvas for toppings like melted cheese, herbs, garlic butter, or even a drizzle of olive oil straight from the pan.

Another beginner-friendly feature of many flatbread recipes is their adaptability to different flours. You can easily start with all-purpose flour, then gradually try incorporating whole wheat, spelt, or even gluten-free blends. Flatbreads respond well to these variations because of their relatively short cooking times and less demanding texture requirements. Getting comfortable working with a variety of flours early on will serve you well as you progress to more advanced loaves and artisan breads in this collection.

While many flatbreads can be cooked on the stovetop, baking them in the oven can add new dimensions of flavor and texture. Baking encourages a tender, uniformly browned crust and allows for toppings to meld into the dough if you choose a focaccia-style approach. When baking, preheat your oven with a baking stone or sheet inside to ensure the bottom reaches a high temperature quickly, replicating a professional bread oven's effect. The results can be surprisingly gourmet and satisfying for a beginner's effort.

Flatbreads are also an excellent way to practice dough hydration and handling. Having fewer steps means you can focus on the feel and look of the dough—learning how hydration affects stickiness, oven spring, and crumb structure. Pay attention to how the dough behaves, how it stretches, and how it reacts to heat applications. This intuitive understanding is crucial and will give you a solid foundation for tackling more intricate bread recipes later.

It's worth noting that many cultural breads fall into the category of flatbreads, from Indian naan and Middle Eastern pita to Mexican tortillas and North African khobz. While those will be explored in later chapters dedicated to international traditions, beginning with basic flatbreads creates a natural stepping stone towards more complex variations. Mastering the foundation recipes presented here will make the transition easier and allow you to appreciate the nuances and techniques each culture has honed over centuries.

Flatbreads are forgiving when it comes to timing, too. Their doughs typically improve with a bit of rest, but don't demand it urgently. This flexibility helps prevent disappointment when schedules get busy or you get distracted during preparation. You can prepare the dough in the morning or the night before, then cook fresh flatbreads in minutes when ready to eat. The convenience factor makes flatbreads consistently appealing as a staple in your home baking repertoire.

Beyond meal-time essentials, flatbreads can be a fun stage for creativity. Kids love helping roll out dough, brush it with olive oil or butter, and sprinkle their favorite herbs or toppings. This hands-on involvement makes baking less intimidating and adds a personal touch to the finished product. Taking pride in simple, honest homemade breads builds confidence faster than tackling complicated loaves right off the bat.

Most importantly, flatbreads show that bread baking doesn't have to be complicated or intimidating. With just a few steps, you get to enjoy the aroma of freshly cooked bread filling your kitchen and share warm, soft bites with those around you. They prove that anyone can bake, and it all starts with a simple mix of flour and water.

Embrace the process, enjoy the tactile experience, and celebrate small successes. Foolproof flatbreads are just the beginning of your journey—a delicious introduction to the world of homemade bread.

OVERNIGHT REFRIGERATOR BREAD

Making bread can feel like a time-consuming process, especially when you're just getting started. That's where overnight refrigerator bread shines. This method lets you mix the dough in the evening, pop it in the fridge, and then bake fresh bread the next day with minimal effort. It's a fantastic way to fit bread baking into a busy lifestyle, allowing the dough to slowly develop flavor and texture while you sleep or go about your day.

The secret to overnight refrigerator bread lies in the slow fermentation caused by cold temperatures. Instead of rushing the process with warm water and quick rises, the dough rests in the fridge for 12 to 24 hours. This extended, gradual fermentation encourages the yeast to work steadily and patiently, producing more complex flavors than a fast-risen loaf. In addition, the longer fermentation helps improve the bread's crumb and creates a slightly chewier, more artisan-like texture—qualities often missing in no-knead breads made within a couple of hours.

One of the biggest advantages of this approach is its simplicity. The basic recipe usually involves just four ingredients: flour, water, yeast, and salt. The no-knead part comes from letting time do the work instead of your hands; the dough is mixed briefly to bring everything together but left undisturbed during its extended rest. This means you don't need any special equipment or complicated techniques, making it ideal for beginners looking to experience the rewarding process of homemade bread.

To get started, you'll combine your flour and water, stir in a small amount of yeast and salt, and then cover the bowl tightly before placing it in the refrigerator overnight. The cold environment slows the yeast's activity, letting the dough mature gradually while you sleep. The next day, you'll notice a bubbly, sticky, and elastic dough waiting for you, signaling that it's ready to transform into a beautiful loaf.

When the time comes to bake, the dough can either be shaped and baked straight from the fridge or allowed to rest at room temperature for 30 minutes to an hour beforehand, depending on your schedule. Shaping is straightforward since the dough will be well-hydrated and forgiving. Because of its softness, gently folding the dough over itself a few times will build enough structure for a round or oval loaf without tearing it. From there, it goes into a preheated Dutch oven or a covered baking vessel that traps steam and encourages a crisp, golden crust.

The aroma and satisfaction of fresh bread wafting through your kitchen after waking up or coming home can't be overstated. It's a small luxury that brightens any meal and feels especially rewarding when it's so easy to accomplish. Plus, since you're using basic pantry staples and no fancy kneading, it's a low-barrier way to start baking your own bread regularly.

One aspect many appreciate about overnight refrigerator bread is the flexibility it offers. Because the dough develops over many hours, you don't have to exactly time your baking. The dough tends to be forgiving if you leave it in the fridge a little longer, typically up to 24 hours, giving you some leeway if your schedule shifts unexpectedly. If you're pressed for time after the fridge, letting it warm up on the counter for 30 minutes makes it much easier to handle and shape.

Another bonus is how versatile the base recipe is. Once you're comfortable with the basic technique, you can experiment by swapping some or all of the white flour with whole wheat or rye for more robust flavors. Adding mix-ins like olives, herbs, or seeds before refrigerating can also elevate your loaf. Just be mindful to keep the hydration balanced so the bread stays moist but isn't too sticky to handle.

A tip to keep in mind is that the dough might be wetter and stickier than traditional bread dough. Don't let this discourage you—it's perfectly normal for no-knead, overnight doughs. Lightly flouring your hands and work surface during shaping will help, as will resisting the urge to overwork the dough. Instead, opt for gentle folds and patting it into shape.

This style of bread baking also reduces waste. Because you prepare dough that stores easily in the refrigerator, it encourages bake-on-demand habits. You can prepare several batches, refrigerate, and bake as needed throughout the week. It's a convenient way to enjoy fresh bread regularly without the pressure to bake multiple loaves at once.

Finally, the crust you get from overnight refrigerator bread is worth mentioning. The slow fermentation deepens the flavor, and baking in a covered pot traps moisture that helps produce a shiny, crisp crust that's hard to beat. Once baked, allowing the bread to cool completely before slicing enhances the texture and flavor, giving you a loaf that's airy with just enough chew.

Starting with overnight refrigerator bread is a smart first step into homemade bread making. It blends patience with ease, offering a satisfying baking experience without any intimidation. For beginners aiming to create delicious, fresh bread with minimal fuss and maximum taste, this method is a perfect foundation.

Beginner's Ciabatta

Ciabatta is a fantastic bread for anyone stepping into the world of baking. This Italian classic has captured the hearts of many with its open crumb, crisp crust, and chewy texture. Although traditional ciabatta is known for being a bit tricky due to its high hydration dough, the beginner's version simplifies the process without sacrificing flavor or character. This makes it an excellent project for bakers who are eager to try something new but still want a recipe that's forgiving and straightforward.

At first glance, ciabatta dough might seem intimidating because it's wetter and looser than typical bread dough. However, that's exactly what gives this bread its signature airy quality inside those irregular holes. The good news is you won't need advanced kneading skills or special equipment. Instead, patience and gentle folding become your best tools. The no-knead method often used here takes advantage of time to develop gluten naturally, which means less effort and more reward.

Getting started involves just a handful of simple ingredients—flour, water, yeast, salt, and a touch of olive oil. The flour typically used is bread flour, which has a higher protein content that helps build structure. Water makes the dough sticky and loose but vital for the open crumb. Yeast breathes life into the dough, creating the bubbles and rise. Salt enhances the flavor while balancing the yeast's activity. Olive oil is optional but adds a subtle richness and helps keep the crust tender. Nothing complicated, just quality basics coming together.

The first important step is mixing everything gently until combined. You'll notice the dough is quite sticky at this point, which is normal. Don't be tempted to add too much flour trying to "fix" the mess—it's part of the process. Instead, the dough is left to rest, usually covered with a damp towel or plastic wrap. Resting allows the gluten strands to form on their own, giving the dough stretchy strength without any hard kneading. This "bulk fermentation" stage can last several hours, during which timing might feel long but yields a wonderfully airy texture.

After the initial rise, the dough needs some gentle handling to shape it properly. Rather than punching it down, you'll perform a series of folds directly in the mixing bowl. Each fold helps align the gluten strands and traps more air bubbles, improving the loaf's final crumb. You can expect the dough to feel soft and sticky, but careful folding gives it better shape and structure. Here, patience pays off, and even beginners can learn to handle wet dough with confidence. Folding might only take a few minutes but greatly influences the bread's character.

Once folded, the dough goes through a second rise, often on a floured surface or parchment paper to prevent sticking. When you're ready to bake, transferring the dough carefully is key since it's not as firm as other breads. Shaped into a rough, slipper-like form—which is actually the origin of the name "ciabatta"—this loaf retains its rustic charm. The texture looks more relaxed and informal, inviting you to enjoy its hearty, open crumb with every bite.

Baking ciabatta requires a hot oven to develop a crust that crackles and crunches under your fingertips. Many home bakers benefit from creating steam in the oven, either by placing a pan with water on the rack or spraying the oven walls during the first few minutes of baking. Steam encourages the crust to expand before setting, producing a beautiful, glossy finish. No fancy equipment needed; these simple tricks bring bakery-style results right into your kitchen.

Cooling your loaf is just as important as baking. Letting ciabatta rest outside the oven ensures the crumb sets properly and prevents it from becoming gummy. Resist the urge to slice right away, even though the smell might be irresistible. Waiting about an hour allows the flavors to develop fully and the texture to become perfect. When you finally cut into your freshly baked ciabatta, the airy holes and chewy crumb will reward your patience.

Besides its delicious texture and flavor, beginner's ciabatta is versatile. It's perfect for sandwiches, toasting, or simply dipping into olive oil or soft cheeses. It pairs beautifully with everything from soups to salads, making it a beloved staple in many households. The open crumb is ideal for soaking up sauces, making it a true all-rounder. Once you've mastered this recipe, you'll find ciabatta popping up at breakfasts, lunches, and dinners with endless possibilities.

One of the greatest joys in baking beginner's ciabatta is how it builds your confidence with wet dough techniques and developing gluten without kneading. Not only does it expand your skills, but it also introduces you to the rewarding patience that bread baking requires. Each loaf you bake builds muscle memory and teaches you more about how dough should feel and behave. Over time, you'll naturally progress to more complex techniques, armed with a solid foundation.

If you're looking for tips to elevate your ciabatta, focus first on the timing of your fermentation stages and the temperature of your kitchen. Warmer environments speed up yeast activity, so adjust rising times accordingly. Humidity can also affect dough hydration, so it's okay to tweak the water amounts slightly to get a dough that's soft but manageable. Remember that no two kitchens are the same, so every bake teaches you a little more about your own baking space.

Keep in mind that flour quality matters, especially in beginner baking. Opting for protein-rich bread flour enhances structure and helps create that classic chewy ciabatta texture. All-purpose flour can be used but might result in a loaf that's softer with a less defined crumb. If you're experimenting, try both types and observe the differences. Baking is as much science as it is art—it invites discovery with every loaf.

Don't be discouraged by the dough's sticky consistency; it's not a mistake but a feature. Working with such dough gets easier the more you do it. Wet dough may seem intimidating at first, but it teaches crucial lessons in handling and shaping bread. Using well-floured hands and surfaces prevents sticking without drying out the dough, while gentle touch avoids deflating the precious air bubbles. These skills carry forward to many other bread recipes.

To sum it up, beginner's ciabatta is a truly approachable bread for budding bakers interested in no-knead techniques paired with rewarding textures. It brings a taste of Italy into your kitchen with minimal fuss and satisfying results. Taking on this loaf will refine your understanding of dough behavior and boost your baking confidence. With every crispy crust and tender crumb, you'll feel more connected to the art of bread making, inspiring you to move forward to new challenges in your baking journey.

Chapter 2
FLAVORFUL YEAST BREADS FOR EVERY OCCASION

Building on the basics of bread baking, this chapter dives into the world of yeast breads packed with character and taste, perfect for any meal or gathering. Here you'll discover how simple additions like herbs, cheese, or dried fruits can transform a basic loaf into something truly memorable, while maintaining straightforward techniques that won't overwhelm beginners. From the comforting warmth of a buttery garlic pull-apart to the subtle sweetness in a honey oat loaf, these breads invite creativity without sacrificing ease. Each recipe is designed to fit smoothly into your baking rhythm, helping you make flavorful bread that stands out at the table—whether it's a casual snack or the centerpiece of a special occasion.

Garlic and Herb Pull-Apart Bread

There's something truly irresistible about the smell of fresh garlic and herbs baking in the oven, filling the kitchen with a warm, inviting aroma that promises comfort and satisfaction. Garlic and Herb Pull-Apart Bread is one of those crowd-pleasing yeast breads that feels both fancy and approachable at the same time. It's perfect for those moments when you want to elevate a simple meal or add a bit of homemade charm to a gathering. This bread isn't just a loaf; it's a convivial experience. Friends and family can pull off pieces one by one, making every bite interactive and fun.

At its core, this bread is about layering flavor and texture. Soft, fluffy dough gets generously brushed and sprinkled with a mixture of minced garlic, fresh herbs like rosemary, thyme, and parsley, plus a touch of butter and seasoning. The pull-apart technique gives you that delightful contrast of crispy edges and tender centers in each segment. No fancy shaping or complicated technique is required, which makes this a fantastic recipe for a beginner baker who wants to impress without feeling overwhelmed.

The dough itself isn't complicated. You're working with simple yeast bread basics — flour, water, yeast, a little sugar, salt, and butter. What really makes this bread shine is the assembly. After the dough's first rise, it's rolled out and cut into squares or strips that are stacked or layered in a loaf pan. Then the magic happens: every layer or stack is coated with the garlicky herb butter, which melts into the dough during baking and creates pockets of flavor that are hard to resist.

One of the best things about this pull-apart bread is how flexible it is. You can easily adjust the herbs based on what you have on hand or like best. Basil, oregano, chives, or tarragon work beautifully if you want a different twist. And if fresh garlic feels too intense, roasted garlic can add a mellower, sweeter note that's just as delightful. This bread pairs perfectly with countless dishes, whether it's alongside a bowl of soup, a fresh salad, or as an appetizer with a dipping sauce.

Taking the step to bake this bread often feels like a mini baking adventure because you get to see the transformation happen in the oven: the dough puffs up and separates into pull-apart sections, and the top turns a gorgeous golden brown, with crispy bits here and there that practically call your name. Visually, it's stunning too — rustic, inviting, and bursting with herbs that peek through the cracks and crevices.

Making Garlic and Herb Pull-Apart Bread also introduces home bakers to some foundational skills without adding complexity. You get familiar with yeast activation, dough kneading or gentle mixing, proofing times, and the rewarding payoff of shaping the loaf. It's a chance to gain confidence and understanding, which helps when you tackle more advanced recipes later on.

The layering technique is especially good practice. It teaches you how butter and flavorings can be incorporated into yeasted dough without being mixed directly into the flour. This helps keep the dough light and airy while packing it with extra taste. Plus, it's wonderfully satisfying to pull the bread apart after baking, as soft pieces melt in your mouth, boosted by the buttery, garlicky, and herby notes.

If you want to serve this bread a little differently, consider tearing it into smaller chunks and toasting them to make garlic croutons. Or slice the finished loaf horizontally and use it for gourmet sandwiches — the layers and seasoning will add a fantastic flavor punch. It's a versatile bread that adapts to plenty of creative uses beyond just being a side.

As you bake this pull-apart bread, keep in mind the importance of proofing. Allowing the dough to rise adequately gives you that wonderfully tender crumb and prevents a dense texture. Though it might feel tempting to rush through, the results are worth the patience. The dough should become noticeably puffy and light to the touch before shaping and layering with the garlic herb butter.

Another helpful tip is to use softened butter for the garlic herb spread, as it spreads more easily and evenly. You want every piece of dough to get a nice, flavorful coating to ensure consistency. If you like, sprinkle a little coarse salt on top before baking — it'll offer a satisfying crunch and make the flavors pop even more.

Choosing the right pan matters too. A standard loaf pan works wonderfully because it supports the layers, helping the bread hold its shape as it rises and bakes. But if you don't have one, a casserole dish or round cake pan can work fine as well. Just make sure the bread has enough room to expand freely without being squished.

When the bread comes out of the oven, it's best enjoyed warm. The aroma is at its peak, and the texture is softest. However, if you want to enjoy leftovers, just reheat individual pull-apart pieces briefly in the toaster or oven to refresh that lovely softness. You'll find that garlic and herb bread tastes even better the next day once the flavors have had time to meld.

For home bakers who want to take one step further, you could experiment by mixing in cheeses like Parmesan or mozzarella between the layers. This will add richness and an additional melty component that complements the herbs and garlic beautifully. Just be mindful of balancing moisture levels so that the dough doesn't become too heavy or dense.

Finally, Garlic and Herb Pull-Apart Bread is one those recipes that invites sharing. It's not just bread — it's a centerpiece on the table, everything from weeknight dinners to holiday feasts can feel a little more festive around a loaf like this. The first pull brings people together, and those simple moments create lasting memories. Baking this bread provides not only a tasty reward but also a touch of joy through the act of making and sharing good food.

CHEDDAR JALAPENO BREAD

When it comes to those flavorful yeast breads that bring a touch of excitement to your table, cheddar jalapeno bread is a standout. It combines the comforting richness of sharp cheddar cheese with the lively kick of fresh jalapenos, creating a loaf that's bursting with personality. Perfect for sandwiches, serving alongside chili, or just enjoying warm from the oven with a slather of butter, this bread has a wonderful way of turning an everyday meal into something memorable.

The magic in this bread starts with the balance of heat and creaminess. Jalapenos provide a bright, spicy pop that contrasts beautifully with the mellow, nutty cheddar. When properly incorporated into the dough, the cheese melts into little pockets of gooey goodness, while diced jalapenos add bursts of biting, fresh heat throughout the crumb. This combination not only boosts the flavor but also adds texture and visual interest with the colorful flecks of green and orange peeking through the crust and crumb.

One of the best things about cheddar jalapeno bread is how approachable it is for bakers at any skill level. The recipe typically begins with a basic yeast dough that you've probably worked with before – flour, water, yeast, salt, and a touch of sugar. From there, it's about gently folding in shredded cheddar and chopped jalapenos so everything is evenly distributed without overworking the dough. The process is straightforward, making it an ideal first step into more adventurous bread baking.

Getting the jalapenos just right is key to the overall success of the loaf. Fresh jalapenos should be finely chopped, but not minced into oblivion, preserving a bit of texture and preventing the bread from turning too spicy. Those who prefer a milder loaf can remove the seeds and membranes, as most of the heat resides there. If you're really after a punch, consider mixing in some pickled jalapenos or even adding a dash of cayenne pepper for an extra layer of warmth.

Cheddar choice also makes a noticeable difference. A sharp, aged cheddar typically melts into the dough beautifully, delivering a deep, tangy flavor that cuts through the heat of the peppers. Mild cheddar works too, but the loaf might feel less bold overall. Whenever possible, opt for freshly shredded cheese rather than pre-shredded, which often contains anti-caking agents that can affect melting and texture.

Your mixing, kneading, and rising times don't change dramatically with this recipe compared to other yeast breads, but the ingredients demand a bit of attention when incorporated. After the initial dough is formed and has had a chance to rest and rise, carefully kneading in the cheddar and jalapenos ensures you get an even flavor throughout without tearing the gluten structure. This gentle incorporation helps the bread maintain a soft yet chewy crumb that holds up well during slicing and eating.

Once shaped, the dough needs to rise a second time, allowing the flavors to meld and the loaf to develop further. This second proofing heralds the creation of pockets where melted cheese and jalapenos will make their home after baking. Don't rush this part – giving the dough enough time to puff up properly guarantees a tender, airy crumb inside.

Baking this bread fills your kitchen with an irresistible aroma that hints at what's to come—a warm, cheesy scent blended with just a hint of peppery spice. The crust should develop a lovely golden-brown color, slightly crisp but not tough. Often, a light sprinkling of extra cheddar on top before baking can turn the crust into a more decadent, crackly layer that's simply hard to resist.

When it's time to enjoy, letting the bread cool only briefly is best. The molten cheese inside stays soft but not runny, and the jalapeno's heat builds slowly on the palate, making each bite interesting. This bread pairs perfectly with soups, stews, and hearty salads, but it's equally delicious slathered with butter or turned into a grilled cheese sandwich for a flavor-packed treat.

For home bakers eager to experiment, cheddar jalapeno bread opens up endless creative possibilities. You can swap in other spicy peppers such as serranos or add herbs like chives or thyme for an aromatic twist. Incorporating nuts like pecans or walnuts adds crunch and complexity, turning the loaf into a centerpiece for casual gatherings or snack time alike.

In terms of storage, this bread keeps well wrapped at room temperature for a couple of days, although it's always best eaten fresh. Leftovers can be toasted the next day and reheated gently in the oven or toaster oven to restore crispness and flavor. Freezing slices individually also works well, allowing you to thaw and enjoy a slice whenever the craving strikes.

Making cheddar jalapeno bread at home offers more than just a delicious loaf—it brings a sense of accomplishment and an invitation to play with flavor combinations. The recipe strikes a sweet spot where simplicity meets bold taste, making it a favorite for those wanting to move beyond basic white bread into something a bit more exciting. You don't have to be an expert baker to nail this one; just a straightforward method, some quality ingredients, and a willingness to enjoy every step of the process.

OLIVE AND ROSEMARY FOCACCIA

When it comes to flavorful yeast breads, few can match the rustic charm and aromatic appeal of olive and rosemary focaccia. This Italian-inspired bread offers an inviting combination of tender crumb, crispy edges, and a fragrant topping that instantly elevates any meal. It's a perfect entry point into artisan-style baking without needing advanced techniques or special equipment. Plus, it's surprisingly versatile—serve it as a side for soups and salads, slice it for sandwiches, or enjoy it simply on its own with a drizzle of good olive oil.

Getting started with focaccia might seem intimidating, but really, it's all about patience and paying attention to the dough's texture. The dough itself is straightforward: flour, water, yeast, a touch of salt, and olive oil. The key is letting the dough rest long enough to develop those lovely air pockets that give focaccia its signature lightness. This bread typically involves a couple of rises, where the dough grows and matures, releasing lovely yeasty aromas. Don't rush these steps; the transformation happening in the bowl is worth the wait.

What makes olive and rosemary focaccia stand out is the topping. Fresh rosemary sprigs combined with whole, briny olives create a wonderful contrast of flavors. The rosemary lends a piney, herbaceous note, while the olives provide bursts of savory richness. Before baking, the dough is generously brushed with olive oil, which helps crisp up the edges and adds a glossy sheen. You'll want to press dimples all over the dough's surface too—this classic touch not only creates focal points for the oil and toppings but also prevents the dough from rising unevenly in the oven.

Although the dough requires time to proof, the actual hands-on work is minimal and very accessible for beginner bakers. Mixing by hand or with a stand mixer is fine, as long as the dough comes together as a slightly sticky but manageable mass. Because focaccia dough contains a fair amount of olive oil, it feels softer and more tender than many other yeasted breads. Handling gently when transferring it to the baking dish helps maintain the airiness built during rising.

One useful tip for home bakers is to use a well-oiled pan or baking sheet. This ensures the focaccia doesn't stick while baking and adds even more olive oil flavor to the bottom crust. It's not unusual for rustic focaccia to have a chewy and slightly crisp bottom, which contrasts nicely with the pillowy interior. If you like, you can sprinkle some coarse sea salt on top before baking—this adds an extra pop of flavor and texture. Feel free to experiment with flakes or grind your own depending on what's on hand.

When it comes time to bake, aim for a hot oven—usually around 425°F (220°C)—to create a golden brown crust while preserving the moist crumb inside. Most ovens vary, so keep an eye during the last 5 to 10 minutes of baking. The finished focaccia should be deep golden with darker browned spots where the rosemary and olives have caramelized. The aroma alone is enough to fill a kitchen with warmth and invite your family or guests to gather around.

If you want to customize your focaccia, there are tons of opportunities to explore different olives or herbs. Kalamata olives provide a rich, fruity bite, while green olives tend to be milder and more briny. Rosemary is the classic herb here, but you can also try thyme, sage, or even rosemary combined with a touch of garlic. This bread beautifully accommodates subtle variations while keeping that essential tender, airy texture.

Serving olive and rosemary focaccia fresh from the oven is always a treat, but leftovers can be equally delicious. Toast slices lightly to refresh the crust, then pair with a soft cheese, hummus, or tapenade. It's also excellent for dipping into soups or stews, soaking up every bit of flavor. You can store focaccia in an airtight container or wrapped tightly in foil for a couple of days at room temperature, or freeze it for longer storage. Reheat in the oven rather than the microwave to keep that bread crust crisp.

For those looking to deepen their bread baking skills, focaccia is an ideal bread to practice dough hydration and fermentation control. The slightly higher hydration (more water than usual) encourages an open crumb and makes the dough more forgiving than denser breads. Learning to recognize when the dough has proofed enough comes with experience but usually involves seeing it double in size and feeling how springy it becomes. These sensory cues are valuable tools that apply to many bread recipes beyond just focaccia.

In many ways, making olive and rosemary focaccia is a gateway to appreciating the simplicity and beauty of classic breadmaking. Despite its rustic nature, it rewards patience and care with delicious complexity. The combination of golden color, tender crumb, and aromatic toppings makes it a bread that feels special, yet approachable for beginner bakers who want to experiment beyond basic white or sandwich bread. It's a keeper recipe that builds confidence and satisfaction in the kitchen.

Beyond the kitchen, focaccia embodies a tradition of communal sharing—an idea baked into every dimpled surface and herb-studded bite. Preparing this bread encourages slow moments of enjoying aromas rising from the oven and celebrating the process of transforming humble ingredients into something memorable. Every step, from mixing the dough to the final brush of olive oil, invites connection with the craft of baking in a way few other breads do.

Whether you're baking for a casual family dinner, a weekend brunch, or a small gathering, olive and rosemary focaccia adds that touch of homemade warmth and genuine flavor. Its forgiving dough and straightforward ingredients make it a natural addition to any home baker's repertoire. With just a little practice, you'll be creating batches of this fragrant, golden bread that fill your kitchen with the scent of fresh rosemary and olives—and the satisfaction of a job well done.

Soft Potato Bread

Soft potato bread holds a special place in the world of yeast breads. What sets it apart is its tender, moist crumb and subtle sweetness, both of which come from the addition of potatoes or potato flour. Unlike typical wheat-based breads, the potato starch in the dough helps retain moisture, resulting in a loaf that stays fresh longer and has a delicate, almost pillow-like texture. This makes it an excellent choice for sandwiches, toast, or simply enjoying with butter and jam on a lazy morning.

For home bakers eager to try something a bit different but not intimidating, potato bread offers a wonderful balance. It's approachable enough for beginners who have already dabbled in basic yeast breads, but it also introduces new ingredients that gently expand baking skills. The process doesn't stray far from classic bread-making techniques; with a little attention to hydrating the potatoes correctly and adjusting the dough's consistency, you'll see how versatile this dough can be.

One of the joys of soft potato bread lies in how forgiving it is during preparation. Potatoes add natural sugars and enzymes that feed the yeast, promoting a quicker and more vigorous rise. This can take a bit of pressure off timing your kneads and proving perfectly. Still, it's important to keep an eye on the dough; it should be soft and slightly tacky but not overly sticky or dense. Using mashed potatoes versus potato flakes will slightly change the crumb: mashed potatoes contribute a creamier softness, while flakes create a lighter loaf with a more uniform texture.

The method starts with cooking and mashing the potatoes—either fresh or frozen work well. For best results, remove any excess moisture as wet potatoes may water down the dough and affect its ability to rise properly. Adding warm mashed potatoes to your basic yeast dough ingredients—flour, water, yeast, salt, and sometimes a bit of sugar or fat—results in a rich dough that's surprisingly straightforward to handle.

Dough hydration is key here. Potato starch holds more water than wheat flour does, so expect doughs to be slightly wetter at first. During kneading, you might notice the dough becomes silkier and stretches easily, which is a good sign. After kneading, letting the dough rest in a warm, draft-free spot encourages the yeast to work its magic, developing flavor while the dough gains strength.

When shaping potato bread, the dough's softness can make it more delicate to handle. If you've baked a simple white loaf before, expect a bit more attention to avoid letting the dough deflate. Using gentle folding motions rather than vigorous kneading during final shaping helps preserve the air pockets inside. Whether you prefer a round boule or a classic sandwich loaf shape, both work beautifully with potato bread dough.

Baking itself is a delightful experience with this bread. As the oven's heat hits the dough, the surface caramelizes gently, forming a thin golden crust that contrasts perfectly with the soft interior. Some bakers like brushing the top with melted butter immediately after baking to add extra richness and keep the crust tender—this step enhances the homemade appeal, making your kitchen smell inviting and warm.

What's especially wonderful about soft potato bread is its versatility. It's a fantastic canvas for flavors and additions without overpowering them. For example, you can mix in herbs, garlic, or even cheese at the dough stage for subtle savory twists. Or, if you lean toward sweet, a sprinkle of cinnamon and sugar on top before baking can turn it into a delightful treat that's ideal for breakfast or snack time.

Beyond flavor, potato bread's texture makes it a favorite for many family kitchens. Kids often enjoy it because it's tender and easy to chew, while adults find it satisfying and comforting. It shines as sandwich bread, whether loaded with fresh deli meats and cheeses or simply layered with peanut butter and jelly. Its softness means it slices beautifully without crumbling, which can sometimes be a challenge with denser whole wheat or artisan styles.

If you're looking to broaden your bread-baking horizons, incorporating potatoes into your dough is an excellent step. Not only does it add moisture and softness, but it also contributes subtle nutrients. Potatoes offer small amounts of vitamins and minerals that, while not enough to make bread a health food, do add a touch of wholesomeness compared to white-only loaves.

As with any bread recipe, patience pays off. Allowing the dough proper time to rise and rest yields the best texture and flavor. Don't rush the proving stages even if the dough seems ready—it can benefit from a bit longer fermentation for a richer taste. The scent of yeast and warm potatoes mingling as the loaf bakes is one of those delightful smells that invites you back to the kitchen again and again.

For those baking in colder environments, a slightly longer proofing time might be needed. Keeping the dough warm but not hot ensures the yeast stays active without producing off flavors. It's helpful to remember that variable factors like humidity, altitude, and even the type of potatoes used can influence the dough's behavior slightly. Experimentation is part of the fun, and once you master soft potato bread, you'll find it a reliable favorite in your baking repertoire.

Keeping fresh potato bread on hand during the week is easy too. Store it wrapped tightly at room temperature, and it will stay moist for several days. You can also slice and freeze leftovers, then toast slices directly from the freezer with excellent results. This convenience makes it a practical option for busy home cooks who still want the joy of fresh-baked bread without daily fuss.

In sum, soft potato bread is an inviting, adaptable yeast bread that's worth adding to your baking lineup. It offers the satisfying experience of making traditional bread but comes with a uniquely tender crumb and moist texture that feel special. Whether you're making daily sandwiches or treating your family to fresh toast, soft potato bread brings warmth, flavor, and a bit of homestyle magic to the table.

CARAMELIZED ONION BREAD

Caramelized onion bread is the perfect pick when you want a loaf that bursts with rich, savory flavor and a touch of sweetness. This bread is nestled comfortably within the broad world of flavorful yeast breads, offering a taste that's both comforting and sophisticated. The slow, gentle cooking of onions until they soften and turn a deep golden brown is what transforms this bread from ordinary to something truly special. This process draws out the natural sugars in the onions, creating layers of complexity that complement the yeasty, fragrant dough.

Getting started with caramelized onion bread might seem like a culinary project, but it's actually quite straightforward—and well worth the effort. Caramelizing onions requires a little patience. You'll want to allow them to cook slowly over medium-low heat, stirring occasionally, until they've darkened and become tender without burning. This step is crucial since undercooked onions won't develop their full sweetness, while burned onions add bitterness that's best avoided. Once your onions are perfectly caramelized, incorporating them into your dough will infuse it with that warm, rich flavor that elevates every bite.

When mixing the dough, consider the balance of moisture and texture. Caramelized onions bring some moisture, so adjusting the flour a little can help achieve the ideal dough consistency. This bread often tends toward a softer crumb while retaining enough structure to hold its shape well. It's a wonderful bread to slice thickly for sandwiches or to enjoy warm with butter as a savory snack. The interplay between the slightly sweet onions and the subtly yeasty bread creates a satisfying experience that's both hearty and elegant.

One of the joys of caramelized onion bread is how versatile it is. It pairs excellently with cheese, making it a fantastic companion to a sharp cheddar or creamy brie. You might also find that it shines alongside robust soups, stews, or even as the foundation for a gourmet grilled cheese sandwich. Using caramelized onion bread in these contexts adds depth that store-bought loaves simply can't match. Plus, the inviting aroma that wafts from your kitchen while baking can practically turn anyone into an enthusiast of homemade bread.

The dough for caramelized onion bread is pretty similar to a basic yeast loaf, which means it's approachable for beginner bakers looking to branch into more flavorful territory. You'll want to use good quality yeast and allow sufficient rising time for the dough to develop both flavor and texture. Patience here pays off big, since rushed proofs often yield bread that's dense or lacks the subtle chewiness that makes this type so enjoyable. For beginners, timing the caramelization and dough preparation together can be a fun challenge that teaches how different components come together.

Some bakers like to add a handful of fresh herbs such as thyme or rosemary to the dough alongside the caramelized onions. This layering of flavors can turn the loaf into something truly memorable. If you prefer a slight tang, a splash of buttermilk in place of some of the liquid can add depth to the crumb without overpowering the onion's sweetness. These tweaks allow you to customize your bread to suit personal tastes or the main dishes you plan to serve.

Of course, the texture of caramelized onion bread is just as important as its flavor. Unlike bread with large chunks of ingredients like nuts or dried fruit, caramelized onions gently fold into the dough, creating subtle pockets of sweetness throughout. When sliced, these little onion-rich veins shine through the crumb, giving every bite a hint of savory bliss. For the best texture, avoid overmixing once the onions are added; this ensures the dough stays tender, rather than becoming tough or overly dense.

Another helpful tip is to consider how you shape your loaf. Some prefer a traditional round boule or an elongated batard, while others enjoy using a loaf pan for a more uniform shape that's perfect for sandwiches. No matter the shape you choose, make sure the dough's final rise is timed to allow enough oven spring—the burst of airiness that happens in the oven before the crust sets. Caramelized onion bread benefits greatly from this, as the rising dough gives it a soft interior that contrasts beautifully with the golden crust.

Crust formation on caramelized onion bread is another area where small details can make a big difference. A light spray of water or a quick steam in your oven just before baking helps create a slightly crisp crust, which contrasts nicely with the tender crumb. The crust color should be a warm amber—not too dark—to complement the golden hues of the caramelized onions inside. If you're baking in a home oven without specialized steam tools, placing a pan of hot water on the oven floor during the first few minutes of baking works wonders in achieving that delicate crust.

Storage and reheating are also worth mentioning. Like many fresh yeast breads, caramelized onion bread is best enjoyed within a couple of days of baking for optimal texture and flavor. To keep it fresh, store the loaf in a paper bag or loosely wrapped in a kitchen towel at room temperature; this prevents the crust from becoming too soft or soggy. If you want to preserve it longer, slicing and freezing portions is a smart choice. When ready to eat, simply toast the slices or warm them gently in the oven to revive that freshly baked aroma and flavor.

What makes caramelized onion bread stand out on the table is its ability to marry simplicity and sophistication. It's a loaf that looks homey and approachable but delivers a taste that speaks to more experienced palates. Whether you're sharing it at a casual family meal or bringing it along to a potluck, this bread offers a little something extra that's sure to impress without requiring complicated ingredients or techniques.

In the journey of learning to bake flavorful yeast breads, this recipe serves as a fantastic milestone. It challenges you to master a technique—caramelizing onions—while reinforcing foundational bread-making skills like kneading, proofing, and shaping. The result is a loaf that's not only delicious but builds confidence and inspiration for your next baking projects.

Once comfortable with the basic caramelized onion bread, home bakers often find themselves experimenting by adding cheese, nuts, or even small bits of crispy bacon to the dough. The possibilities are endless when you start with a solid, flavorful base like this one. Each variation offers learning opportunities and new delicious experiences, helping develop your baking intuition.

Overall, caramelized onion bread is a must-try in the repertoire of flavorful yeast breads. It stands out as a crowd-pleaser that's surprisingly easy to make, with a rich flavor profile that awake your senses. There's something uniquely satisfying about pulling a warm loaf laden with sweet, golden onions from your own oven and slicing it fresh. This bread beckons you to slow down and appreciate the craft of baking, rewarding patience with every bite.

SUN-DRIED TOMATO LOAF

When it comes to flavor-packed yeast breads, the sun-dried tomato loaf stands out as a beloved choice for those wanting to add a little Mediterranean flair to their baking repertoire. This loaf balances the tangy sweetness of sun-dried tomatoes with the earthy goodness of herbs, creating a bread that's bursting with character and perfect for sandwiches, toasts, or just on its own. It's approachable for home bakers, even beginners, since the method largely follows classic yeast bread techniques, but with a flavorful twist that rewards patience and attention to detail.

First, it's worth highlighting why sun-dried tomatoes are such a fantastic addition to bread. These tomatoes, dried either in the sun or via dehydrators, concentrate sugars and acids, lending an intense, savory taste that can brighten up the whole loaf. Unlike fresh tomatoes, which might release water and cause sogginess in baked goods, sun-dried tomatoes maintain a chewy texture and robust flavor after being incorporated and baked into the dough. Their savory nature pairs beautifully with various herbs such as basil, oregano, or thyme, which you'll often find added alongside the tomatoes to deepen the loaf's aromatic qualities.

Making this loaf starts with creating a dough that has a soft, slightly elastic crumb, allowing the chunks or chopped sun-dried tomatoes to fully integrate without falling apart or drying out during baking. The base dough is typically a straightforward mix of all-purpose or bread flour, yeast, water, a bit of sugar to feed the yeast, and salt. What sets it apart is the addition of finely chopped sun-dried tomatoes folded gently into the dough once it's had a chance to develop some gluten. This gives the tomatoes space to distribute evenly throughout the loaf.

Another tip is to choose your tomatoes based on preference for texture and flavor intensity. Tomatoes packed in oil offer a richer, silkier profile that imparts extra moisture and richness to the bread. Those dried without oil produce a more concentrated intensity, albeit slightly drier, so soaking them briefly in warm water before chopping can rehydrate and mellow their chewy bite. If you're aiming for a milder tomato presence, smaller amounts work well, but don't hesitate to get generous—the flavors meld well with each bite.

Herbs are a common companion and can be introduced either mixed in with the tomatoes or sprinkled over the loaf before baking. Fresh basil or dried Italian seasoning provide herby bursts that complement the tomato's tartness. Some bakers also add a splash of garlic powder or even a pinch of crushed red pepper flakes if they want a sneak of heat. This loaf's versatility means you can customize it to suit your tastes without adding complexity to the process.

After mixing the dough and folding in the tomatoes and herbs, you'll allow it to rise until doubled in size. During this time, the yeast ferments sugars, producing that wonderful airy texture that helps the loaf remain soft while still offering a satisfying chew. The fermentation also enhances the bread's flavor, allowing the tomatoes and herbs to infuse subtly throughout the crumb. Rising times might vary depending on room temperature or yeast activity, but expect about one to two hours, or until the dough looks noticeably puffy.

Shaping the loaf usually involves forming it into a round boule or a more traditional elongated shape, depending on your preference or what fits best on your baking sheet. One approachable method is to gently shape the dough into a tight ball, ensuring the tomatoes stay enveloped within the dough rather than sticking out and risking burning during baking. A light dusting of flour on top before the oven helps it develop a rustic crust.

Baking the sun-dried tomato loaf requires moderate oven heat, generally around 375°F (190°C). Baking at this temperature strikes a nice balance between creating a golden, crusty exterior and a tender, moist interior. You can bake on a preheated baking stone or a regular sheet, but a stone often helps achieve that artisan-style crisp bottom. For an extra boost in crust development, some bakers add a pan of water in the oven to generate steam during the first 10 minutes, mimicking traditional bread ovens and resulting in a shiny, crackly crust.

One of the joys of this bread is how flexible it is to serve. Warm slices slathered with good butter, a smear of cream cheese, or even a drizzle of olive oil feel indulgent and fresh. Try it alongside soups, salads, or charcuterie boards for a complementary pop of flavor. It also makes for incredible sandwiches; think roasted vegetables, fresh mozzarella, or thinly sliced meats—the sun-dried tomato loaf stands up and enhances those tastes without overpowering them.

As you bake more of these, you might experiment with variations. Adding shredded cheese like parmesan or mozzarella into the dough elevates richness and introduces an extra layer of texture. Nuts, such as pine nuts or walnuts, can bring crunch and earthiness to the loaf. You could also try mixing olives for a briny counterpoint or even a touch of roasted garlic for deeper savoriness.

One common challenge with this bread is ensuring the tomatoes don't clump together or settle at the bottom of the loaf, which can sometimes happen if they're too moist or chopped unevenly. To avoid this, try chopping tomatoes uniformly and gently folding them into the dough at the right time. Overworking the dough can cause the tomatoes to break down too quickly or release excess moisture, so timing and gentle handling are key.

Storage is straightforward—once cooled, the loaf keeps well wrapped at room temperature for up to two days. Because of the tomatoes' moisture content, longer storage is best handled in the fridge, wrapped tightly, to prevent mold. Slicing and freezing the loaf works wonderfully too; just toast slices straight from the freezer for a fresh-baked taste anytime.

If you're seeking an easy way to add a gourmet touch to your home baking, this sun-dried tomato loaf hits the mark. Its vibrant flavors make it a crowd-pleaser, and the techniques involved build confidence in handling flavorful doughs. With practice, the balance of herbs, tomatoes, and a well-crumbed loaf become second nature, inspiring you to explore even more creative yeast bread recipes.

Embrace this loaf as a pantry-friendly staple that pairs beautifully with many meals or stands proudly alone with a drizzle of olive oil or a sprinkle of flaky sea salt. It's a simple step beyond basic white bread that offers both delicious flavor and a rich baking experience.

Honey Oat Bread

If you're looking to add a wholesome, subtly sweet loaf to your baking repertoire, honey oat bread is a perfect choice. It manages to strike a beautiful balance between hearty and soft, making it suitable for breakfast toast, sandwiches, or even just plain snacking. This bread is all about combining the warm nuttiness of oats with the gentle floral sweetness of honey, creating a loaf that's inviting and comforting.

One of the special things about honey oat bread is its texture. The oats give the crumb a slight chewiness and a rustic feel, while the honey contributes moisture and tenderness. Unlike a basic white bread, this loaf feels rich and satisfying without being heavy or dense. This recipe is especially friendly for bakers who want to experiment beyond simple white or whole wheat loaves but aren't quite ready to dive into complex artisan formulas.

Getting started with honey oat bread involves working with a few staple ingredients: rolled oats, whole milk or buttermilk, honey, yeast, and all-purpose or bread flour. The oats, both inside the dough and sprinkled on top, add more than just texture—they also bring a bit of earthy flavor that enhances the overall bread experience. The honey plays a dual role, sweetening the dough while also helping to feed the yeast during fermentation, which encourages a beautiful rise.

In terms of the process, this bread is fairly straightforward. After an initial mixing of the wet and dry ingredients, expect to spend some time kneading to develop gluten. However, since honey oat bread usually incorporates a moderate amount of whole grains and oats, kneading gently and not excessively is advisable to keep the crumb tender rather than tough. You'll want a dough that's soft, slightly sticky, but still manageable. If you're new to bread baking, don't worry—a little stickiness is normal with oat-based doughs.

Letting the dough rise allows the yeast to create those lovely air pockets that make bread so light and fluffy. Given the presence of honey, which can speed up yeast activity, watch your dough carefully during the first rise. It may take less time than your typical white bread. Overproofing can cause the bread to collapse or become dense, especially with the added weight of oats. Aim for the dough to roughly double in size—touching it lightly should leave a slight indent that springs back slowly.

Shaping honey oat bread can be as simple as forming a classic loaf shape or even a round boule. If you prefer sandwich bread, a standard rectangular pan works well. Before placing the dough into the pan or onto the baking surface, a light brush of honey-water and a sprinkle of oats add a lovely finishing touch both visually and flavor-wise. When baked, these oats toast slightly and add a welcoming aroma.

One of the perks of baking honey oat bread at home is the delightful crust it produces. Unlike some crusts that harden into tough shells, the combination of milk and honey in this loaf encourages a soft and slightly chewy crust, which pairs perfectly with the tender interior. Though it's not a bread you'd expect a super-crispy crust from, the crust on a honey oat loaf is satisfying—pleasant to bite into, with a golden sheen that hints at the care put into baking.

Storage is straightforward. Honey oat bread tends to keep its moisture well, thanks to the sugars and fats in honey and milk, but like all fresh bread, it's best consumed within a few days for optimal flavor and texture. Wrapping the loaf in a clean tea towel or paper bag helps maintain the crust's texture, while storing it in a plastic bag keeps it softer but sacrifices crunch. If you need to save some for later, slices freeze beautifully—just wrap them tightly to prevent freezer burn.

Aside from eating it plain or with butter, honey oat bread is incredibly versatile. It pairs beautifully with fruit preserves, nut butters, or savory toppings like cheese and ham. The mild sweetness opens up possibilities for sandwiches that are a little bit different—think turkey and cranberry or smoked salmon with cream cheese and cucumber. For breakfast lovers, toasting this bread and topping it with avocado or eggs is a quick and tasty way to start the day.

If you've hesitated to include oats or honey in bread baking, honey oat bread makes a great introduction. It's forgiving enough for beginners to handle but sophisticated enough to impress guests or elevate your weeknight meals. Over time, you might even find yourself swapping it for regular sandwich bread due to its richer flavor and more complex texture.

Mastering honey oat bread also opens the door to customizing the loaf with your favorite add-ins. Want to add a sprinkle of cinnamon or a handful of chopped nuts? Go for it. Some bakers incorporate seeds like flax or sunflower for extra crunch and nutrition. Each small tweak lets you make this bread your own, tailored perfectly to your tastes while still enjoying the straightforward joy of baking at home.

In summary, honey oat bread is a lovely, nourishing loaf that combines simplicity and flavor with a touch of rustic charm. For home bakers who want to branch out from plain white bread but aren't ready to tackle artisan sourdoughs or multi-step enriched recipes, this is a reliable, rewarding option. It offers a tasty way to feed your family or guests something comforting and homemade with minimal fuss.

Whether you're enjoying thick slices slathered with butter at breakfast, or stacking it high for a satisfying sandwich, honey oat bread is an excellent choice. It brings a natural sweetness and a lovely hearty texture without being overwhelming, making every bite feel just right. As you get comfortable with this loaf, you'll gain confidence that sets the stage for experimenting with even more exciting flavor combinations in the future.

Remember, the joy of baking honey oat bread isn't just about the final product—it's in the process itself. Mixing, kneading, watching the dough rise, and finally pulling a golden, fragrant loaf from your oven is a gratifying experience. You'll find that this recipe is one that becomes a regular part of your baking rotation, a trusty companion when you want something a little special but not complicated.

CINNAMON SWIRL BREAD

Cinnamon Swirl Bread is a timeless classic that brings warmth and comfort to any kitchen. This bread isn't just another loaf; it's a flavorful experience wrapped up in tender dough and a luscious cinnamon-sugar spiral. Perfect for breakfast, afternoon tea, or even a simple snack, it's a versatile bread that caters to both novices and those ready to experiment beyond plain loaves. Unlike basic white bread, what sets this recipe apart is the captivating swirl that adds a beautiful pattern and a burst of flavor in every bite.

The magic of Cinnamon Swirl Bread lies in its balance. The dough is soft yet sturdy enough to hold the cinnamon-sugar filling without losing structure during baking. This means you get a loaf that slices beautifully, revealing that enticing, candy-striped interior. It's a wonderful way to elevate your bread-baking skills because the technique encourages you to practice dough rolling, spreading, and shaping—a step up from simple loaf pans or free-form rounds.

When embarking on this recipe, pay close attention to your ingredients. Using fresh ground cinnamon makes a noticeable difference; it infuses a deep, spicy aroma that pre-ground, older cinnamon might lack. The sugar you select also matters—traditionally, granulated white sugar is used in the swirl, but mixing in brown sugar provides a richer, molasses-like depth to the flavor. Some bakers add a pinch of nutmeg or cardamom to enhance the warmth of the cinnamon. Small tweaks here allow you to personalize the loaf while keeping the core concept intact.

One of the best things about Cinnamon Swirl Bread is how adaptable it is for everyday baking. While some enriched dough recipes require butter, eggs, or milk, this bread can be made lighter or richer depending on your preferences. For a basic version, simple yeast dough with a touch of sugar and oil is enough, and you'll still get a tender crumb. Adding milk or butter enriches the dough, making it softer and longer-lasting. If you're looking for an easier version, you can even use a no-knead dough technique and refrigerate it overnight for better flavor development without extra effort.

The shaping step deserves special consideration because it directly impacts the final look and texture. After rolling out the dough into a rectangle, spreading the cinnamon-sugar mixture evenly is key. Try not to overfill, as this can cause the filling to leak or burn, but don't be stingy either—each bite should be packed with that luscious cinnamon flavor. Once spread, the dough is rolled tightly like a jelly roll, then placed seam-side down in your loaf pan. This ensures the swirl stays intact and the loaf rises evenly. If you want to take it a step further, experimenting with a braided shape or a "pull-apart" style loaf can make your Cinnamon Swirl Bread an impressive centerpiece.

Proofing time here is vital. Allow the dough to rise until it's noticeably puffy but not overproofed. Overproofed dough can lose its shape or yield a crumb that's overly airy and fragile. Underproofed dough means your bread will be dense and won't have the ideal texture. Learn to read the dough's signs—when it springs back slowly after a gentle poke, it's ready to bake. Watching the dough closely helps avoid common pitfalls and leads to a perfectly tender crumb with a golden, shiny crust.

Baking Cinnamon Swirl Bread fills your home with an inviting aroma that's hard to beat. The sweet scent of cinnamon and sugar mingling in the oven feels almost therapeutic. Baking time usually ranges between 30 to 40 minutes, though oven differences mean checking the loaf's color and internal temperature is important. Using an instant-read thermometer, look for an internal temperature around 190°F (88°C) to ensure the bread is fully baked but still soft. Once cooled, slicing into this bread reveals the beautiful swirl, and each piece offers a delightful bite where crust and sweet filling meet crumbs that are light yet pleasantly chewy.

Serving Cinnamon Swirl Bread fresh from the oven feels special, but an unexpected bonus is how well it keeps. Wrapped tightly in plastic wrap or stored in an airtight container, it stays fresh for several days—perfect for making ahead or stretching your bake over a few breakfasts. Toasting slices gives the cinnamon sugar a slight caramelization and a crispy edge that lovely contrasts the soft interior. Spread a bit of butter or cream cheese, and you've got an easy treat that appeals to all ages.

For those who want to play with flavor, Cinnamon Swirl Bread provides an excellent canvas. Adding raisins or chopped nuts to the cinnamon mixture creates extra texture and bursts of sweetness. Alternatively, a drizzle of simple glaze made from powdered sugar and milk can dress it up for special occasions or gift-giving. Changing the type of flour, such as incorporating some whole wheat, alters the loaf's character with a nuttier taste and denser crumb while keeping that irresistible cinnamon ribbon. This flexibility makes Cinnamon Swirl Bread a favorite for home bakers who enjoy customizing familiar recipes.

In the broader scope of yeast breads, Cinnamon Swirl Bread offers a satisfying step beyond basic loaves. It introduces important techniques like dough shaping, filling incorporation, and managing enriched doughs while still staying accessible. This bread rewards patience and attention with a stunning final product that's as delicious as it is visually inviting. Whether you're making it for a family breakfast or to impress friends, Cinnamon Swirl Bread has a place in your baking repertoire ready to be mastered.

Finally, baking this bread reminds us why the simplest ingredients can become extraordinary with a little care and creativity. Flour, yeast, sugar, cinnamon—they're common pantry staples transformed into something comforting and memorable. By perfecting this recipe, you build confidence to try more adventurous doughs or variations, deepening your understanding of bread baking. So, grab your rolling pin, warm up the oven, and enjoy the wonderful process of creating Cinnamon Swirl Bread—your future self will thank you with every delicious slice.

RAISIN WALNUT LOAF

Moving on from the tangy warmth of breads packed with herbs and cheeses, the Raisin Walnut Loaf offers a sweeter, heartier option that still fits beautifully into the flavorful yeast breads category. This loaf strikes a lovely balance between soft, tender crumbs and just the right amount of crunch from the walnuts. With juicy raisins scattered throughout, it's a versatile bread that works equally well for breakfast, an afternoon snack, or alongside a savory meal. Whether toasted with butter or enjoyed as-is, this loaf brings a welcomed touch of natural sweetness combined with nutty depth.

One of the first things to appreciate about the Raisin Walnut Loaf is how accessible it is for bakers at all levels. If you're a beginner, crafting this loaf is a great way to get comfortable working with enriched dough that contains mix-ins—those handfuls of raisins and walnuts—without overwhelming complexity. The recipe encourages hands-on learning about proper kneading techniques to develop gluten, which gives the bread its characteristic chew and structure. Plus, it's forgiving enough that a slight variation in rise times won't ruin your final product.

This bread starts with a classic yeast dough base made from bread flour, sugar, salt, and a touch of butter or oil to enrich the texture. What sets it apart is how those raisins and chopped walnuts are incorporated in just the right amounts, introducing bursts of flavor without making the dough too heavy or dense. Careful folding of the nuts and fruit during the mixing stage ensures even distribution, which is key because no one wants raisins clumped awkwardly on one side or walnuts packed into a tight cluster that disrupts the loaf's tender crumb.

Using warm liquid—often milk or water—with the yeast jumpstarts the fermentation process, encouraging that delightful rise that results in a loaf with an inviting crumb structure. In fact, proper proofing is critical here. The dough needs enough time to double, allowing the yeast to work its magic and create air pockets that lighten the loaf. It's a rewarding step to watch as the dough swells gently, like a soft pillow ready to be baked into golden perfection.

Speaking of baking, the Raisin Walnut Loaf bakes up into a deeply aromatic bread with a golden-brown crust that's just firm enough to hold shape while remaining soft inside. The scent filling your kitchen as it bakes is a cozy mix of toasted walnuts, sweet raisins, and yeasty warmth. When you slice into the loaf after it cools slightly, you'll notice the beautiful swirl of nestled fruit and nuts against a warm-hued, soft crumb. It's the kind of bread that looks as good as it tastes.

As you experiment with this bread, feel free to adjust the ratio of raisins to walnuts to suit your preferences. Some like a more pronounced nutty bite and may prefer to toss in an extra handful of walnuts or even substitute pecans for a slightly different flavor profile. Others prefer sweeter notes and might add a few more raisins or combine them with dried cherries or cranberries for a tart contrast. This loaf is forgiving and fun to customize, making it a perfect canvas for creative baking.

One practical tip to keep this loaf moist and soft is to watch your baking time carefully. Overbaking can dry out breads enriched with nuts and fruit, so removing it from the oven just as the crust reaches a rich golden color helps preserve that tender crumb. If you have a kitchen thermometer handy, aim for an internal temperature around 190°F (88°C) to know it's perfectly done. Letting it cool on a rack before slicing also prevents the crumb from becoming gummy—patience here really pays off.

Beyond the sensory enjoyment, this bread also lends itself well to versatile serving ideas. Try it lightly toasted with a spread of cream cheese or almond butter for breakfast. For lunch, it pairs wonderfully with hearty cheese and charcuterie boards, its sweetness offsetting sharp or savory accompaniments. It even works as a base for open-faced sandwiches topped with roasted vegetables or smoked turkey. No matter how you slice it, the Raisin Walnut Loaf feels like a special indulgence made simply in your own kitchen.

For those aiming to include healthier touches without sacrificing flavor, consider slightly reducing the sugar or opting for unrefined sweeteners like honey or maple syrup. Whole wheat flour blends can be used in part to lend more fiber and complexity, though you might want to increase hydration slightly to keep the dough from stiffening. Toasting the walnuts before adding them can also boost the bread's nutty aroma while adding depth to every bite.

Making your own Raisin Walnut Loaf extends beyond the recipe itself—it's about mastering foundational bread baking skills such as dough handling, shaping, and timing fermentations. These lessons will build your confidence and prepare you for more advanced doughs and intricate formulas down the road. And while it delivers on taste and texture, it's also a delightful project that yields a rewarding sense of accomplishment when you pull the loaf fresh from the oven.

In summary, the Raisin Walnut Loaf stands out as a beloved addition to the flavorful yeast bread collection for good reason. It seamlessly blends sweet and nutty elements into a bread that's as practical as it is delicious. With approachable techniques and adaptable ingredients, it invites beginner bakers and experienced home cooks alike to explore the satisfying art of yeast baking. Fresh from your oven, it promises more than just nourishment—it offers moments of comfort, creativity, and joy at the heart of every meal.

CHEESE AND HERB BREADSTICKS

Breadsticks might seem simple at first glance, but when you add layers of cheese and fragrant herbs, they transform into something truly special. These Cheese and Herb Breadsticks offer a deliciously savory twist on a classic bread treat, perfect for pairing with soups, salads, or enjoying on their own as a snack. Their golden crust, flecked with melted cheese and bright green herbs, makes them as pleasing to the eye as they are to the palate. Whether you're prepping for a casual family dinner or looking for an easy appetizer to impress guests, this recipe brings the warmth and comfort of homemade breadsticks with a flavorful punch.

The good news is these breadsticks are beginner-friendly. You don't need intricate techniques or fancy equipment to get soft, airy results with a satisfying crust. A few simple ingredients—flour, yeast, olive oil, cheese, and herbs—are all you need to get started. The dough is stretchy and forgiving, making it a great project for someone new to yeast breads who wants to build confidence while learning fundamental skills such as kneading, shaping, and proofing.

One of the key benefits of this recipe is its flexibility. You can experiment with your favorite cheese varieties, from sharp cheddar to mellow mozzarella or even a tangy

Parmesan. Fresh herbs like rosemary, thyme, or parsley add fragrant notes that elevate the breadsticks without overwhelming the dough's delicate crumb. For an easy way to boost flavor, finely chop fresh herbs and fold them right into the dough or sprinkle them on top before baking.

When preparing the dough, be mindful of the temperature of your liquids and the environment since yeast is sensitive to heat and cold. Using warm water helps activate the yeast quickly, encouraging a good rise, but water that's too hot can kill the yeast and prevent proper fermentation. Once the dough comes together, allowing it to rest in a warm spot lets the yeast work its magic, creating those irresistible airy pockets inside the breadsticks. Don't rush this stage; patience rewards you with texture that's both tender and delightfully chewy.

Shaping these breadsticks can be a fun part of the process. You can stick with classic long, slender fingers or play around with twists, knots, or braided shapes that look impressive but aren't tricky to pull off. Remember to give a light brushing of olive oil or melted butter before baking—this not only enriches the flavor but also encourages a golden brown crust with just the right crunch.

Oven temperature matters here as well. Baking at a moderately high heat helps the breadsticks rise quickly and develop a crisp exterior without drying out. Placing them on a preheated baking stone or an inverted baking sheet can simulate the hot surface of a professional oven, yielding a better crust. Keep an eye during the last few minutes of baking; those edges, especially where the cheese melts and crisps, turn beautifully golden and slightly caramelized, signaling they're ready to enjoy.

Once out of the oven, these breadsticks are best served warm so you can enjoy the gooey cheese and aromatic herbs at their peak. They pair wonderfully with marinara, garlic butter, or even a simple extra drizzle of olive oil for dipping. If you want to prepare them ahead of time, you can freeze unbaked breadsticks shaped on the baking sheet and pop them into the oven straight from the freezer when you're ready. This method saves prep time and keeps your kitchen smelling amazing whenever you bake a batch.

Aside from being delicious and versatile, cheese and herb breadsticks are often crowd-pleasers at parties, potlucks, and family gatherings. They invite creativity—different cheeses, herb blends, and even an occasional sprinkle of chili flakes or garlic powder can customize the flavor profile to fit your mood or season. They also help build important bread-making techniques that set the foundation for tackling more advanced recipes later on.

This recipe encourages bakers to embrace experimentation while keeping things simple and manageable. Follow the steps, trust the ingredients, and know that every batch improves with practice and care. Once you master these cheese and herb breadsticks, you'll find they become a reliable go-to for quick, satisfying homemade bread that elevates any meal.

Chapter 3
WHOLE GRAIN AND HEALTHY BREAD CREATIONS

Moving into whole grain and healthier bread options brings exciting opportunities to nourish your body and delight your taste buds at the same time. These breads often combine hearty textures and rich flavors packed with nutrients, making them perfect for those focused on wellness without sacrificing the joy of fresh-baked bread. From the nutty bite of multigrain harvest loaves to the subtle earthiness of spelt and flaxseed, you'll find breads that suit various dietary needs and preferences. This chapter offers practical recipes that are approachable for beginners while encouraging experimentation with diverse grains and seeds. Whether you're aiming for high fiber, gluten-free, or simply a wholesome sandwich staple, these creations prove that healthy baking can be simple, satisfying, and downright delicious.

% WHOLE WHEAT BREAD

When it comes to baking whole wheat bread, using 100% whole wheat flour is both a rewarding and challenging choice. Whole wheat flour offers a richer flavor, a denser texture, and more nutrition compared to white flour, thanks to the bran and germ it retains. For home bakers eager to dive deeper into wholesome baking, mastering a fully whole wheat loaf is an essential milestone. It lets you fully embrace the hearty, nutty taste while developing a more satisfying crumb structure in your bread.

One of the biggest adjustments when baking with 100% whole wheat flour is handling the dough's density and hydration. Unlike white flour, whole wheat flour absorbs significantly more water, thanks to its bran particles. This means you'll need to increase the water content in your recipes, often by 10 to 20 percent or more, to achieve a dough that's soft and extensible. Underestimating hydration will likely result in a dry, crumbly loaf with less rise, so don't skimp on the water. A wetter dough might feel intimidating at first, but it actually helps the gluten develop and gives the bread a lighter texture in the end.

Gluten development in 100% whole wheat dough also behaves differently than in white dough. The bran and germ pieces cut into gluten strands, weakening the dough's structure. Because of this, the kneading process might feel a little different—you won't get that smooth, silky dough you expect with white bread. Instead, whole wheat dough tends to be stickier and rougher. To overcome this, many bakers use a technique called autolyse, where flour and water rest together before kneading begins. This resting period hydrates the bran and germ fully, allowing the flour to absorb moisture more thoroughly, which helps build stronger gluten networks. It also softens the dough, making it easier to work with.

Patience becomes a baker's best friend when working with 100% whole wheat bread. The dough often requires longer fermentation times to fully develop flavor and rise properly. You can take advantage of cooler, slower rises by letting the dough sit in the refrigerator overnight. This not only improves the flavor—allowing natural enzymes and yeast to enhance the wheat's earthy character—but also makes the dough easier to handle when you're ready to shape and bake.

Shaping whole wheat dough demands just a bit more care, too. Because the dough is denser and may tear more easily, gentle handling is important to retain as much gas as possible, which contributes to a better crumb and oven spring. Avoid excessive punching down or rough manipulation; instead, use a gentle folding technique to strengthen the dough without losing its volume. Proper shaping helps create a loaf that looks appetizing and bakes evenly from crust to crumb.

Another helpful tip is to consider blending a small percentage of vital wheat gluten into your flour. Adding just 1 to 2 tablespoons per cup of whole wheat flour enhances gluten strength and elasticity, which can help combat the natural weakening caused by bran. While not always necessary for every baker, it's a great trick when you want consistently fluffy loaves without losing the nutritional benefits of 100% whole wheat.

Temperature control also plays a role in success with whole wheat bread. Because whole wheat ferments faster due to its nutrient-rich composition, warmer temperatures can accelerate proofing times. Keep an eye on your dough during fermentation so it doesn't overproof, which can lead to collapsed loaves or dense crumb. Conversely, cooler proofing slows fermentation, helping manage your schedule and develop deeper flavor.

The crust of a 100% whole wheat bread tends to be slightly thicker and chewier than white bread, which adds to its rustic appeal. If you prefer a lighter crust, you can try covering your dough with a damp towel during the first rise or experimenting with steam in your oven during baking. Creating a moist environment helps the crust stay tender while still forming that appealing golden color and slight crunch.

When it comes to flavor, whole wheat bread offers a complex, nutty, and slightly sweet profile. Unlike the mild taste of white bread, this enriched flavor stands up well to savory or sweet toppings alike. Honey, molasses, or malt syrup added to the dough give it a subtle sweetness that complements the whole grain's natural tones. Some bakers enjoy mixing in toasted wheat germ or cracked wheat for added texture and flavor dimension.

Because 100% whole wheat bread can sometimes feel intimidating, a good approach is to start with small loaves or rolls to practice the nuances of handling and baking. Once you're comfortable with hydration, kneading, and proofing times, you can scale up to larger sandwich loaves or artisan-style breads with confidence.

Using 100% whole wheat flour in your breads is also a terrific way to boost the nutritional value of your baking. Whole wheat contains more fiber, vitamins, and minerals compared to highly refined white flour. Eating breads made only with whole wheat can contribute positively to digestive health and provide sustained energy throughout the day. It's a delicious way to eat clean and nurture your body without sacrificing the comfort and aroma of fresh-baked bread.

In this journey toward 100% whole wheat bread mastery, don't hesitate to experiment with different brands and types of whole wheat flour. Some mills produce stronger, higher-protein whole wheat, which can impact how your dough behaves. Red wheat varieties tend to have a robust flavor, while white whole wheat offers a milder, sweeter taste with all the benefits intact. Trying these variations can help you find the perfect loaf adapted to your personal preferences.

In sum, baking a loaf made entirely from whole wheat flour takes some attention to detail, but it's incredibly worth it. The result is a bread that embodies wholesome goodness, rich flavor, and old-fashioned heartiness. With practice, you'll soon be slicing into warm, freshly baked 100% whole wheat bread that fills your kitchen with irresistible aroma and delivers satisfying nourishment one slice at a time.

MULTIGRAIN HARVEST LOAF

The Multigrain Harvest Loaf is a shining example of how wholesome ingredients come together to create a satisfying and nutritious bread that's perfect for any time of day. It strikes a beautiful balance between hearty grains and tender crumb, delivering a loaf that's both flavorful and packed with texture. This bread is an excellent choice for home bakers looking to expand beyond basic whole wheat bread and add variety to their baking repertoire with something that feels both rustic and refined.

What sets this loaf apart is its rich blend of grains and seeds, which give each slice a delightful complexity. Incorporating a combination of whole wheat flour along with oats, millet, sunflower seeds, flaxseeds, and sometimes barley or rye creates a loaf bursting with character. These grains not only enhance taste but also boost the nutritional profile significantly. You get a great dose of fiber, vitamins, and minerals, plus the added bonus of satisfying crunch from the seeds that bake into the crust.

Because of its diverse grain content, the Multigrain Harvest Loaf has a denser crumb than simple white or even standard whole wheat breads. This density means the loaf holds up beautifully to hearty sandwich fillings without falling apart, yet it remains soft enough to enjoy toasted or with a spread of butter and jam. Its nutty flavor profile is subtle yet distinct, lending itself perfectly to both savory and sweet accompaniments.

When you decide to bake this loaf at home, it's reassuring to know that while it might seem complex due to the variety of ingredients, the process itself is very approachable. Many recipes use an easy yeast method with a straightforward mixing and resting routine, so you can avoid any intimidating techniques. The relaxed mixing method also helps to preserve the texture of the grains and seeds, ensuring they stay pleasantly chewy after baking.

One key to a successful multigrain loaf is soaking some of the grains or seeds beforehand, often referred to as a "soaker." This step might feel like an extra task, but it's worth it for the enhanced moisture and tenderness it imparts. Without soaking, the grains can absorb water from the dough after baking, leaving the crumb dry and crumbly. By hydrating them ahead of time, you help the loaf retain softness and improve flavor development during fermentation.

You'll notice the loaf's crust emerges beautifully caramelized due to the natural sugars present in whole grains and seeds. The crust crisps up nicely while the inside stays moist. Home bakers often appreciate how this bread can be enjoyed fresh or even a day or two later, either toasted or straight from the loaf. Storing it properly by wrapping in a clean kitchen towel or placing in a paper bag helps maintain that fresh-baked quality without letting it get soggy.

This bread is a canvas for many variations. For instance, you might add dried cranberries or raisins for a touch of sweetness, or toss in some finely chopped nuts like walnuts or pecans for extra crunch. Herbs like rosemary or thyme can also enhance the flavor without overpowering the natural grain character. The flexibility of the recipe means you can tailor the loaf to your favorite tastes and pantry staples.

Another rewarding aspect of baking a Multigrain Harvest Loaf is its wholesome aroma filling your kitchen as it bakes. The heady smell of toasted grains combined with a warm yeast undertone makes it nearly impossible to wait until the loaf cools. This sensory experience brings a sense of accomplishment and comfort, which is why so many bakers return to multigrain recipes for everyday enjoyment.

For early bakers or those experimenting with whole grains for the first time, starting with a Multigrain Harvest Loaf teaches valuable lessons in dough hydration and timing. Balancing the flour and grain ratios, observing how the dough feels after mixing, and noticing the rising patterns all help build intuition that applies to countless other bread recipes. Patience is key here, as multigrain dough typically benefits from a slightly longer bulk fermentation to develop full flavor and structure.

Once baked, this loaf brings versatility to your homemade bread table. It's excellent for sandwiches because its firm crumb holds up well against moist ingredients like tomatoes and spreads. At breakfast, it pairs wonderfully with avocado or nut butter and a sprinkle of seeds for added texture. And it makes an excellent accompaniment to soups, stews, or roasted vegetables at lunchtime or dinner, adding a nourishing element to your meal.

In terms of ingredients, most home bakers will find everything readily available at their local grocery or natural foods store, especially if they keep a small stash of whole grains and seeds on hand. You don't need specialty flours or exotic grains to succeed in this recipe—simplicity and quality of ingredients make a huge difference. Choosing freshly milled whole wheat flour or freshly purchased seeds will naturally elevate your loaf.

Don't be discouraged if your first attempts aren't perfect. Working with multigrain doughs can be a little different than white flour doughs, mostly because of the heavier bran and rougher texture of the grains. The dough might feel sticky or sluggish at times, but gentle kneading and longer rest periods will help it become more elastic and manageable. Remember, every loaf you bake is a step closer to mastery.

One technique worth trying is the use of a Dutch oven or heavy lidded pot for baking. This method traps steam, helping the loaf develop a deep, glossy crust and a wonderful rise. The loaf gains both aesthetic appeal and a satisfying mouthfeel, which makes the extra effort entirely worth it. Even if you don't have one, placing a small pan of water in the oven can create steam and improve crust formation.

In the broader scope of healthy bread baking, the Multigrain Harvest Loaf is a crowd-pleaser that fits seamlessly into various dietary preferences. Whether you're seeking to boost fiber intake, incorporate more seeds and whole grains, or simply enjoy a more complex flavor, this recipe delivers. It's also a fantastic choice for family baking projects since the ingredients are safe and familiar, resulting in a wholesome treat everyone can enjoy.

As you continue exploring whole grain and healthy bread creations, the Multigrain Harvest Loaf serves as a reliable foundation. Its approachable method and satisfying results encourage you to experiment further with ancient grains, natural sweeteners, and creative add-ins. Each loaf you bake not only nourishes the body but also nurtures your growing confidence as a home baker dedicated to wholesome, delicious breads.

Spelt and Flaxseed Bread

Spelt and flaxseed bread stands out as one of those wonderfully wholesome loaves that feels both nourishing and satisfying with every bite. If you haven't yet experimented with spelt flour or flaxseeds in your baking, this is a fantastic way to bring something a little different to your breadbasket. Spelt is an ancient grain, closely related to wheat but with a nuttier, slightly sweet flavor that adds depth without overpowering other ingredients. When combined with flaxseeds, which are packed with omega-3 fatty acids and fiber, you get a bread that's not only tasty but also incredibly good for you.

One of the best things about baking spelt and flaxseed bread at home is its versatility. Whether you're making a simple everyday loaf or a more rustic artisan-style bread, the combination actually performs quite well without the need for complicated techniques. Spelt flour contains gluten, but it's more delicate than regular wheat gluten, so it's important to handle the dough a bit more gently. You'll want to avoid over-kneading to keep your loaf light and tender, yet well-structured.

The flaxseeds offer both texture and nutrition. When added whole, they provide a pleasant chew and a subtle crunch. Ground flaxseeds, on the other hand, integrate more fully into the dough, enriching it and helping to retain moisture. Both forms are worth trying depending on your preference, though ground flaxseed also works as a binding agent and can slightly improve the shelf life of your loaf.

Getting the hydration right in this bread is crucial. Spelt flour tends to absorb less water compared to traditional wheat flour, so you'll often find you need a bit less liquid in your dough. That said, flaxseeds absorb moisture quite well, particularly when ground, which can counterbalance the spelt's lower absorption. A good approach is to start with a slightly lower amount of water, then add more as you mix until the dough feels soft but not sticky.

When stirring in flaxseeds, some bakers like to soak them first in a bit of warm water to release their natural mucilage, a gel-like substance that can help improve dough texture and keep your bread moist for longer. Even soaking for 10 to 15 minutes can make a difference. This technique is especially handy when making spelt and flaxseed bread without additional fats or eggs, keeping the loaf tender and chewy.

Baking spelt and flaxseed bread also opens the door for experimenting with flavor add-ins. Toasted nuts, dried fruits, or even a few herbs can complement the natural nuttiness of spelt and the subtle earthiness of flaxseeds. Sunflower seeds, pumpkin seeds, or chopped walnuts all make excellent companions. However, if you prefer to keep it simple, letting the natural flavors shine through is a wonderful option too.

Handling the dough gently during shaping is something that should be emphasized. Because spelt gluten is more fragile, dough elasticity won't develop quite as robustly as with regular bread wheat. When you shape your loaf, try to use a light touch—press and fold rather than stretch vigorously. This helps prevent the dough from tearing and losing gas that the yeast has produced, which is essential for a good rise.

Rising times can also be a bit quicker with spelt flour. Keep an eye on your dough rather than the clock, aiming for it to roughly double in size before baking. Spelt's sugars and proteins feed the yeast well, encouraging a good rise, but because gluten is less strong, over-proofing can quickly cause your loaf to collapse. A shorter, well-monitored proof usually yields the best results.

Once baked, expect spelt and flaxseed bread to have a golden crust that's slightly crisp, with a crumb that's moist and tender but pleasantly chewy. The aroma during baking is warm and inviting, thanks to those nutty undertones. This bread makes a perfect canvas for everything from simple butter and jam to heartier sandwiches packed with fresh vegetables, cheeses, or smoked meats.

For those interested in nutrition, spelt and flaxseed bread is a winning choice. Spelt is rich in protein, B vitamins, and fiber, while flaxseeds are known for their anti-inflammatory properties and ability to support digestive health. Together, they create a loaf that feels both hearty and healthful without any sacrifice to taste or texture.

While spelt is often touted as easier to digest than modern wheat varieties, it's worth noting that it still contains gluten. So, if gluten sensitivity or celiac disease is a concern, this bread would not be appropriate. However, for most home bakers looking to elevate their whole grain options, spelt and flaxseed bread fits right in with a balanced diet.

If you're new to spelt, begin by substituting spelt flour for up to half of the wheat flour in your usual bread recipes to get a feel for how the dough behaves. Once comfortable, you can try recipes that call for 100% spelt flour. Similarly, flaxseeds can be added gradually, starting with two to three tablespoons per loaf, before experimenting with larger quantities for more nutritional punch and texture.

One practical tip for storing this bread is to keep it in a paper bag or bread box at room temperature for a day or two to maintain its crust. For longer storage, slicing and freezing is best. Simply thaw at room temperature or toast slices straight from the freezer for fresh taste and texture. This way, the wholesome goodness of your spelt and flaxseed bread can last without waste.

Baking your own spelt and flaxseed bread also gives you a chance to feel connected to the ingredients and process. The aroma filling your kitchen, the satisfying feel of kneading gentle dough, and finally slicing into a beautiful loaf lend a comforting rhythm to your baking routine. As you gain confidence, you might find yourself tweaking hydration or introducing new mix-ins, making this bread truly your own.

In summary, spelt and flaxseed bread offers a wonderful balance of nutrition, flavor, and texture that's accessible for bakers of all skill levels. Whether you're aiming to expand your whole grain repertoire or seeking a healthier option for everyday bread, this loaf delivers on all fronts. With a bit of practice and attention to detail, you'll enjoy fresh, homemade spelt and flaxseed bread that's delicious in every way.

QUINOA OAT BREAD

Adding quinoa and oats to your bread dough brings more than just hearty texture and flavor—it introduces a powerful nutrition boost that's perfect for home bakers craving wholesome, satisfying loaves. Quinoa, often dubbed a supergrain, is rich in protein and essential amino acids, which complement the fiber-packed oats to create a bread that's as nourishing as it is delicious. This combination lends a slightly nutty flavor and wonderful chewiness, elevating your everyday loaf into something special without complicating the process.

One of the best parts about baking quinoa oat bread is how adaptable it is. Whether you're new to bread baking or have several batches under your belt, this recipe fits smoothly into your routine. The oats add moisture and tenderness, while quinoa offers a subtle earthiness that pairs beautifully with whole wheat or all-purpose flour. Plus, the vibrant little quinoa seeds sprinkled throughout give the crust a lovely visual interest that suggests care and artistry in your homemade bread.

Quinoa oat bread also stands up well to a variety of uses. It's sturdy enough to hold hearty sandwich fillings without falling apart, yet tender enough to enjoy with a simple pat of butter or jam at breakfast. Because of its balanced flavor profile, it pairs wonderfully with both savory and sweet accompaniments, making it a versatile staple in your bread lineup. Imagine fresh slices toasted alongside eggs and avocado for a nourishing start to your day, or piled with roasted vegetables and hummus for a satisfying lunch.

Baking with quinoa requires some special attention, mainly because the seeds need to be cooked before adding them to the dough. This step unlocks their digestibility and softness, ensuring the final loaf isn't gritty or dry. Once cooked and cooled, the quinoa mixes right into the dough, imparting moisture that keeps the bread fresh longer than many traditional loaves. That means fewer wasted leftovers and more delicious homemade bread ready to enjoy.

Oats in bread do more than just add flavor—they contribute to a perfect crumb and crust that stays tender over time. Rolled oats or old-fashioned oats work best here, offering a balance between structure and chew without overwhelming the loaf. You can even sprinkle oats on top before baking for a rustic touch that enhances the bread's appearance. Integrating oats into the dough also subtly sweetens the bread, making it especially appealing if you prefer your bread on the milder, naturally sweet side.

One challenge you might run into when baking quinoa oat bread is finding the right balance of hydration. Both quinoa and oats absorb water differently compared to plain flour, so the dough feels a bit stickier at first. Don't be discouraged. With practice, you'll develop a feel for when the dough has come together just right—smooth, slightly tacky to the touch, and elastic. Remember to keep your flour measurements flexible, adding a little more or less depending on your working environment and exact ingredients.

Don't shy away from letting the dough rise a bit longer than usual. Whole grain ingredients tend to slow down yeast activity, so patience pays off here. A longer rise encourages better flavor development and allows the natural sweetness of the grains to shine through. When baked, the crust browns to a tempting golden hue, crisp but not hard, creating a perfect contrast to the tender crumb within.

To make your first quinoa oat bread, start by gathering quality ingredients: cooked quinoa, rolled oats, your choice of flour, yeast, salt, a bit of honey or maple syrup for subtle sweetness, and warm water to bring everything together. Don't rush the mixing and kneading stages; these ensure your loaf rises evenly and gains the ideal texture. Since this bread benefits from a more deliberate approach, set aside some focused time, and enjoy the calming rhythm of working dough between your hands.

Once you slide your loaf into the oven, the warm aroma that fills your kitchen hints at the wholesome goodness inside. As the crust crisps and browns, you'll notice hints of nuttiness and oats melding with the slight toastiness of bread baking to perfection. When it's done, allow it to cool completely so the crumb firms up; slicing too early can squash the delicate structure, so patience here makes all the difference.

Slices of quinoa oat bread keep well stored in a bread box or wrapped in a clean towel, maintaining their freshness for several days. If you want to extend the life even further, freezing individual slices works wonderfully—just pop them in the toaster when ready for a quick, fresh taste. This makes quinoa oat bread an excellent choice for busy households, where convenience and nutrition need to go hand in hand.

Experimenting with mix-ins like seeds or nuts can take this bread up another notch. Sunflower seeds, flaxseeds, or chopped walnuts complement the nutty flavor of quinoa and oats, adding extra texture and nutritional value. You can sprinkle these on top or knead them into the dough, tailoring the loaf to your personal taste and dietary preferences. These tweaks make quinoa oat bread not just a nourishing choice but a canvas for creativity.

Beyond the taste and nutrition, baking quinoa oat bread is a reminder that healthy eating doesn't mean sacrificing flavor or the joy of baking from scratch. Each loaf you pull from the oven reinforces the satisfying connection between hands-on crafting and nourishing your body. For beginners, this bread is approachable yet rewarding, offering straightforward steps that build confidence while teaching valuable skills.

In the larger picture of whole grain and healthy bread creations, quinoa oat bread stands out for its balance of nutrients and its welcoming texture. It shows how thoughtful ingredient combinations can transform basic bread-making into a mindful act of self-care. As you continue exploring different whole grain breads, this recipe offers a dependable favorite that makes wholesome baking feel effortless and genuinely enjoyable.

CHIA SEED SANDWICH BREAD

In the world of whole grain and healthy bread baking, chia seed sandwich bread holds a unique place. It combines the nutritional powerhouse of chia seeds with the familiar comfort of a soft, sandwich-ready loaf. This bread isn't just about health benefits—it's about flavor and texture, too. The tiny chia seeds add a subtle nutty crunch that lifts the bread's character without overpowering it. Plus, they bring a boost of fiber, omega-3 fatty acids, and a nice dose of protein, making every slice a little more nourishing.

Many home bakers might hesitate when they see the word "chia" in a recipe, thinking it's complicated or the seeds will disrupt the loaf's texture. But that's far from the truth. Chia seed sandwich bread is surprisingly easy to make, even if you're new to baking whole grain loaves. What makes it approachable is that you start with a classic sandwich bread base—flour, yeast, water, salt, and a touch of sweetener—and simply incorporate the chia seeds during the mixing stage. This gives you the chance to enjoy the familiar process of making bread while embracing healthier ingredients.

One of chia's standout qualities is its ability to absorb a lot of liquid and form a gel-like consistency. This means that when chia seeds hydrate in the dough, they help retain moisture, resulting in a tender, soft crumb that stays fresh longer than many other whole grain breads. For home bakers, this quality is especially valuable because it keeps your bread from drying out too quickly, so each sandwich stays moist and pleasant to eat for days.

When mixing the dough, it's best to soak your chia seeds in water beforehand. This simple step activates their gelatinous nature and integrates them smoothly into your dough, avoiding any gritty pockets. A quick soak of 10 to 15 minutes before combining with the flour and yeast makes a huge difference. Once the dough comes together, you'll notice it's slightly tackier compared to plain white bread dough, but don't be alarmed. This dough behaves differently because of the gelled chia seeds, so handling it with a bit more care during kneading and shaping leads to the best results.

Speaking of kneading, this recipe benefits from gentle, mindful kneading rather than vigorous action. The chia's moisture retention means the dough remains softer and less elastic than typical sandwich dough, so too much kneading can break down the structure. Aim for a kneading time just long enough for the dough to become smooth and a little springy—about 5 to 7 minutes by hand or a few minutes in a stand mixer on low speed.

After kneading, you'll let the dough rise. It's a good idea to watch the dough's fermentation carefully here. Because chia seeds change the dough's hydration, rising times can be somewhat shorter or longer than classic sandwich bread. Usually, one rise lasting around 1 to 1 ½ hours at room temperature should double the dough's size comfortably. Check for a light, airy feel when pressing a finger gently into the dough—if it springs back slowly and leaves a small indentation, it's ready to shape.

When it comes to shaping the loaf, use a standard bread pan for perfectly sized slices ideal for sandwiches. The dough is soft, so try to handle it delicately. Form it into a smooth, tight log before placing it into the greased pan, then cover and allow a second rise. This proof should take roughly 45 minutes to 1 hour, or until the dough rises about halfway above the edge of the pan.

One subtle trick that can elevate your chia seed sandwich bread is brushing the top with a bit of milk or egg wash before baking. This adds a gentle sheen and encourages a nicely browned crust. The crust should remain tender but with a slight chew—ideal for sandwich bread that holds up well to spreads and fillings without crumbling or snapping.

Baking typically occurs at 350°F (175°C), with the loaf going in the oven for about 30 to 35 minutes. You'll know the bread is done when it's beautifully golden and sounds hollow when tapped on the bottom. Using an instant-read thermometer is a great idea if you want to be precise: the internal temperature should hit about 190°F (88°C). Once baked, the bread needs to cool completely on a wire rack before slicing. This final step allows the crumb to set, so you get clean, even slices without squishing the loaf.

The versatility of this chia seed sandwich bread really shines through after baking. It pairs wonderfully with everything from classic peanut butter and jelly to savory fillings like turkey and avocado. Because the bread is lightly flavored with the mild nuttiness of chia, it complements a wide variety of tastes without overwhelming your favorite sandwich ingredients.

Chia seed sandwich bread also shines as a base for toasts or open-faced sandwiches. A simple smear of cream cheese topped with fresh tomatoes or avocado and a sprinkle of salt reveals the bread's gentle texture and wholesome nature. It toasts evenly, developing a crisp crust while maintaining a soft, chewy center.

For bakers looking to customize the recipe, chia seeds open doors to creative additions. You might mix in whole flaxseeds, sunflower seeds, or even rolled oats to the dough for extra texture and nutrition. Just remember to balance hydration if you add more dry ingredients. The chia seeds' absorbency means you might need to tweak the water a little to keep the dough comfortable, but this is easily managed with small adjustments.

A final note for busy bakers: chia seed sandwich bread is an excellent candidate for dough preparation ahead of time. You can prepare your dough in the evening, allow for a slow, refrigerated fermentation overnight, and then bake fresh bread first thing in the morning. Chilling the dough enhances flavor complexity and helps control rising times, which is especially helpful when you're juggling schedules.

In summary, chia seed sandwich bread is a fantastic entry point into whole grain and healthy loaf baking. It brings impressive nutritional benefits without sacrificing texture or taste. With some simple preparation and a few little tweaks to your standard sandwich bread technique, you'll soon have a loaf that's as hearty and healthful as it is delicious and versatile. Whether you're packing sandwiches for lunch, setting a wholesome breakfast table, or simply enjoying a fresh slice with homemade jam, this bread blends tradition and nutrition effortlessly.

So, give this recipe a try and enjoy how chia seeds elevate your everyday bread baking experience. It's the perfect way to bring more whole grains and superfoods right into your kitchen with each warm, inviting loaf.

HIGH-FIBER BREAKFAST LOAF

When it comes to maximizing nutrition in the first meal of the day, a high-fiber breakfast loaf stands out as an excellent choice. This type of bread not only fuels your morning with sustained energy but also supports digestive health, thanks to its rich fiber content. Unlike typical white breads, which are usually low in dietary fiber, a high-fiber loaf incorporates whole grains, seeds, and sometimes nuts that offer a flavorful and hearty start to your day. This loaf is perfect for toasting and pairing with simple toppings like nut butter, fresh fruit preserves, or even a soft scrambled egg.

Creating a high-fiber breakfast loaf might sound intimidating at first, especially if you're new to baking, but it doesn't have to be. The key is in balancing the ingredients so the loaf remains moist and tender while delivering a dense dose of fiber. Whole wheat flour forms the base here, often combined with other grains or flours such as oat, rye, or spelt. Adding flaxseeds, chia seeds, or sunflower seeds not only increases the fiber content but also introduces delightful texture contrasts. These seeds provide crunch and subtle nutty nuances that make every bite interesting.

One of the great things about this loaf is its versatility. You can easily tweak the recipe depending on what you have on hand or your nutritional goals. For instance, swapping some of the whole wheat flour with rolled oats or oat bran can boost the soluble fiber, which helps manage cholesterol levels. Incorporating ground flaxseed means you're adding omega-3 fats alongside fiber, enhancing the overall health benefits. Plus, the natural sweetness that comes from honey or maple syrup melts into the crust during baking, adding just a touch of indulgence without overwhelming the wholesome flavor.

From a practical standpoint, mixing the dough for a high-fiber breakfast loaf follows much of the same process as other whole grain breads, but there are some things you should keep in mind. High-fiber flours tend to absorb more liquid than refined flours, so adjusting the hydration level is crucial to avoid ending up with a dry or crumbly finish. Start with slightly more water or milk in the recipe and add it gradually, paying close attention to how the dough feels. A moist, tacky dough is a good sign that you're on the right track. You'll also want to give the dough sufficient time to rise; slower fermentation at a cooler room temperature can develop better flavor and texture, especially when working with denser whole grains.

Baking this loaf at home also offers the chance to simplify your morning routine. Instead of reaching for packaged, processed breads with added sugars and preservatives, making your own means you control every ingredient. It's an empowering process that encourages healthier choices without sacrificing ease or taste. Plus, the aroma of freshly baked bread wafting through your kitchen is both comforting and motivating, setting a positive tone for the day ahead.

One piece of advice for those trying this loaf for the first time is to experiment with mix-ins that add extra fiber while enhancing flavor. Chopped nuts like walnuts or pecans bring crunch and subtle richness, while dried fruits such as raisins, apricots, or cranberries introduce bursts of natural sweetness. You can even toss in shredded carrot or zucchini for moisture and nutrition, making the loaf a near-complete breakfast by itself. These additions are especially welcome for picky eaters or anyone wanting to sneak in additional servings of whole foods.

When it's time to bake, aim for a golden-brown crust with a slight sheen, which indicates proper caramelization of the natural sugars and a well-developed crust. The loaf should sound hollow when tapped at the bottom, signaling it's fully baked. Once out of the oven, give it ample time to cool on a wire rack. Cooling allows the crumb to set properly, making slicing easier and preventing your loaf from turning gummy inside.

Storing the high-fiber breakfast loaf is straightforward. Since it contains whole grains and seeds, it will keep well at room temperature for a couple of days if wrapped in a clean tea towel or kept in a bread box that encourages airflow to prevent excess moisture buildup. For longer storage, slicing and freezing individual pieces works wonderfully—you can pull out just what you need each morning and toast it straight from the freezer, saving time without compromising freshness.

For those who love a hands-off approach, try preparing the dough the evening before and letting it ferment slowly in the refrigerator overnight. This method not only fits neatly into a busy lifestyle but also develops deeper flavor and improves the loaf's texture. The next morning, you just shape it and pop it into the oven. It's a win-win for freshness and convenience.

Let's also talk about the nutritional aspects. A well-crafted high-fiber breakfast loaf can pack between 3 to 6 grams of fiber per serving, depending on ingredients and portion size. This contributes significantly to the daily recommended fiber intake, which many people fall short of. Fiber helps regulate blood sugar levels, supports gut health, and can aid in weight management by promoting feelings of fullness. Starting your day with a fiber-rich loaf can improve overall digestion and energy levels throughout the morning, making it more than just a tasty treat.

Another reason this particular loaf makes a fantastic morning choice is its compatibility with an array of spreads and toppings. Nut butters, cream cheese, avocado, or even simply olive oil and sea salt work beautifully. The wholesome nature of the bread complements savory or sweet flavors equally well, giving you endless possibilities to keep breakfast exciting. Feel free to adorn your slices with fresh seasonal herbs or a sprinkle of cinnamon for variety.

Experimenting with this loaf can also be a perfect way to introduce nutritious ingredients that might otherwise be overlooked. For example, using wheat bran or oat bran in small amounts will enrich the loaf with insoluble fiber without drastically changing the taste or structure. Similarly, a modest amount of psyllium husk powder can boost fiber content and improve crumb softness, which many home bakers appreciate when working with dense whole grain flours.

Finally, don't shy away from making this recipe your own. Measure carefully but listen to your instincts about dough texture and flavor balance. Baking bread is as much about developing your intuition as it is following ingredients precisely. The high-fiber breakfast loaf is incredibly forgiving and adaptable, making it the ideal project for a home cook eager to step beyond basic white or sandwich breads. With a little practice, you'll have a reliable, delicious loaf that not only tastes great but also makes mornings healthier and more rewarding.

GLUTEN-FREE ARTISAN BREAD

Creating gluten-free artisan bread is an exciting challenge that rewards patience and creativity. For home bakers eager to enjoy the rich, satisfying texture and flavor of an artisan loaf without gluten, it's a journey worth taking. The goal here isn't just to replicate traditional bread but to embrace the uniqueness of gluten-free ingredients and methods. This section will guide you through the essentials, helping you craft beautiful, crusty, and flavorful gluten-free artisan breads from scratch.

Unlike wheat-based artisan breads, gluten-free versions rely heavily on the properties of alternative flours and starches to mimic that ideal chewy crumb and crispy crust. Blending flours like brown rice, sorghum, or millet with binding agents such as xanthan gum or psyllium husk is crucial. These ingredients help provide structure and elasticity, both of which gluten naturally imparts. Understanding these building blocks sets the foundation for a loaf that not only holds together but also delights the senses.

One thing many home bakers find encouraging about gluten-free artisan bread is how forgiving the process can be. Because gluten-free doughs lack the elasticity that requires kneading, you'll usually work with batters or very soft dough. This means less kneading, less mess, and often, less frustration. Instead, most of the work comes in mixing well, allowing enough rise time, and mastering the baking techniques to develop that sought-after crust.

Hydration plays a different, but equally important role in gluten-free bread. These doughs absorb water differently — often requiring higher hydration levels to achieve the right consistency. The dough will appear wetter and looser compared to traditional wheat doughs, but this is expected and necessary. Over time, as you gain experience, you'll learn how to gauge when the dough is just right. Using a kitchen scale becomes indispensable here because precise measurements help you get reliable results every time.

Patience is key during the rising phase. Gluten-free breads usually demand longer fermentation times to develop flavor and improve texture. You might notice that these doughs don't double in size the way their wheat counterparts do. Instead, subtle changes like increased puffiness and a slight spring when pressed indicate readiness. It helps to keep your dough in a warm, draft-free environment to encourage the yeast's work, and in cooler kitchens, a proofer or turned-off oven with just the light on can provide steady warmth.

Shaping gluten-free artisan bread is less about tight formation and more about gentle handling. Because these doughs lack elasticity, trying to shape them like traditional bread might cause them to collapse. Instead, transferring the dough carefully onto parchment paper or a well-floured surface will set it up for baking without deflating it. Some bakers turn to proofing baskets lined with cloth to help hold the shape during the final rise. The results are loaves with rustic, charming imperfections that only add to their artisan appeal.

Getting the crust right is one of the biggest rewards when baking gluten-free artisan bread. You'll want a deep golden-brown color with a crisp, crackling exterior. Achieving this often involves baking the bread with steam during the first part of the bake. You can create steam by placing a pan of hot water in the oven or spritzing the oven walls with water right after sliding the loaf in. This moisture delays the crust formation just enough to allow the interior to expand fully. Once the steam phase is over, the heat begins to dry out the surface, encouraging that satisfying crunch.

Because gluten-free breads can dry out faster than wheat bread, it's common to bake slowly and at slightly lower temperatures to preserve moisture inside while crisping the crust. If you own a baking stone or steel, this is the time to use it—it helps create that radiant heat from below which encourages a better oven spring and crust texture. Keeping an eye, or better yet, using a digital thermometer to check the loaf's internal temp can take the guesswork out of doneness. Aim for around 205°F to 210°F to ensure the crumb is well set without being gummy.

Flavor development in gluten-free artisan bread is where you can really let your style shine. Because you're working with different grains and blends, the taste profile can be quite distinct and interesting. Adding ingredients like roasted nuts, seeds, or herbs introduces delightful textures and aromas. Many bakers enjoy incorporating a sourdough starter to bring complexity and tang to the loaf. If you choose to go the sourdough route, just remember that gluten-free starters behave differently, often needing more frequent feeding and hydration adjustments.

One practical tip for beginners is to prepare your gluten-free flours in advance through toasting or blending batches. Toasting enhances the nutty flavors of grains like quinoa or millet and can elevate your bread's taste significantly. Plus, making your own flour blends tailored to your preferences means you'll start with a custom mix that suits your baking style and dietary needs.

Gluten-free artisan baking can seem intimidating at first, especially when comparing loaves side-by-side with traditional bread. However, the magic lies in embracing the differences rather than forcing a direct comparison. Over time, you'll develop a feel for the dough — its looks, its smells, its behavior during fermentation, and finally, its bake. This connection fosters a deeper appreciation of each loaf that comes out of your oven, knowing it's crafted with care and intention.

Finally, don't hesitate to experiment. Switch up flours to discover new flavor combinations, try different hydration levels, or add unique ingredients like dried fruits or spices. Every loaf is an opportunity to learn and create something uniquely yours. The world of gluten-free artisan bread is vast and rewarding for those willing to explore without fear of the occasional misstep.

With the guidance provided so far and plentiful recipes throughout this book, you have everything needed to embark on your own gluten-free artisan baking adventure. Each loaf is more than just nourishment—it's a labor of love that brings the craft and joy of home baking to life, free from gluten yet full of character and flavor.

Low-Carb Almond Flour Bread

Finding a satisfying low-carb bread can be a challenge, especially for home bakers new to alternative flours and grain substitutes. Almond flour bread offers a fantastic option for anyone looking to cut carbs but still enjoy the comforting texture and flavor of freshly baked bread. Unlike traditional wheat-based breads, this recipe relies on almond flour, which is naturally gluten-free and packed with protein, healthy fats, and fiber. It provides a moist crumb and a subtly nutty taste that works beautifully for sandwiches, toast, or simply served warm with a pat of butter.

What makes almond flour bread so appealing is how approachable it is, even if you're just starting to explore low-carb or gluten-free baking. The ingredients list is straightforward—primarily almond flour, eggs, a little baking powder, and some salt with optional flavor boosters like herbs or seeds. Since almond flour lacks gluten, which normally gives bread its structure, this recipe compensates by using eggs to bind and leaven the dough. The result is a loaf that's dense but tender, with a satisfying bite and a slightly crisp crust.

You won't need a stand mixer or special equipment to whip up this loaf. A sturdy mixing bowl, a whisk or fork, and a loaf pan are all it takes. This makes it perfect for anyone aiming to keep their bread baking process simple. The dough itself is much more batter-like than traditional yeast doughs, so kneading isn't necessary—just mix and pour.

Because it doesn't rely on yeast, almond flour bread stays fresh much longer than some gluten-free yeasted breads that can stale quickly. After baking, allow the bread to cool completely before slicing to ensure the best texture.

Store leftovers in an airtight container at room temperature, or keep them in the fridge for up to a week. It also freezes very well, slicing easily once thawed. This means you can bake a large batch on the weekend and enjoy fresh low-carb slices throughout the week.

One common concern when baking with almond flour is how moist the bread can sometimes turn out. Balancing the right wet-to-dry ingredient ratio is key to preventing a gummy or overly dense loaf. Too many eggs or wet ingredients will weigh the bread down, while too little can result in a crumbly texture. In this recipe, proportions have been carefully tested to hit the ideal sweet spot.

Flavors are another area where almond flour bread really shines. While the base recipe yields a subtle nutty taste, it's an excellent canvas for customization. Feel free to stir in chopped fresh herbs like rosemary or thyme, or add a handful of toasted seeds for extra texture and flavor dimension. Crushed garlic or grated Parmesan can make an enticing savory twist, perfect for pairing with soups or cheeses. If you prefer a hint of sweetness, consider adding a teaspoon of honey or a sprinkle of cinnamon and nutmeg for a comforting morning bread.

Adaptability is a hallmark of this loaf. For bakers who need a grain-free option, it's naturally gluten-free when using pure almond flour. It's also suitable for paleo and keto diets, which makes it a versatile choice for various nutritional needs. Just double-check that any add-ins you choose align with your dietary preferences.

When baking almond flour bread, oven temperature and baking time matter quite a bit. Typically, the bread bakes at a moderate temperature—around 350°F—to allow even cooking without burning the crust. Baking longer at a lower heat helps develop that light crust while giving the inside time to set properly without drying out. Keeping an eye on the bread during the last 10 minutes of baking can make the difference between a perfectly baked loaf and one that's either too moist or too dry.

Unlike yeast breads, almond flour bread doesn't undergo a rise, so expect a dense but tender crumb rather than a fluffy one. This makes it ideal for toast since the bread holds its shape without crumbling. It's excellent for open-faced sandwiches or as a base for avocado toast, where you want a firm yet soft texture that won't sag under the weight of toppings.

Another tip for success is to use blanched almond flour, which is lighter in color and finer in texture than natural almond meal. This subtle difference results in a smoother crumb and avoids any gritty mouthfeel. If you only have almond meal on hand, it may still work, but expect a slightly coarser bread with a darker color and nuttier intensity.

One of the perks of making this bread yourself is control over what goes into it. Many store-bought low-carb breads include preservatives, fillers, or unfamiliar additives that might not fit everyone's preferences. Baking at home lets you use all-natural ingredients and customize flavors without compromise. Plus, warm homemade bread fresh from the oven is hard to beat.

This bread pairs well with breakfast favorites like scrambled eggs or smoked salmon and cream cheese. It's also a wonderful base for sandwiches filled with grilled vegetables, roasted turkey, or even a classic BLT. Its dense structure supports hearty fillings without falling apart, so it's quite versatile for daily meals and snacks alike.

The step-by-step approach is simple: mix wet ingredients thoroughly, then gently fold in the almond flour and baking powder blend. Be careful not to overmix; just combine until no large lumps remain. Pour the batter into a greased loaf pan and bake until a toothpick inserted near the center comes out clean. The bread will pull away slightly from the edges of the pan when ready.

Keep in mind that almond flour bread's flavor is inherently different from wheat-based loaves. It's not about replicating the light, airy crumb of traditional bread but embracing a new texture and taste that's nourishing and delicious in its own right. By celebrating these differences, you open up new possibilities in your bread baking repertoire.

In conclusion, low-carb almond flour bread is a fantastic bread baking adventure for those wanting to explore healthier options without sacrificing homemade quality. Its easy preparation, rich nutrition, and versatility make it a worthy addition to any home baker's collection. Whether you're managing dietary restrictions or just curious about alternative flours, this loaf offers a gratifying, reliable option that's both delicious and wholesome. Give it a try—you might just find a new favorite to keep on hand for everyday enjoyment.

BUCKWHEAT HONEY BREAD

Buckwheat Honey Bread stands out as a delightful twist on traditional whole grain loaves, offering a rich, nutty flavor complemented by the gentle sweetness of honey. This bread is a fantastic choice for those looking to explore hearty, flavorful baked goods without relying solely on wheat flours. Buckwheat, although often mistaken for a grain, is actually a seed—related to rhubarb and sorrel—which gives the bread a unique texture and a slightly earthy taste that pairs beautifully with the warmth of honey. The result is a loaf that feels wholesome and comforting but also carries an intriguing depth of flavor that will keep you coming back for more.

Incorporating buckwheat flour into your bread baking repertoire has several benefits. For one, it's gluten-free, making it a valuable addition for those experimenting with blending flours to reduce gluten content without sacrificing structure entirely. When combined with wheat flour or other whole grain flours, buckwheat enhances nutritional value, providing a good source of protein, fiber, and minerals like magnesium and manganese. Meanwhile, the honey brings not just sweetness but also moisture, allowing the crumb to stay soft longer. This makes the bread wonderful for sandwiches, toasting, or enjoying simply with a pat of butter.

One thing to keep in mind is that buckwheat flour behaves differently than wheat flour in bread dough. It lacks gluten-forming proteins, so a 100% buckwheat loaf tends to be dense and crumbly. Most recipes for Buckwheat Honey Bread blend buckwheat with bread flour or whole wheat flour to strike a balance between nutty flavor and a pleasant, slightly chewy texture. This combination helps achieve a loaf that rises adequately, holds together well, and still has that signature taste. If you're new to working with buckwheat, expect the dough to be stickier and less elastic compared to doughs made from just wheat flour, which makes the kneading and shaping process a bit gentler and more forgiving.

Starting with the recipe, the foundational ingredients include buckwheat flour, bread flour, active dry yeast, honey, warm water, and a touch of salt. The honey should be raw or unprocessed if possible, as it has a more vibrant flavor and also contributes to the bread's moist crumb. When mixing, it's best to dissolve the honey in warm water along with the yeast to give the yeast a small energy boost. This step ensures a lively fermentation, which is crucial because the added density of buckwheat flour can slow down the rise.

Let the dough rest and rise in a warm spot until it doubles in size—a timeframe that may take a bit longer than typical wheat-based doughs, especially if your kitchen is cool. Once risen, the dough is gently shaped into a loaf or placed into a bread pan. A final rise follows, which sets the stage for a tender crumb and nicely formed structure. Baking typically happens at a moderate temperature to ensure the loaf cooks evenly without burning the crust, and it usually needs about 35 to 40 minutes in the oven.

The aroma that fills your kitchen while baking Buckwheat Honey Bread is inviting in itself—the sweet, slightly toasted scent paired with notes of honey and earthiness is comforting in a way that makes it perfect for weekend mornings, lazy brunches, or anytime you want a versatile bread with personality. Once cooled, this loaf offers a beautiful, medium-brown crust and a crumb that's moist with well-distributed air pockets, giving it a satisfying chew without being overly dense.

Serving suggestions are abundant with this bread. It pairs beautifully with fruit preserves, cream cheese, or avocado for breakfast or snacks. For dinner, try it alongside stews or hearty soups; its robust flavor stands up well to strong, savory dishes. Toasting enhances the honey notes and adds a pleasant crispness to each slice. Many home bakers also enjoy slicing and freezing this bread to keep it fresh for longer periods—just toast the slices directly from the freezer to revive their warmth and texture.

As you get comfortable baking Buckwheat Honey Bread, feel free to experiment with additions that complement its natural flavors. Toasted walnuts, sunflower seeds, or a sprinkle of rolled oats on top before baking add interesting texture contrasts. Some bakers like to fold in dried fruits like raisins or chopped dates to deepen the loaf's sweetness without overpowering the buckwheat's earthiness. These small tweaks make the recipe your own and provide room for creativity as you deepen your skills.

One of the most rewarding aspects of baking this bread is how accessible it is for home bakers who want to try a wholesome bread outside the usual wheat-based options. It introduces you to a broader palette of flavors and textures and broadens your baking horizons. Since the recipe doesn't require complicated techniques or specialty equipment, it's just as suitable for beginners as it is for those more experienced who want to add healthy variety to their bread baking routine.

While baking Buckwheat Honey Bread, it's also helpful to pay attention to the moisture content as buckwheat flour can absorb water differently depending on its freshness and brand. Sometimes a little extra water or honey might be necessary to keep the dough from becoming too stiff. Likewise, ensuring your yeast is fresh and your water temperature is ideal (around 100 to 110 degrees Fahrenheit) helps build a lively, well-risen loaf.

With its balance of nutrition, flavor, and ease, Buckwheat Honey Bread encourages home bakers to lean into whole grains without sacrificing taste or texture. Its slightly sweet, deeply satisfying profile makes it a versatile bread worth mastering. Baking this loaf regularly helps build confidence in working with alternative flours and teaches valuable lessons about hydration, fermentation, and crumb texture that apply to many other healthy bread recipes.

Ultimately, Buckwheat Honey Bread is more than just a loaf—it's a gateway to wholesome baking that feels approachable and rewarding. Its rustic appeal and lovely flavor invite you to explore the world of whole grain breads while making something deliciously homemade. Whether eaten fresh from the oven or toasted with a drizzle of honey or a smear of nut butter, this bread consistently delights and inspires home bakers to keep creating fresh loaves packed with taste and nutrition.

RYE AND CARAWAY SEED BREAD

Rye and caraway seed bread holds a special place among whole grain and healthy bread creations. Unlike typical wheat breads, rye offers a distinct flavor profile and denser crumb that many home bakers find both challenging and rewarding. If you're looking for a bread that's rich in taste and complexity but still approachable, this loaf is an excellent choice to add to your repertoire. The earthiness of rye flour combined with the slightly spicy, anise-like aroma of caraway seeds makes for a satisfying bread that pairs beautifully with both savory and sweet accompaniments.

One of the key things to understand about rye bread is the composition of the flour itself. Rye flour doesn't behave the same way wheat flour does. It has less gluten, which results in a denser and moister loaf. This characteristic can initially throw off beginner bakers who are used to lighter, fluffier wheat breads. However, with the right technique and a few pointers, making rye and caraway seed bread at home becomes less intimidating. A well-made rye loaf has a wonderfully moist crumb, chewy texture, and a flavor depth that often surprises those who expect a simple hearty bread.

When it comes to caraway seeds, they're not just a garnish but an essential component bringing flavor and aroma that elevates the bread. These tiny seeds release their oils slowly during the baking process, infusing the loaf with a nutty, slightly peppery, and aromatic note. Caraway is a traditional spice for rye bread that balances the naturally tangy flavor developed during fermentation. While it might be tempting to add a lot of seeds, a balanced amount ensures they enhance rather than overpower the rye's subtle flavors.

The mixing and proofing stages of rye and caraway bread demand special attention. Rye dough is stickier and less elastic than wheat dough, partly because of the different protein structure and high water absorption of rye flour. It's important not to overwork the dough, as excess kneading can cause the crumb to tighten up excessively, resulting in a dry loaf. Instead, a gentle mix combined with a longer fermentation lets the flavors mature, some gluten form, and the dough develop the desired rise and texture.

One practical tip for working with rye dough is to incorporate a small percentage of bread flour or a higher-gluten flour. This blend supports better structure and improves handling without diluting rye's characteristic flavor too much. You'll often find recipes call for a mix of rye and wheat flours, giving you a bread that's both authentic and easier to work with than 100% rye flour. Using this combination allows the loaf to achieve a nice rise and crumb while retaining that signature rye taste and dense, moist quality.

Caraway seeds can be incorporated into the dough either whole or lightly crushed. Crushing them slightly releases their essential oils, which intensifies the flavor in the finished bread. Some bakers like to toast the seeds briefly before mixing them in to deepen their aroma, but this step is optional. Both methods yield delicious results, so it comes down to personal preference. It's also nice to sprinkle a handful of caraway seeds on top of the dough before baking for an inviting aroma and decorative touch.

Fermentation plays a vital role in developing rye bread's full potential. Unlike many wheat bread recipes that emphasize quick rising times, rye bread benefits significantly from longer, slower fermentation. This process encourages the natural sourness that balances the sweetness of the grain and the sharpness of the caraway. Letting the dough proof slowly, ideally in a cool place or even refrigerated overnight, deepens its flavor and improves the bread's texture.

When you shape your rye and caraway seed loaf, remember that your goal is to handle the dough gently. Because of the rye's lower gluten content, it doesn't hold air as well as wheat dough, so the loaf will be denser. A traditional shaping method is to create a rounded loaf or an oblong shape, depending on your baking vessel or preferences. Don't worry if the dough feels sticky or doesn't maintain a perfect shape; rye bread often bakes with a rustic, artisanal appearance that's part of its charm.

Baking rye bread requires some adjustments, especially in temperature and time. Rye absorbs more moisture, and a slightly longer bake at moderate heat ensures the crumb cooks through without drying out the crust. If you have a baking stone or Dutch oven, those tools excel at retaining heat and creating a moist yet crusty loaf. You'll notice a beautiful dark patina on the crust after baking, which contrasts wonderfully with the tender interior. The rich aroma that fills your kitchen during this process is rewarding on its own.

One of the best things about rye and caraway bread is its versatility. It's a superb sandwich base for strong, savory fillings like smoked meats, sharp cheeses, or pickled vegetables. It's equally enjoyable just toasted and slathered with good butter, honey, or jam. The dense, chewy texture holds up well to hearty toppings and dips, making it a staple in many households around the world. Over time, many bakers grow attached to this loaf because it has a comforting, homey feel and a sense of tradition that connects you to centuries of baking history.

As a home baker, you'll find that rye and caraway seed bread opens up exciting new horizons beyond the usual wheat loaves. This bread encourages you to experiment with flavors and textures and to develop a deeper appreciation for whole grain baking. Because it requires some patience and a gentle touch, it's an excellent bread for improving your skills and understanding dough behavior. By mastering it, you build confidence and diversify your bread baking abilities.

One final piece of advice: don't be discouraged if your first rye loaf isn't perfect. The density, flavor, and crumb of rye bread are quite different from typical wheat breads, so the learning curve can be steep at first. Each loaf teaches you more about hydration levels, fermentation times, and handling techniques. Your senses will become attuned to rye dough's nuances, helping you adjust and improve with practice. Eventually, you'll develop your own rhythm and preferences that make rye and caraway seed bread a regular feature in your baking routine.

Incorporating this recipe into your baking repertoire not only expands your skills but also adds a wholesome, flavorful bread option to your table. Rye and caraway seed bread is the perfect choice for those who love hearty, nutritious breads with character. With minimal fuss and some patience, you'll be rewarded with loaves that offer both a satisfying chew and complex taste. Whether you're making sandwiches or enjoying a simple slice with butter, this bread is bound to become a comforting favorite in your kitchen.

Chapter 4
SOURDOUGH MASTERY AND SIGNATURE LOAVES

Building on the basics you've already learned, mastering sourdough opens up a whole new world of flavor and texture that can elevate your baking to artisan levels without overwhelming complexity. Creating and nurturing your own sourdough starter becomes a rewarding ritual, connecting you to the natural fermentation process that brings bread to life with tangy depth and crusty beauty. As you practice, you'll discover that sourdough isn't just about technique but about patience, timing, and experimentation with signature loaves that suit your taste—from classic boules and crusty baguettes to soft focaccia and even creative uses for discard like crackers and cinnamon rolls. This chapter guides you through the essential principles to confidently bake these breads at home, inspiring you to develop your personal sourdough style effortlessly and consistently.

How to Make a Sourdough Starter

If you're serious about mastering sourdough and creating your own signature loaves, starting with a vibrant, healthy sourdough starter is absolutely crucial. This living culture is the very heart of sourdough baking. It's a simple mixture of flour and water that captures wild yeast and friendly bacteria from the environment. Over time, these microscopic organisms grow and ferment the mixture, producing the unique tang and natural rise that defines sourdough bread.

The beauty of making your own starter is that it connects you directly to the process and allows you to bake bread with a depth of flavor that commercial yeast just can't match. While it may seem intimidating at first, creating a starter is actually quite straightforward. The key is patience and consistency. You're cultivating life, so it takes time for the right balance of wild yeast and lactic acid bacteria to develop. Generally, the process takes about five to seven days, though it can vary depending on your kitchen environment.

To begin, you'll need only two ingredients: flour and water. Whole wheat or rye flour is a great choice to kickstart fermentation because it contains plenty of natural nutrients and wild yeasts. However, all-purpose flour can work just fine once your starter is established. Use filtered or bottled water if your tap water is high in chlorine, as chlorine can slow down or inhibit yeast growth.

Start by mixing equal parts flour and water by weight (not volume) in a clean jar or container. For example, 50 grams of flour and 50 grams of water work well as a starting point. Stir the mixture until it's smooth and no dry bits remain. The consistency should be like a thick batter or pancake mix. Cover the jar loosely with a cloth or a breathable lid—this allows air to circulate while preventing dust or bugs from contaminating your starter.

Once your initial mixture is ready, it's time to create a daily feeding routine. Every 24 hours, you'll discard about half of your starter and feed it fresh flour and water in equal parts by weight. Discarding part of the starter may seem wasteful, but it's essential to maintain a healthy balance and manageable volume. Feeding replenishes nutrients for the yeast and bacteria, encouraging growth and activity.

In the first two or three days, you might not see much bubbling or aroma. Don't worry—this is perfectly normal. Wild yeast populations are gradually waking up and multiplying. By day four or five, you should notice bubbles forming throughout the starter and a pleasantly tangy, fruity smell developing. These are reliable signs your starter is becoming active and ready for baking.

During this fermentation period, the temperature of your kitchen plays a big role in how fast your starter matures. Ideal temperatures range between 70-75°F (21-24°C). If your space is cooler, the process will slow down, so be patient or consider placing the starter in a slightly warmer spot, such as near a radiator or inside an oven with just the light on. Conversely, warmer temperatures speed up activity but require more vigilant feeding to avoid over-fermentation.

Once your starter consistently doubles in size within 4 to 6 hours after a feeding and displays plenty of bubbles and a mild, pleasant sour aroma, congratulations! You have a mature sourdough starter ready for baking. At this point, you can use it to make everything from rustic boules to soft sandwich loaves, imbuing your bread with layers of flavor that come from natural fermentation.

There's an art to maintaining your starter over the long term. If you bake frequently (daily or several times a week), you can keep your starter at room temperature and feed it every 12 to 24 hours. For less frequent baking, storing it in the refrigerator slows its activity, so you only need to feed it once a week or so. Before using refrigerated starters, get them back to room temperature and feed them a couple of times to reactivate the yeast and bacteria for best results.

Remember, your starter is a living thing and can vary depending on your local environment—the flour you use, the water quality, and even your kitchen's microbes all impact the final flavor and rise. Don't stress about minor changes or fluctuations. With consistent care and attention, your starter will become a reliable baking companion that improves with age.

One of the best parts about creating a sourdough starter is that it opens the door to a whole world of bread baking possibilities. Once you have a robust starter, you have the foundation needed to tackle classic sourdough loaves, country-style breads, and creative signature recipes that reflect your personal taste. The natural leavening process gives your bread a chewy crumb, crisp crust, and complex flavor you won't find anywhere else.

It's also worth noting that you can share your starter with friends and family. Because a sourdough starter is essentially a culture, it can be passed along and kept alive across generations. Many bakers cherish their starters as a symbol of their baking journey, sometimes naming them or tracking their age—some starter cultures have been maintained for decades!

If at any point your starter develops an off smell (like rotten or cheesy odors), or if you see any pink or fuzzy mold spots, it's best to start fresh. Cleanliness is important, but don't aim for sterile—wild yeast thrives best in a clean but everyday kitchen environment. Clear signs of health include a tangy aroma, lots of bubbles, and consistent growth after feeding.

Finally, trust your senses while nurturing your starter. The smell and texture are great indicators of health. As it matures, your starter will guide you instinctively when it's ready to use. Whether you're aiming for a mild sourdough flavor or something more tangy and pronounced, your starter's personality can evolve over time, allowing you to tailor your baking toward your preferences.

Starting your own sourdough culture transforms bread baking from a simple recipe-following exercise into a soulful, rewarding craft. It offers a glimpse into traditional baking methods and connects you to an age-old cycle of fermentation that's both natural and fascinating. With patience, a few basic ingredients, and care, you'll soon be nurturing a lively starter that unlocks the magic of artisan sourdough right in your own kitchen.

CLASSIC SOURDOUGH LOAF

The classic sourdough loaf represents the heart of traditional bread baking, a staple that every home baker dreams of mastering. Its signature tangy flavor, chewy crumb, and crisp, crackling crust tell the story of natural fermentation, patience, and a little bit of magic. While it might seem intimidating at first, creating a classic sourdough loaf is well within reach—even if you're just starting out. The key lies in understanding the essential components and respecting the rhythms of the process rather than rushing through it.

At its core, sourdough is simply flour, water, salt, and a living culture—known as a starter—that naturally ferments the dough. This starter is a wild yeast and bacteria ecosystem that breaks down sugars in the flour, producing those lovely bubbles that make your bread rise, plus the signature sour note that sets sourdough apart from breads made with commercial yeast. The beauty of a starter is that it's very forgiving, evolving and strengthening with each feed. In that sense, it's not just an ingredient, but a partner in your baking journey.

When preparing your dough, the process starts with mixing the flour and water to create what's called an autolyse, allowing the flour to fully hydrate and enzymes to activate. This simple resting step heightens gluten development and results in better texture without needing intense kneading. After autolyse, you add your sourdough starter and salt, which are crucial for flavor and structure. Salt tightens the gluten network and controls fermentation speed, balancing everything perfectly.

Mixing and folding the dough is an art in itself. Instead of heavy kneading, which beginners often associate with bread-making, sourdough benefits from gentle stretch-and-fold techniques during bulk fermentation. This approach preserves the delicate gas bubbles formed by ferments, yielding an open, airy crumb once baked. Folding the dough every 30 to 45 minutes during the first few hours deepens gluten development and evenly distributes the yeast without knocking out too much air.

The fermentation timing will vary based on your kitchen's temperature and the strength of your starter, so learning to read the dough's readiness is essential. A well-fermented sourdough will have a fluffy, pillowy appearance sprinkled with air bubbles right beneath the surface. It should feel soft and slightly jiggly when gently shaken in the bowl. These signs indicate the wild yeast has done its job, feeding generously and creating enough carbon dioxide to produce an excellent rise.

Once fermentation is complete, shaping the loaf is your chance to build structure and prepare it for a beautiful bake. There's a satisfying simplicity here: a tight round boule or a classic elongated batard—either shape helps support the dough's expansion while baking. Pulling the dough taut across the surface traps air within and encourages impressive oven spring. A few practice runs will sharpen your skills, revealing how gentle hands go a long way in delivering stunning results.

Proofing is the next important step. The final rise, often done in a banneton or a bowl lined with a towel, slows fermentation to develop complex flavors and strengthen the dough's final form. Many home bakers find success with a cold overnight proof in the fridge, which enhances sourness and controls timing. While it requires planning ahead, this slow proof makes it easier to manage busy schedules and achieves the deep flavor profiles sourdough is known for.

Baking the loaf is where all your patience pays off. Transferring the dough to a hot Dutch oven or baking stone traps steam, which keeps the crust moist during the first crucial minutes, letting it expand fully before the surface hardens. This technique gives rise to that trademark glossy, artisan crust with dramatic, crackling ears—the flour-dusted seams you score right before baking. The aroma that fills the kitchen as it bakes is irresistible, promising fresh, wholesome goodness.

The crumb of a well-made classic sourdough loaf boasts an irregular, open structure with chewy, tender pockets that soak up butter or soak into soups beautifully. Every slice carries the balance of tangy flavor with mild sweetness from the flour's natural sugars, making it a versatile companion at breakfast, lunch, or dinner. Slice it thin for toasts and sandwiches, or thick for hearty bread bowls—the classic sourdough loaf adapts seamlessly to many meals.

From a practical standpoint, mastering this classic loaf teaches valuable skills that transfer to countless other sourdough recipes. Understanding fermentation, gluten development, hydration, and baking dynamics builds foundational confidence. You'll find yourself more in tune with dough, learning to trust your senses and instincts rather than relying solely on clocks and thermometers. It's a rewarding process that cultivates a deeper connection to your food and origins of baking itself.

While many associate sourdough with rustic, complex artisan loaves, this classic version remains surprisingly accessible. It doesn't require fancy equipment—just patience, consistency, and fresh ingredients. The starter you nurture today can last a lifetime and provide endless creative opportunities with various hydration levels, different flours, or enriched variations down the line.

In essence, the classic sourdough loaf is more than a recipe. It's a gateway to bread-making mastery, inviting you to slow down, experiment, and ultimately enjoy the rewards of truly homemade bread. Those crackling crusts and tangy, moist interiors make every effort worthwhile, reminding us why baking remains an enduring, beloved tradition in kitchens worldwide.

So as you take on your first classic sourdough loaf, remember that mistakes are part of the learning curve. Each loaf teaches something new—whether it's timing, shaping, or just patience. Keep working your starter, observe your dough, and relish the incredible transformation from humble ingredients to a loaf bursting with life and flavor. With each bake, you get closer to that perfect crust and crumb, and become part of a centuries-old craft.

COUNTRY SOURDOUGH BREAD

Stepping into the world of country sourdough bread is like taking a deep breath of fresh air from a rustic farmhouse kitchen. This loaf captures the heart of traditional bread baking, where simplicity meets flavor in the most satisfying way. It's a bread that feels wholesome, with a crust that crackles under your fingers and a tender crumb dotted with irregular holes—each slice telling a story of patience and craft.

What sets country sourdough apart is its wonderfully rustic texture and deep, tangy flavor that comes from a confident sourdough starter nurtured over time. Unlike more delicate or sweetened breads, country sourdough embraces natural fermentation and long proofing times, which bring out complex notes that balance sourness with subtle sweetness. The aroma alone is enough to make you eager to get your hands floury and your oven warm.

Making a country sourdough loaf at home is surprisingly approachable, especially for beginners willing to commit to a little planning and care. The process encourages you to slow down and get in tune with your dough—hydration levels, fermentation stages, and the way the dough feels at every step. That hands-on involvement is rewarding, not just because it yields delicious results, but because it teaches you the fundamentals of bread that can be applied across various styles.

One of the beauties of country sourdough bread is its natural versatility. The basic ingredients—flour, water, salt, and starter—are staples you likely already have or can easily acquire. There's no need for fancy additives or complex mixing techniques. The magic happens through fermentation, as wild yeast and beneficial bacteria develop flavor and lift the loaf. With just a few simple tools and a little patience, you can achieve bakery-quality bread right in your kitchen.

Getting started, you'll want to use a high-hydration dough, typically around 75% to 80% water relative to flour weight, to encourage an open crumb and moist texture. The flour itself is often a blend of all-purpose or bread flour with some whole wheat or rye for extra character. The whole wheat or rye contributes nutrients that feed the starter and add a hearty depth to the loaf. Mixing until just combined and then letting the dough rest allows the flour to fully hydrate, which is critical for a light, airy crumb.

Fermentation takes center stage here. After an initial bulk rise at room temperature, the dough benefits from a series of gentle stretch-and-folds that strengthen its gluten network without kneading. Stretching and folding the dough every 30 to 45 minutes during the first few hours encourages structure and improves gas retention, which are essential for a well-risen bread. This part of the process also gives you a chance to observe the dough's development, feeling it become smoother and more elastic.

Following this, a slow, cool fermentation—often an overnight rise in the refrigerator—allows flavors to deepen considerably. This extended fermentation phase is where country sourdough earns its complex, mildly tangy profile. The cool temperature slows down yeast activity but keeps bacterial fermentation steady, which produces lactic and acetic acids contributing subtle sour notes without overwhelming sharpness.

Shaping the loaf after refrigeration requires a gentle hand. You'll want to handle the dough delicately to preserve the airy pockets forged during fermentation. The classic country sourdough loaf often takes on a round or oval shape, known as a boule or bâtard, respectively. These shapes help create an even bake and a satisfying crust-to-crumb ratio. Light dusting with flour not only prevents sticking but also adds that iconic rustic look once baked.

When it comes to baking, high heat and steam play vital roles. Preheating your oven to at least 450°F ensures a strong initial oven spring—the rapid rise bread experiences during the first minutes in the oven. Introducing steam during the first 15 to 20 minutes of baking keeps the crust soft, allowing full expansion, while eventually contributing to a deep golden color and crisp exterior. You can create steam by placing a cast iron skillet with hot water in the oven or using a covered Dutch oven, which traps moisture and heat efficiently.

The result of this baking method is a country sourdough loaf with a crunchy, blistered crust that's as satisfying to bite into as it is to look at. The crumb inside is tender yet chewy, with irregular holes indicating a well-fermented, well-handled dough. Each slice carries the warm, smoky tang that's signature to sourdough bread, perfect for sandwich making, toasting, or simply savoring with butter.

Beyond taste and texture, country sourdough bread serves as a canvas for creativity in the kitchen. While the traditional loaf is delightful on its own, you can experiment with mix-ins like cracked grains, seeds, or herbs to personalize your bread. Adding sunflower seeds or cracked wheat during the initial mix introduces fascinating textures and nutty flavors. Herbs like rosemary or thyme lend a fresh, aromatic twist that complements the sour tang.

It's common for beginner bakers to initially worry about getting the crust just right or fermenting the dough perfectly. But with country sourdough, every batch is a learning opportunity. The more you bake, the better you become at reading your dough's behavior—knowing when it's ready to shape, how your environment affects fermentation, and how your oven responds during baking. This evolving knowledge builds confidence, making bread baking less a mystery and more a fulfilling routine.

When you share a fresh country sourdough loaf with family or friends, you're sharing more than just bread—you're sharing time, effort, and tradition. The loaf represents a return to basics with a modern appreciation for craft and quality. Despite its artisanal feel, it's a loaf anyone can make at home, turning your kitchen into a small bakery and your daily meals into little celebrations.

Finally, country sourdough bread is a gateway into deeper sourdough mastery. It introduces essential skills like managing hydration, temperature, and fermentation times that apply to all sourdough projects. Learning to handle this loaf well paves the way for more complex endeavors, from whole wheat variants to fragrant baguettes. Your journey through sourdough begins here, with something beautifully simple yet endlessly rewarding.

WHOLE WHEAT SOURDOUGH BREAD

Whole wheat sourdough bread brings together the rustic charm of sourdough's natural fermentation with the hearty, nutty flavors of whole grain flour. For home bakers eager to add a wholesome touch to their loaf repertoire, this bread stands out as both nourishing and delicious. Unlike white sourdough, whole wheat sourdough has a deeper flavor profile and denser crumb. The bran and germ in whole wheat flour contribute texture and complexity, but also introduce challenges like reduced gluten development and quicker fermentation times that need gentle handling.

Starting with whole wheat sourdough means embracing a longer, patient process. The natural wild yeast and lactic bacteria in your starter work together to break down the bran's tough outer layers, making nutrients more accessible and softening the loaf's crumb. This slow fermentation enhances digestibility and gives the bread its signature tang. It's common to feel a bit intimidated at first, but once you understand how to balance hydration, fermentation, and shaping, baking this bread is rewarding.

A key tip is hydration. Whole wheat flour demands more water compared to white flour because of its bran content. The bran soaks up moisture rapidly, leaving your dough drier if you don't adjust water levels. Aim for a hydration level between 75-85% of the flour weight. You'll notice the dough feels wetter and stickier than a classic white sourdough loaf. This stickiness can be a challenge, but learning to work with it rather than fight it is part of mastering the craft.

Fermentation times must also be tuned carefully. Whole wheat dough often ferments faster due to extra nutrients that feed your starter's microorganisms. This can be a great advantage but requires keeping a watchful eye. Overfermentation can lead to a collapsed loaf with a gummy texture. To avoid this, bulk rise times are usually shorter—often around 3 to 4 hours at room temperature—though temperature and starter activity can vary this. Cold fermentation in the fridge overnight is another beneficial step. It slows fermentation, allowing flavors to further develop and making the dough easier to handle the next day.

When it comes to mixing whole wheat sourdough dough, gentle folding during bulk fermentation helps build gluten strength without tearing the bran strands and flattening your loaf's structure. Performing a series of stretch-and-folds every 30 to 45 minutes keeps the dough aerated, develops gluten, and manages its tacky nature. Don't over-knead; instead, focus on rhythm and feeling the dough's transformation from shaggy to smooth and elastic.

Shaping a whole wheat sourdough loaf calls for a light touch because of the denser flour. When shaping, aim to create surface tension while not deflating the dough too much. A tight, well-shaped boule or batard will hold its form and produce an open crumb with a chewy crust. Dust your banneton or proofing basket with rice flour or a mix of all-purpose and whole wheat to prevent sticking. Proof times—again—will be shorter than white sourdough, usually between 1 to 2 hours depending on your kitchen's warmth.

Baking whole wheat sourdough achieves its best crust and crumb in a hot, steamy oven environment. Preheat your Dutch oven or baking stone to 450°F or higher and introduce steam by covering the dough during the first 20 minutes of baking. Steam encourages oven spring and caramelizes the crust, leading to that perfect crackly finish. After uncovering, the loaf browns beautifully without drying out. Expect your loaf to bake for roughly 35 to 45 minutes, but always check for an internal temperature of about 205°F to ensure it's fully baked.

Texture-wise, whole wheat sourdough bread has a more substantial crumb than its white counterpart. The crumb often is moist and slightly chewy with a dense but open structure, dotted with flecks of bran adding rustic character. Flavors are complex, showcasing the earthy nuttiness of toasted wheat combined with the signature tang of sourdough's natural fermentation. This bread pairs beautifully with savory toppings like avocado, cheese, or roasted vegetables but also holds up well for sandwiches and toast.

For bakers interested in boosting nutrition and flavor, incorporating a small percentage of whole wheat starter or adding soaked grains and seeds can enhance the loaf's character. Some like to mix whole wheat flour with bread flour to find balance—this approach improves rise and lightness without sacrificing wholesomeness. Experimenting is part of the fun with sourdough, and even slight tweaks in flour blends or fermentation times can create notable differences in the final bread.

Maintaining a healthy, active whole wheat starter can make all the difference when baking this bread regularly. Whole wheat flours tend to ferment faster and generate more acids, so paying attention to the starter's feeding routine will keep it bubbly and ready to produce lively dough. Feeding the starter with some whole wheat flour can also promote a more robust microbial community that thrives on whole grain sugars, enhancing flavor complexity.

While it can take a few tries to get comfortable with whole wheat sourdough, the learning curve is part of the rewarding journey. Each loaf is a little experiment, teaching you to read your dough's feel, timing, and response to your home environment. With practice, you'll develop confidence to troubleshoot fermentation issues, adjust hydration, and fine-tune your shaping technique.

In summary, whole wheat sourdough bread is an excellent way to dive deeper into sourdough baking with a healthful twist. Its rich flavors, chewy texture, and impressive crust make it a standout in any bread collection. Whether enjoyed fresh with a smear of butter or used for hearty sandwiches, this bread offers nourishment and satisfaction baked right in your kitchen. Embrace patience, respect the process, and enjoy the beautiful complexity that whole wheat and sourdough combine to deliver.

Sourdough Baguettes

Among the many loaves you'll explore in this journey through sourdough baking, sourdough baguettes hold a special place. These elegant, slender loaves combine the rustic tang and complex flavors of sourdough with the crisp, crackling crust and airy crumb that baguettes are known for. They might seem intimidating at first glance, but once you grasp the techniques behind them, you'll find they're incredibly rewarding and well within reach of any home baker.

At its core, a sourdough baguette is a marriage of traditional French bread-making and natural fermentation. The slow fermentation process with a reliable sourdough starter enhances flavor and texture, giving the baguette a distinct depth absent from quick-rise breads. Because the starter replaces commercial yeast, your dough will develop nuanced acidity and a thicker, chewier crust that's positively addictive. Despite their seeming sophistication, making sourdough baguettes doesn't require fancy equipment—just patience, practice, and a little know-how.

What makes sourdough baguettes stand out is their lightness. Unlike dense, heavy loaves sometimes associated with homemade bread, these baguettes are known for a delicate, open crumb filled with irregular holes. Achieving that airy texture comes down to proper hydration, skillful folding, and the magic of a well-fed starter. When handled carefully, the dough stretches and traps gas bubbles during fermentation, creating the signature open structure. Once baked, the result is a loaf with a thin, shatteringly crisp crust surrounding a tender, springy interior that sings with sourdough complexity.

Working with high hydration dough is a big part of mastering sourdough baguettes. Typically, these doughs have water content around 75% or higher, which can feel sticky and challenging to handle at first. However, embracing this wet dough is key—it encourages gluten development and helps achieve the light crumb. Expect some initial messiness, but with practice, your hands will learn to manage the softness, folding and shaping gently to maintain those precious air pockets.

One baking tip worth emphasizing revolves around the shaping process. Unlike round loaves or boules, baguettes require a streamlined, elongated shape that's slim and uniform. Proper tension on the surface of the dough helps it keep its form and allows the loaf to expand upward during baking rather than spreading out flat. Achieving this tension comes from careful folding and rolling; avoid pressing too hard, which can degas the dough. Instead, think of the dough as delicate—supporting its structure with soft, deliberate motions.

Proofing is another crucial step in your sourdough baguette journey. Depending on your kitchen environment and the strength of your starter, this final rise can take anywhere from one to three hours. The dough's readiness is revealed by a gentle spring back when poked lightly but still holding some indentation—a sign that it's risen fully but won't collapse in the oven. Maintaining the right temperature and humidity during proofing can make a big difference, so consider covering your dough with a damp cloth or placing it inside a proofing box if your kitchen tends to be dry.

Baking sourdough baguettes requires creating steam in the oven, which helps develop that characteristic shiny, blistered crust. You can achieve this by placing a pan of hot water on the oven floor or spritzing water inside just before sliding in the loaves. Steam keeps the crust moist long enough for the dough to expand fully before setting, resulting in a light, crackly exterior. Using a baking stone or steel also promotes even heat distribution and better oven spring, bringing your baguettes closer to those bakery-quality loaves.

The beauty of sourdough baguettes is their versatility. These loaves shine at the breakfast table sliced thin with butter or jam but also make a perfect companion for sandwiches, cheese boards, and hearty soups. Their tangy flavor balances rich and savory fillings exceptionally well, making leftovers just as delightful the next day. If you're aiming to impress at a gathering, nothing rivals the rustic charm and mouthwatering aroma of freshly baked sourdough baguettes.

For beginners, the idea of mastering sourdough baguettes might feel like a steep climb, but the payoff is huge. Start by familiarizing yourself with your starter's activity levels and practice the hydration and folding techniques discussed. Don't be discouraged by early imperfections—each loaf teaches you something new about timing, temperature, and texture. Over time, you'll gain confidence, and your baguettes will become more reliable and expressive of your personal style.

One of the joys of sourdough baking is its adaptability, and baguettes are no exception. You can experiment by adding a bit of whole wheat or rye flour into the mix for earthier notes or tweaking hydration slightly to suit your climate and ingredients. Playing with fermentation times—longer cold proofing overnight or shorter, warmer rises—

will yield different flavor profiles and textures. Keep notes on your experiments, and you'll steadily build a learning curve that makes the process feel less mysterious and more like a rhythm you can trust.

To sum it up, sourdough baguettes are a masterclass in patience and technique, wrapped up in a loaf that delivers big on flavor and texture. The combination of tangy starter, wet dough, careful shaping, and steam baking creates an irresistible bread you'll reach for time and again. They might take more time than a basic loaf, but the satisfaction of pulling a golden, crusty baguette from your oven transforms your baking from simple routine to rewarding craft.

When you decide to embark on baking sourdough baguettes, remember that every loaf is a step closer to mastery. The process teaches you how to read dough, adjust to your environment, and appreciate the beauty of slow, natural fermentation. With practice, these loaves won't just fill your home with warm aroma—they'll become treasured staples in your bread-baking repertoire.

Sourdough Boules

Among the many iconic shapes in the sourdough world, the boule stands out both for its simplicity and classic appeal. The term "boule" comes from the French word for ball, describing the round, rustic loaf that's instantly recognizable with its thick crust and open crumb. For home bakers eager to elevate their sourdough skills, mastering the boule offers a rewarding experience that combines straightforward techniques with impressive results.

What makes a sourdough boule special isn't just its form—though that perfect dome-shaped crust is undeniably stunning. It's the balance of texture, flavor, and crumb structure that defines a great boule. You want a loaf with a deeply caramelized crust that crackles when you tap it, while the inside stays open and airy yet moist, showcasing the tangy complexity typical of a sourdough fermentation. This harmony is exactly what you'll achieve when you understand the nuances of hydration, fermentation, shaping, and baking specific to boules.

One of the first considerations in baking a sourdough boule is dough hydration. Boules typically benefit from a medium to high hydration, often around 75 percent or slightly more. Higher hydration encourages a looser dough, which helps develop the open crumb bubbles many bakers admire. That said, handling wetter doughs can be a challenge at first, so it's perfectly fine to start a bit lower, around 70 percent, and gradually increase hydration as you become more comfortable with shaping and scoring.

Fermentation is equally critical. Because sourdough relies on wild yeast and lactic acid bacteria, patience plays a big role in the development of flavor and texture. During the bulk fermentation phase, your dough should rise noticeably but not double completely, preserving the delicate gluten structure. Watch for a dough that's soft and bubbly to the touch, signaling it's ready for the next step. If you rush this stage, the crumb may end up dense; wait too long, and you risk over-fermentation which weakens the dough's ability to hold shape.

Shaping a boule is almost an art form. It's about creating surface tension on the dough to encourage it to rise upward and maintain a round, domed shape. Start by gently deflating your dough, then use a technique called "stretch and fold" to pull the edges under the loaf, slowly building tension on the surface. This tight skin traps gas produced during the final rise, which helps the boule achieve that prized oven spring—dramatic expansion during baking that gives the loaf its height and light crumb.

Proofing the boule correctly is another vital phase. You'll notice many bakers prefer to do a cold proof in the refrigerator for 12 to 24 hours. This slow, cold fermentation deepens flavor and makes the dough easier to score and handle before baking. If pressed for time, a room temperature proof is acceptable, but the flavor may not develop as richly. Remember that the boule's texture depends heavily on how well the dough has fermented during proofing.

Proper scoring is the final skill to learn. Scoring isn't just decorative; it allows the loaf to expand predictably during the initial moments in the oven. For boules, a simple cross or an ornamental spiral can direct the oven spring elegantly, producing the characteristic ear and cratered crust texture. Use a very sharp blade or bread lame, slicing swiftly but gently through the loaf's skin without deflating it. With practice, you'll find scoring can become both a creative outlet and a confidence booster.

Baking sourdough boules requires a hot, steamy oven environment. Steam is essential to keep the crust from setting too early, allowing the loaf to expand fully and develop a crisp, shiny exterior. For home ovens, this is often achieved by adding a pan of boiling water on the oven floor or using specialized Dutch ovens or baking cloches. If using a Dutch oven, it helps trap moisture released by the dough while providing intense, even heat—ideal conditions for that brilliant oven spring.

Once baked, the boule should rest on a cooling rack for at least an hour before slicing. This resting time lets the crumb finish its transformation, allowing moisture to redistribute evenly throughout the bread. Cutting too soon often results in a gummy texture, disappointing after all the effort you've put in. Resist the temptation, knowing the reward will be a perfectly textured slice bursting with flavor.

One of the most inspiring aspects of baking sourdough boules at home is the chance to experiment with flours. While white bread flour is popular for its gluten strength, mixing in whole wheat, rye, or spelt can enhance complexity and nutrition in your loaves. Each flour behaves differently—whole wheat, for example, absorbs more water and can produce a denser crumb, while rye adds earthiness and a unique tang. Playing with blends lets you find a signature flavor that speaks to your personal taste and local ingredients.

As you advance, you might explore different fermentation timings and starter maintenance routines to fine-tune your boule's flavor profile. Adjusting your starter's feeding schedule or hydration can introduce subtle changes. Some bakers favor a longer cold fermentation to intensify sour notes, while others prefer a milder taste with shorter fermentation. The beauty of sourdough is the control it offers—you're both a scientist and artist shaping each loaf.

Remember, even the most skilled bakers face unexpected results sometimes. Sourdough is a living process, influenced by variables like room temperature, flour quality, and humidity. If your first boule falls flat or lacks the open crumb you hoped for, don't be discouraged. Each attempt teaches you more about your dough's behavior and helps build intuition. Keep notes of your process so you can tweak factors gradually—baking, in essence, is a continuous learning adventure.

Beyond technique, baking sourdough boules connects you to centuries of bread-making tradition and offers a tangible way to slow down and appreciate simple craftsmanship. Pulling a warm, fragrant boule from your oven is deeply satisfying. It transforms your kitchen into a bakery and your home into a place where friends and family gather, making every loaf feel like a shared celebration.

To sum up, the sourdough boule is a perfect entry point into artisan bread baking. It combines timeless simplicity with rich complexity. By focusing on hydration, fermentation, shaping, and baking methods tailored for the boule, home bakers can achieve consistent, delicious results. The skills you develop here lay a solid foundation for more adventurous bread projects down the line.

So, ready your flour and starter. Embrace patience, apply the techniques patiently, and treat each boule as a step toward sourdough mastery. Whether enjoyed fresh with butter or transformed into sandwiches, your homemade boule will undoubtedly become a cherished classic in your baking repertoire.

SOURDOUGH FOCACCIA

Focaccia has become synonymous with comfort bread. Its golden crust, airy crumb, and aromatic surface make it a favorite for many home bakers. Incorporating sourdough starter into focaccia elevates this already delightful bread by adding subtle tang and complexity, giving it a depth of flavor that commercial yeast versions often can't replicate. If you have mastered basic sourdough loaves, diving into sourdough focaccia will feel like a rewarding next step.

What makes sourdough focaccia stand apart is the way the natural fermentation interacts with olive oil, herbs, and sea salt. The dough, rich with hydration, creates those signature dimpled pockets on the surface, allowing oil and seasoning to collect beautifully. Though it looks rustic, sourdough focaccia offers flexibility—whether it's a simple salted bread or a canvas for creative toppings like caramelized onions, olives, or rosemary sprigs.

The key foundation lies in hydration percentage. In sourdough focaccia, expect a fairly high hydration dough—often around 75% or more—which contributes to its softness and surprising chew. It can initially seem sticky and loose compared to your traditional bread dough, but this is exactly what you want. Trust the process: generous use of olive oil on the baking surface and dough will prevent sticking. Proper stretching and folding during bulk fermentation develop gluten without heavy kneading, making the dough manageable.

Timing the fermentation stages is essential. Unlike lean sourdough loaves where you seek a very tight crumb, focaccia benefits from a lighter aeration inside. Using your mature, bubbly starter, begin by mixing flour, water, starter, and salt, then let it rest for about 30 minutes to an hour for autolyse—this helps the flour hydrate and improves gluten structure. Following this, gently stretch and fold the dough a few times over the next two to three hours during bulk fermentation. Patience during this phase rewards you with a dough that holds air pockets without deflating.

Once your dough has risen, turn your attention to the pan. Use an oily baking sheet or a rimmed cast iron skillet; extra virgin olive oil is ideal here because it not only prevents sticking but also crisps the bottom crust just right. Gently transfer the dough, then spread and stretch it using your fingertips, creating those characteristic dimples across the entire surface. Don't worry if the dough resists a little—that tension helps build structure.

Seasoning is the moment to get creative and personalize your focaccia. Sea salt flakes, cracked black pepper, and fresh rosemary are classic choices, but feel free to experiment. Thinly sliced garlic, cherry tomatoes, sauteed leeks, or kalamata olives make wonderful additions. Sprinkle toppings evenly, pressing them lightly into the surface so they adhere during baking and don't burn.

Proofing after shaping is crucial. Let the dough rest in its oiled pan for at least 45 minutes to an hour, or until it visibly puffs up. This relaxes the gluten and allows the dough to regain some spring, ensuring a lighter crumb after baking. Meanwhile, preheat your oven to a high temperature—usually around 450°F. A hot oven jumpstarts oven spring and helps create that crisp exterior while keeping the interior soft.

Baking sourdough focaccia is a balance of crust development and crumb texture. You want the exterior to be golden and crisp but not too dark or hard. As the dough bakes, the olive oil melds with the dough and toppings, infusing those pockets of flavor that keep you coming back for more. Typically, baking takes 20 to 30 minutes, depending on your oven and pan. Keep an eye after 15 minutes; if the top is browning unevenly, rotate the pan to promote even cooking.

Once out of the oven, give the focaccia a few minutes to cool in the pan before transferring it to a wire rack. This prevents sogginess on the bottom and allows the crust to firm up without losing moisture. The aroma of fresh baked sourdough focaccia is irresistible—crispy edges, tender crumb, and an inviting olive oil fragrance. It's perfect for slicing thick and serving alongside soup, or as the base for an unforgettable sandwich.

One of the best parts about sourdough focaccia is how forgiving it is. Unlike certain intricate breads needing precise shaping or temperature control, focaccia's rustic nature means slight variations won't ruin the final product. If your dough feels too slack, try cold fermenting it overnight in the fridge for more structure and flavor. If you forget to make a starter in advance, a portion of active starter from a regular bread batch works well here, too.

Storage is simple because sourdough focaccia keeps well for a couple of days at room temperature, sealed in an airtight container or loosely wrapped in foil. For longer storage, freezing individual portions can ensure you enjoy that fresh-baked taste anytime. Reheating in a toaster oven or skillet with a dusting of olive oil keeps the crust lively and fragrant.

Incorporating sourdough into your focaccia baking opens doors to explore various flavor pairings and textures. You might try swapping some of the all-purpose flour for whole grain or rye to add earthiness. Herbs like thyme, sage, or basil can be mixed into the dough or sprinkled on top. Even finishing with a drizzle of balsamic glaze after baking introduces delightful contrast.

Mastering sourdough focaccia also deepens your intuition for dough handling and fermentation timing. As you observe how hydration levels affect crumb openness, or how olive oil influences browning, you build transferable skills useful across many bread projects. This bread embodies the joy of baking—simple ingredients, time-honored technique, and room for your personal touch.

From casual weeknight dinners to leisurely weekend brunches, sourdough focaccia fits beautifully into homemade meals. Its versatility makes it a staple worth perfecting in your bread baking arsenal. Whether topped simply or elaborately, it offers a fresh, flavorful way to enjoy sourdough's signature tang and texture. Take your sourdough starter from the jar to the pan and bake a focaccia that's sure to impress friends and family alike.

Sourdough Dinner Rolls

Sourdough dinner rolls are a charming addition to any meal, offering that classic tang and chewiness that only natural fermentation can deliver. While bigger sourdough loaves tend to steal the spotlight, these soft, fluffy little rounds deserve just as much attention. They're perfect for sandwiches, alongside soups, or simply slathered with butter. Making sourdough dinner rolls at home is rewarding, especially once you discover how straightforward the process can be when you understand the basics of working with your starter and dough.

One of the great things about sourdough dinner rolls is how adaptable the recipe is. You can tweak hydration levels, flour types, or even mix in herbs, garlic, or cheese for extra flavor. The key lies in balancing the fermentation time so that you retain the subtle sour notes without overwhelming the tender crumb with too much tang. The beauty of these rolls is in this balance: a slightly tangy crust with a light, fluffy interior that melts in your mouth.

Getting the dough right starts with your sourdough starter. It should be active and bubbly, ready to lend its natural yeast and bacteria to leaven your rolls. Unlike many quick-rising dinner roll recipes that rely on commercial yeast, sourdough rolls take a bit longer to rise. But this slower fermentation is where the complex flavors develop, and the texture improves. Plan ahead and make sure your starter is fed and at its peak activity before mixing your dough.

Once you mix your dough—usually a blend of bread flour and a bit of whole wheat or rye for flavor complexity—you'll want to incorporate enough water to hydrate the flour well but not so much that the dough becomes unmanageable. Hydration around 65% to 70% usually hits the sweet spot for soft rolls. After mixing, the dough undergoes a bulk fermentation period that can range from 4 to 6 hours at room temperature or longer if you chill it overnight, which slows fermentation and adds even more depth of flavor.

Handling sourdough dinner roll dough is a little different than working with stiffer bread dough. You'll want to practice gentle stretches and folds every 30 minutes during the bulk fermentation to strengthen the gluten network without deflating the dough. This technique makes the dough more elastic and better able to trap the natural gases produced by the starter. Those gases help give your rolls their lift and airy crumb.

Shaping the rolls is where you decide their final form. Whether you opt for small, round balls, tight knots, or even mini baguette shapes, you'll find the shaping process fun and creative. A simple, classic round shape is achieved by pulling the edges of a dough piece underneath itself to form a smooth top surface. This tension helps the rolls keep their shape as they rise and bake.

Next comes the proofing step, which is critical for achieving that perfect spring when the rolls bake. After shaping, the rolls generally need about 1 to 2 hours to proof at room temperature. You'll want to cover them lightly with a damp cloth or plastic wrap to avoid drying the surface. Avoid rushing this process—underproofed rolls can end up dense, while overproofed rolls might collapse or spread too flat during baking.

Baking sourdough dinner rolls is simpler than many imagine but knowing a few tricks will set your rolls apart. Preheat your oven thoroughly, ideally to around 400°F. Using a baking stone or a steel helps create radiant heat that encourages even browning on the bottom crust. Adding steam in the first 10 minutes of baking also helps develop a soft crust, which contrasts nicely with the tender crumb inside.

Steam can be introduced in several ways. Some bakers like to place a small, oven-safe pan with hot water in the oven or quickly spritz water onto the oven walls right after loading the rolls. The extra moisture keeps the crust from hardening too fast and promotes a delicate, glossy exterior. After that initial steaming period, remove the water and let the rolls finish baking uncovered. This lets them brown evenly and develop a slight chewiness on the crust without becoming tough.

When your sourdough dinner rolls come out of the oven, resist the urge to dive in immediately. Allowing them to cool on a wire rack for at least 20 minutes finishes the cooking process inside and prevents the crumb from turning gummy. Cooling also helps the crust settle into its ideal texture—a thin crust that's soft but still has a little bit of a snap when you bite into it.

Many bakers find sourdough dinner rolls a perfect entry point into working with live starters because the batch sizes are manageable and forgiving. Plus, they're extremely versatile. You can use leftover starter to add flavor, experiment with whole grain flours for extra nutrition, or incorporate mix-ins like caramelized onions or herbs for a twist. Because they're small, each baking session feels rewarding without the pressure of producing a large loaf.

Keeping sourdough dinner rolls fresh can be straightforward, too. While they're best on the day they're baked, you can store cooled rolls in an airtight container at room temperature for a couple of days. If you want to keep them longer, freezing works wonderfully. When it's time to eat, thaw rolls at room temperature and warm them in a low oven to bring back some of that fresh-baked softness.

One more helpful tip is to remember that baking sourdough dinner rolls is a journey full of small learning moments. Even if your first batch isn't exactly textbook perfect, each try improves your understanding of dough hydration, fermentation timing, and shaping technique. It's worth keeping notes with each bake to track what worked and what didn't because every kitchen environment is unique.

With practice, sourdough dinner rolls will become a staple in your baking routine. They aren't just a side dish; they can elevate your meals and impress family and friends alike. From holiday gatherings to casual weeknight suppers, these rolls bring a homey warmth and a slice of traditional bread artistry to your table.

Ultimately, mastering sourdough dinner rolls is about patience and respect for the dough's natural fermentation process. When you embrace that rhythm, your baking results will consistently reflect a balance of texture and taste that only true sourdough can offer.

DISCARD CRACKERS AND PANCAKES

One of the most rewarding parts of sourdough baking is learning how to make the most of every bit of your starter—especially the discard. Instead of tossing out that excess sourdough starter, you can transform it into some truly delightful goodies. Discard crackers and pancakes are simple, practical, and delicious ways to make use of sourdough that might otherwise go to waste. These recipes not only save you money but also add new dimensions of flavor and texture to your baking routine.

The key to working with sourdough discard is understanding its characteristics. Since discard hasn't been refreshed with new flour and water, it's a bit more acidic and less active than your feeding starter. However, that tartness gives discard-based snacks a unique tang that can really brighten up your taste buds. When you turn discard into crackers or pancakes, you're basically giving it a second life that highlights its lively, fermented flavors without the wait that bread needs.

Discard crackers are probably the easiest and most versatile project to start with. They're crunchy, crispy, and make a perfect snack or appetizer base. All you really need is some sourdough discard, flour, oil, and seasonings. From there, you can experiment with binding flavors like garlic, herb blends, cheese, or even a touch of sweetness with honey or maple syrup. Rolling the dough out thinly and scoring it before baking is key to getting those perfect cracker shapes and textures. Baking times can vary, so keeping an eye on them as they golden is essential to avoid any burnt bits.

Because cracker dough is quite forgiving, it's a great way to get comfortable handling discard-based batters. Plus, these crackers are a fantastic alternative to store-bought snacks, offering a homemade twist and better ingredients. Pair them with cheese, dips, or just enjoy them on their own. They're also great to keep on hand for unexpected guests or a simple, crunchy addition to a lunchbox.

On the flip side, discard pancakes provide a soft and fluffy route to savoring your starter's extra life. Unlike traditional pancakes, these have a subtle tang and depth thanks to the fermentation process. Making discard pancakes is incredibly straightforward and doesn't require a ton of extra ingredients. You can mix your discard with some basic pantry staples like flour, eggs, a little sugar, and baking soda or powder for lift. The real magic happens when the tang of the sourdough blend meets the warmth of a griddle or skillet.

Discard pancakes are perfect for a cozy weekend breakfast or a quick, nutritious snack any time of day. Their unique texture — slightly chewy with a light, tender crumb — makes them stand out from everyday pancake recipes. They're also a fantastic blank canvas. Try adding fresh fruit, nuts, or even a touch of cinnamon or vanilla to elevate your morning stack. Serving these with classic toppings like butter and maple syrup plays well with that gentle sourness.

While discard pancakes don't require much effort, timing can make a difference. Letting the batter rest for a few minutes before cooking enhances the flavor. This little pause allows the starter to meld with the other ingredients, boosting the depth and character of each bite. Cooking discard pancakes over a medium heat ensures they develop a golden exterior while staying tender inside — a trick that's easy to master with a bit of practice.

Both discard crackers and pancakes show how sourdough discard is far from waste. These recipes demonstrate resourcefulness in the kitchen, which is a cornerstone of handmade bread making. Using every part of your starter creates less waste and makes your baking adventure even more satisfying. You don't have to be an expert to try these ideas—they're accessible, forgiving, and versatile enough to suit any skill level.

Some bakers like to keep a stash of discard in the fridge between baking days, making it quick and convenient to whip up crackers or pancakes when hunger strikes. This practice is a handy solution for managing your starter without pressure. It also means you're always ready with a fresh batch of sourdough snacks that carry the unmistakable tangy charm of fermented flour.

On top of being convenient, discard crackers and pancakes bring a tasty way to introduce friends and family to the flavors of sourdough without the challenge or time investment that loaves require. They're also fantastic conversation starters—people often ask about the unique taste, and that's a great opportunity to share your newfound love for sourdough culture.

For home bakers eager to expand beyond the usual loaves, incorporating discard recipes into your routine encourages creativity. You're not just following a formula; you're experimenting with flavor combinations and kitchen techniques. Whether you're using herbs plucked fresh from your garden in your crackers or adding blueberries to your discard pancakes, these recipes embrace the joy of baking as an adventure.

It's important to remember that discard is best when used within a few days of feeding your starter. Older discard can become overly sour or less pleasant in flavor, which might affect how your final crackers or pancakes taste. Keeping an eye on the freshness of your discard ensures that your snacks will have that signature bright, tangy flavor without any off-putting notes.

Discard crackers and pancakes also open a door to healthy baking. Sourdough fermentation breaks down some of the gluten and naturally occurring phytic acid in flour, improving digestibility. This means your discard treats can be gentle on the stomach, making them a wholesome choice for many people. Plus, they're typically lower in sugar and additives than commercial crackers or pancakes, which aligns with a home cook's desire for clean, wholesome food.

Another benefit of discard recipes is their quick turnaround. Unlike traditional sourdough bread, which needs hours or overnight fermentation, you can prepare and bake crackers in under an hour. Pancakes cook up even faster, making both options ideal for busy mornings or last-minute snacks. This immediacy adds to the fun of sourdough baking, showing how it doesn't always have to be a long, slow process to yield amazing results.

If you like to personalize your baking, discard snacks let you tailor flavors to your mood and pantry. Experiment with spicy chili flakes, parmesan cheese, or even sesame seeds pressed into the crackers. You can sweeten pancakes naturally with honey, mashed banana, or cinnamon for a breakfast that feels a bit special without extra fuss.

In short, discard crackers and pancakes aren't just clever ways to reduce waste—they're a celebration of sourdough's versatility and flavor. These recipes are simple enough for beginners but satisfying enough to delight any home baker wanting more from their starter. They're the perfect complement to the signature loaves and artisan breads covered in other chapters, rounding out the sourdough experience with practical, delicious, and easy options.

Next time you feed your sourdough starter and find yourself with discard, don't toss it away. Instead, think of it as a new ingredient brimming with potential. Whether crunchy, savory crackers or fluffy, tangy pancakes, you'll find that using your discard adds a fresh angle to your baking skills and proves just how adaptable sourdough baking can be.

Sweet Sourdough Cinnamon Rolls

There's something undeniably magical about cinnamon rolls, especially when infused with the tangy complexity that sourdough brings to the table. These sweet sourdough cinnamon rolls elevate a classic favorite by layering in the depth and nuance of natural fermentation. The result? Rolls that are not only soft and pillowy but also boast a subtle sour note that balances perfectly with the sweet, spicy swirl inside.

Working with sourdough in a sweet roll recipe might seem intimidating at first, but it's surprisingly approachable once you understand the basics. Unlike traditional cinnamon rolls made with commercial yeast, using sourdough starter adds flavor that develops slowly, offering a richer profile. Plus, the fermentation process helps create exceptional texture—soft, tender crumb with a slight chew that's incredibly satisfying.

One of the key differences here is the dough's hydration and rising time. Since sourdough ferments more gradually, you'll find that timing plays a more critical role. Giving the dough the right amount of time to bulk ferment not only builds flavor but also affects how easy it is to work with during shaping. Patience here rewards you with a dough that's elastic enough to roll out thinly without tearing and sturdy enough to hold those luscious cinnamon swirls intact.

In addition to the dough itself, the filling is ripe for customization. The traditional blend of cinnamon and brown sugar provides warmth and sweetness, but adding a touch of nutmeg, a pinch of cloves, or even a little cardamom can take these rolls to the next level. Some bakers like to stir softened butter into the filling mixture, which helps everything meld together into a glossy, sticky layer once baked. Don't hesitate to sprinkle chopped nuts like pecans or walnuts too—these add crunch that contrasts beautifully with the soft dough.

One practical tip when it comes to sourdough cinnamon rolls is how to handle the proofing stage after the rolls are shaped. Due to the natural acidity in sourdough, these rolls generally need a longer, slower final rise to unlock their full flavor potential. This rise can happen at room temperature or in the refrigerator overnight. The cold proofing option not only fits nicely into a home baker's schedule but also enhances the tang in the dough, deepening complexity without overwhelming the sweetness.

The baking process itself is straightforward but requires close attention. Baking in a preheated oven ensures those rolls develop a beautiful golden-brown crust without drying out. You'll notice the scent of cinnamon filling your kitchen, accompanied by that toasty, slightly nutty aroma common to well-baked sourdough. Once out of the oven, it's best to let the rolls cool just enough so the filling can settle, but warm enough that the icing or glaze melts into the nooks and crannies.

Speaking of glaze, the finishing touch on these rolls usually involves either a classic cream cheese frosting or a simple powdered sugar glaze. Both options complement the fermented sourdough flavors while highlighting the cinnamon's warmth. For a more decadent experience, a cream cheese frosting with a hint of vanilla and lemon zest adds a pleasantly tangy sweetness. Meanwhile, a vanilla or even maple syrup glaze can keep things lighter and let the sourdough shine.

These sweet sourdough cinnamon rolls make a perfect weekend project. Their leisurely fermentation fits well with relaxed baking days, and the aroma fills your home with comforting scents that create a cozy atmosphere. Serve them fresh from the oven with a cup of coffee or tea, and you've got a breakfast or dessert that feels special without requiring complicated techniques or hard-to-find ingredients.

One of the best things about sourdough cinnamon rolls is how forgiving they can be for beginner bakers willing to experiment. While sourdough starters demand care and timing, you don't need to aim for perfection with every batch. Variations in rising time and hydration will simply add subtle differences to the flavor and texture, which makes the baking process both educational and satisfying. Each batch deepens your understanding of how sourdough behaves, so the next time you prepare them, you'll feel even more confident.

Of course, mastering these rolls also opens up numerous creative possibilities. You can try swapping out the classic cinnamon for a blend of spices inspired by chai tea or pumpkin pie. Adding dried fruits such as raisins or cranberries swirled in with the cinnamon sugar is another way to personalize your rolls. For a nutty twist, incorporate almond or hazelnut butter into the filling or swirl a ribbon of chocolate hazelnut spread for a sweet surprise.

When it comes to dough handling, gentle folding during the bulk fermentation helps keep the dough airy and open, contributing to that tender texture we all love in cinnamon rolls. Avoid over-flouring your work surface; a lightly floured board allows the dough to stretch nicely without sticking or becoming stiff. Rolling the dough evenly ensures consistent layers and prevents thin spots that might tear during shaping.

Storage and reheating are also straightforward. These rolls stay soft when stored in an airtight container at room temperature for a couple of days or frozen for longer storage. Reheating in a low oven or microwave restores that freshly baked feel, making them a convenient sweet treat anytime. They also make excellent gifts—homemade, warm cinnamon rolls say a lot about care and hospitality.

Learned well, sweet sourdough cinnamon rolls embody what this book is all about: simple techniques merged with rich flavors that anyone can bake with confidence. They're a testament to how just a few ingredients and thoughtful, patient preparation can transform everyday bread into an extraordinary experience. Whether you're baking for family gatherings, lazy weekend mornings, or a special occasion, these cinnamon rolls remind us that sourdough baking isn't just about crusty loaves and tangy bread—it's an art form that can be sweet, decadent, and deeply satisfying too.

Chapter 5
INTERNATIONAL BREAD TRADITIONS

Exploring international bread traditions opens up a world of flavors and techniques that can inspire every home baker. Each culture brings its own unique touch—from Italy's rustic ciabatta with its airy crumb to the crisp crust of the classic French baguette, and from the hearty German Bauernbrot to the soft, pillowy Indian naan perfect for scooping up curries. You'll find that breads like Greek pita, Moroccan khobz, and Turkish simit offer surprising versatility for everyday meals, while Ireland's soda bread and Scandinavian rye reconnect us with simple, nourishing ingredients. Even Mexican bolillo rolls, with their light, fluffy interiors, have a place at the table alongside these storied loaves. By understanding these traditions, you gain more than recipes—you get a chance to bring the spirit of global baking into your own kitchen with straightforward methods that deliver impressive results.

Italian Ciabatta Bread

Ciabatta, which means "slipper" in Italian, is one of those breads that instantly evokes the warmth and rustic charm of the Italian countryside. Its name describes the loaf's distinctive shape: long and flat with a slightly curved sole, resembling a slipper or a casual house shoe. This bread has become a beloved classic far beyond Italy, admired for its light, open crumb and crackly, golden crust—a texture that's both chewy and airy at once. If you're just starting out with artisan-style bread baking, ciabatta offers a rewarding challenge with its unique dough characteristics and rustic aesthetic.

Unlike some more compact bread varieties, ciabatta dough is quite wet, often described as a "high-hydration" dough. This means it contains a relatively large amount of water compared to flour, making the dough sticky and loose. While this can initially feel intimidating, the resulting crumb is well worth the effort. That open, holey texture is the hallmark of ciabatta, achieved thanks to the generous hydration and careful handling during the shaping process. The moisture in the dough encourages a soft, springy interior, full of those delightful irregular air pockets.

One of the secrets to ciabatta's distinctive texture lies in its fermentation method. Traditionally, a pre-ferment called biga is used, which adds complexity to the flavor and improves the dough's extensibility. Bigas are stiff starters made by mixing flour, water, and a pinch of yeast and letting them ferment slowly. This method boosts the bread's aroma and taste, giving it that slightly nutty, mildly tangy note that pairs perfectly with savory fillings or simple dipping oils.

Modern home bakers, especially beginners, often adapt the biga method to suit their schedules with overnight rises or refrigerated fermentation. This not only deepens the flavor but also makes handling easier come bake day. In fact, working with ciabatta dough encourages bakers to embrace some patience and gentle techniques rather than aggressive kneading. Instead of kneading vigorously, the dough is often folded and stretched gently—sometimes multiple times—to develop gluten strands without deflating the precious air bubbles.

Before shaping, the dough is usually allowed to ferment until doubled in size, becoming bubbly and alive. When ready, it's transferred to a well-floured surface to maintain its structure during shaping. Because the dough is sticky, using plenty of flour on your hands and the work surface is essential to prevent sticking. The goal isn't to knead the dough flat but to gently fold and shape it into an elongated loaf that will proof again before hitting the oven.

Baking ciabatta traditionally involves placing the loaf on a hot baking stone or steel to simulate stone oven conditions. This helps develop that iconic crust—a thin, crisp shell that shatters deliciously when bitten into. Steam is also introduced either by misting water into the oven or by creating a humid environment, which delays crust formation just long enough for the bread to rise fully and develop that beautiful, rustic surface. This technique ensures the crust holds a slight crunch while the interior remains moist and tender.

The flavor balance of ciabatta makes it incredibly versatile. With its mild wheat aroma and subtle tang from fermentation, it pairs wonderfully with a variety of ingredients. It's the perfect vessel for classic Italian sandwiches layered with fresh mozzarella, ripe tomatoes, and fragrant basil. But it's just as good as a simple accompaniment to soups or olive oil for dipping. Even toasted, ciabatta retains its charm—light, crispy, but still chewy inside.

For home bakers, ciabatta offers a fantastic introduction to artisan doughs that require a bit of finesse and timing. It teaches you how hydration affects dough texture and how gentle folding can develop structure without losing precious air pockets. Don't be discouraged by the initial stickiness; once you get the feel of managing wet dough, you'll find the process quite meditative and satisfying. Plus, pulling your own golden ciabatta from the oven, with its rustic imperfections and warm aroma, never gets old.

When it comes to ingredients, ciabatta is refreshingly straightforward. Quality flour—typically bread flour with a higher protein content—is key for developing gluten and supporting that open crumb. Water should ideally be filtered or at least room temperature to avoid interfering with yeast activity. Salt enhances flavor, while commercial yeast or wild yeast in the biga starter provides the lift. Because the dough relies on fermentation for flavor, resist the temptation to rush it. Letting the dough rise slowly, even overnight, will reward you with a bread that truly sings with character.

One tip for ensuring a beautiful crust is to avoid over-flouring the surface when shaping, which can create dry patches. Instead, use enough flour to prevent sticking but keep the loaf's exterior lightly coated and sticky in places. This helps the crust caramelize more evenly during baking. Also, if your kitchen is cool or drafty, try creating a warm, humid proofing environment by placing your dough bowl near a turned-off stove or covering it with a damp towel, encouraging consistent fermentation.

As you get comfortable, experimenting with add-ins like olives, sun-dried tomatoes, or fresh herbs can turn a straightforward ciabatta into a flavorful showstopper. The bread's light crumb absorbs moisture and flavors well without becoming soggy, making it a fantastic base for numerous variations. However, the classic plain ciabatta remains a timeless favorite—its rustic simplicity a testament to the art of bread making.

Ultimately, baking Italian ciabatta at home is about embracing the dough's natural qualities and working with it gently and patiently. It's a bridge between no-knead beginner breads and more advanced artisanal loaves, offering invaluable lessons about hydration, fermentation, and shaping. With practice, you'll find ciabatta an enjoyable and rewarding addition to your baking repertoire—a bread that's as versatile in the kitchen as it is inviting on your table.

FRENCH BAGUETTE BREAD

Few breads carry the unmistakable charm and cultural cachet of the French baguette. Often seen peeking out of market baskets and enjoyed as a staple on French tables, the baguette's iconic shape and irresistible crust have inspired home bakers worldwide. Despite its seemingly simple composition—just flour, water, salt, and yeast—the baguette demands respect and a little technique to truly master. This section explores the essence of the French baguette, its unique baking characteristics, and practical tips to bring a slice of France into your kitchen.

At first glance, the baguette appears straightforward: a long, slender loaf with a golden-brown crust and a tender crumb inside. However, achieving the perfect baguette crust and crumb is an art learned through understanding fermentation, dough hydration, and baking conditions. Traditionally, French bakers use a high-protein wheat flour that gives the bread its characteristic chewiness and structure. While American all-purpose flour can work in a pinch, opting for bread flour will deliver a more authentic result. The flour's protein content helps develop gluten strength, which is essential for the baguette's shape and airy interior.

Water and yeast are just as critical. The baguette dough usually has a slightly high hydration level, meaning the dough feels a bit sticky and soft compared to denser breads. This moisture encourages an open crumb structure dotted with irregular holes—a hallmark of well-made baguettes. Yeast works its magic during fermentation, creating carbon dioxide that puffs up the dough and adds flavor. A key part of the process lies in giving the dough enough time to ferment slowly, often with a bulk fermentation that lasts a few hours or even some cold fermentation in the fridge overnight. This slow rise enhances flavor complexity, allowing the natural sweetness of the wheat and subtle tang from fermentation to shine through.

Shaping the baguette is where skill really comes into play. The dough must be handled gently to preserve the gas bubbles inside, yet stretched carefully to reach the traditional elongated form. The technique involves flattening the dough into a rectangle, folding it with precision, and rolling it tightly before setting it on a baking sheet or couche—a linen cloth that helps maintain its shape during the final rise. The final proofing stage is crucial: the dough should rise until just puffed, avoiding overproofing which can lead to flat, dense loaves.

One defining characteristic of the French baguette is its crust. Achieving that crisp, crackly exterior requires a hot oven and steam during the initial phase of baking. Home bakers can mimic this by placing a pan of boiling water or ice cubes at the bottom of the oven or spritzing the dough with water just before baking. The steam delays crust formation, allowing the dough to expand fully before a thick crust sets in. This results in a loaf with a shiny, blistered crust that snaps when broken, contrasting beautifully with the soft interior.

Flavor is another aspect where baguettes stand out. Because the recipe is minimalist, each ingredient has a starring role. Quality flour, pure water, and natural fermentation create subtle nutty and slightly sweet notes. It's worth experimenting with hydration levels and fermentation times to find what works best in your environment—humidity, temperature, and flour vary widely from kitchen to kitchen. Patience and observation are key. Don't rush the process; respecting fermentation will reward you with richer taste and better texture.

For home bakers testing this technique, there are simplified baguette recipes that skip kneading or use commercial yeast with shorter fermentation times. These versions offer a great starting point to build confidence. Even with basic ingredients and equipment, you can craft fresh baguettes that smell irresistible and taste far superior to store-bought options. Mastering the baguette also provides a solid foundation to expand into more complex French breads and artisan-style baking.

Given the baguette's universal appeal, you can customize it slightly without losing its character. Adding seeds like sesame or poppy on the crust before baking creates enticing variation, or brushing a touch of olive oil on the loaf after baking enhances the crust's sheen and flavor. However, it's best to get comfortable with the classic formula before experimenting too much, as the joy of a true French baguette lies in its simplicity and balance.

Baking baguettes at home brings more than just a tasty loaf to your table; it connects you to a centuries-old tradition. The process encourages mindfulness and skill, reminding us why fresh bread remains an essential, comforting part of daily life. With practice, you'll gain the confidence to create baguettes that crackle when you slice them, offering a beautiful combination of crunchy crust and pillowy crumb that pairs beautifully with butter, cheese, soups, and more.

Before jumping in, consider these practical tips: use a sharp blade or bread lame for scoring the dough just before baking. This not only gives baguettes their classic tiger-stripe look but also controls where the bread expands in the oven. Keep your workspace lightly floured but avoid adding too much extra flour to the dough, which can stiffen the crumb. And make sure your oven is fully preheated—baking in a hot environment encourages an excellent rise and crust formation.

Finally, the beauty of baking French baguettes lies in the ritual itself—the mixing, fermenting, shaping, and baking become a rewarding process that fills your home with delicious aromas and ends with the satisfaction of making something truly authentic. Whether you're aiming to impress guests or simply treat yourself to fresh bread, the baguette holds a timeless allure and offers endlessly rewarding results for the home baker.

German Bauernbrot (Farmer's Bread)

German Bauernbrot, which translates to "farmer's bread," is a hearty, rustic loaf deeply rooted in Germany's baking traditions. It's the kind of bread that feels grounded and wholesome—perfect for those who want a satisfying loaf with a robust flavor and chewy texture. Unlike delicate brioche or fluffy sandwich bread, Bauernbrot carries the essence of countryside baking, often made with a mix of rye and wheat flours that give it both substance and that characteristic slightly tangy taste. If you're looking to add variety to your baking repertoire, this bread is an excellent choice that delivers rustic charm straight to your kitchen.

One of the defining features of Bauernbrot is its dense crumb and thick crust. The structure comes mainly from the rye flour, which doesn't contain as much gluten as wheat flour, making the dough heavier and less elastic. Many traditional recipes combine about 40-60% rye flour with wheat flour to provide enough gluten for rise and structure, while maintaining that deep flavor rye is known for. The wheat flour helps lighten the loaf and adds a tender bite without losing the rustic feel that Bauernbrot is famous for. This balance of flours is crucial and often the secret behind a truly authentic result.

Malty, nutty, and slightly sour—thanks to long fermentation or the addition of sourdough starter—Bauernbrot offers a complex flavor that's miles away from ordinary bread. Some bakers choose to use a sourdough starter to ferment the dough, which naturally enhances the bread's tanginess and improves shelf life. Even with a simple commercial yeast version, a slow, cold ferment in the refrigerator for 12 to 24 hours can develop more nuanced flavors and a chewy, moist crumb. Patience certainly pays off with this bread, and once you get the process down, it turns into a reliable favorite for sandwiches, with cheese, or just slathered with butter.

The crust of Bauernbrot also deserves a moment of appreciation. It's usually thick, crackly, and deeply browned, which comes from baking the loaf in a hot oven with steam during the first part of the bake. This steam helps the crust form slowly, allowing the bread to expand fully before setting into a crunchy, golden shell. You don't need fancy equipment to achieve this at home—simply toss a few ice cubes or pour water onto a preheated baking tray to create steam inside your oven. Watching the crust turn from pale dough to perfectly crackling bread is very satisfying and hints at the rich flavors lurking inside.

Making Bauernbrot at home might sound intimidating at first because of the rye flour and sometimes the sourdough component. However, it can be surprisingly simple if you stick to a straightforward recipe and don't rush the fermentation steps. Beginner bakers are encouraged to try a version using a mix of rye and wheat with commercial yeast first. This approach allows you to familiarize yourself with the dough's texture, which will be much denser than typical white bread dough. One key tip: rye dough feels stickier and less stretchy, so resist the urge to add too much flour. Instead, work gently and embrace that slightly tacky sensation—it's part of what makes Bauernbrot authentic.

Another neat aspect of Bauernbrot is its shape and scoring. Traditionally, loaves are shaped into rounds or oblongs, then dusted generously with flour before being scored with a sharp blade. The flour dusting adds to the rustic look, while scoring helps control how the dough expands during baking, preventing it from bursting unpredictably. The patterns can be simple slashes or more decorative cuts depending on your mood. The ritual of scoring is a moment to take pride in craftsmanship, encouraging bakers to be both creative and precise.

When it comes to serving Bauernbrot, it pairs beautifully with bold flavors. Think slices topped with sharp German cheeses, cured meats, or a thick spread of mustard. Its sturdy nature also makes it a great companion to soups and stews—perfect for dipping and soaking up savory broths. Because it's filling and packed with complex carbohydrates, it's often enjoyed as a mainstay in rustic German households, where meals highlight practicality and nourishment alongside flavor.

For home bakers interested in experimenting, try adding caraway seeds to the dough for an aromatic twist. Caraway is classic in German rye breads and lends a distinctive licorice-like hint that complements the sourdough tang and hearty rye base beautifully. Just a teaspoon or two stirred into the flour before mixing can transform the loaf subtly but noticeably. A clove of crushed garlic or some cracked black pepper can also add another layer of personality, but these variations work best after mastering the basic Bauernbrot formula first.

One of the surprises of making Bauernbrot is how forgiving it is once you understand its nature. The dough won't behave like a soft wheat loaf, but its robust character means it can handle some unevenness in shaping or timing without losing appeal. It's the kind of bread that welcomes imperfection; small cracks, slightly irregular shapes, or a thicker crust all add to the charm. Baking this loaf regularly lets you develop a rhythm, and you'll soon get a feel for the dough's behavior—how it smells, stretches, and looks ready for the oven.

In terms of equipment, Bauernbrot doesn't require much beyond a large mixing bowl, a sturdy wooden spoon or dough scraper, and a baking sheet or Dutch oven if you want to mimic the traditional steam environment. A kitchen scale to measure flour accurately is helpful but not mandatory if you're comfortable eyeballing common baking volumes. The key ingredient that might take some searching is good-quality rye flour—ideally fresh and finely milled. Without rye flour, the bread wouldn't have the signature flavor and density that truly puts Bauernbrot apart in the world of breads.

For anyone aiming to develop their bread baking beyond simple white or whole wheat loaves, German Bauernbrot represents a wonderful next step. It introduces you to new ingredients, fermentation techniques, and shaping skills while delivering a loaf that feels genuinely connected to a rich cultural tradition. Plus, the bread's hearty nature means it stores well, staying fresh for days if wrapped properly. This makes it a smart choice for meal prepping or enjoying over several breakfasts and lunches without rushing to finish.

Trying out Bauernbrot also allows a peek into the role bread plays in German everyday life. Unlike fancy artisan loaves that might be reserved for special occasions, Bauernbrot is practical, filling, and meant to be shared abundantly at the family table. It reflects the idea that bread is fuel and comfort all in one, an essential daily ritual rather than just food. Embracing this mindset can transform your approach to baking—from a chore into a satisfying, slow craft where the sensory joys of touch, smell, and taste come together beautifully.

Finally, don't be discouraged if your first Bauernbrot isn't exactly as pictured in cookbooks or bakeries. Rustic breads involve variables such as fermentation time, humidity, and flour type, which all affect the final loaf. Each bake teaches you something new, whether it's about dough hydration or crust color, so keep notes and enjoy the process. Soon enough, your kitchen will fill with the smell of baking bread that calls to mind German countryside kitchens and simple wholesome living—a truly rewarding experience for any home baker.

INDIAN NAAN BREAD

Among the rich tapestry of international bread traditions, Indian naan bread holds a special place, renowned for its soft texture, slightly smoky flavor, and its unparalleled versatility at the table. Naan is much more than just an accompaniment; it's a cultural icon deeply woven into Indian cuisine and beloved in kitchens worldwide. Traditionally cooked in a tandoor, a cylindrical clay oven heated to very high temperatures, naan develops those signature charred spots and a pillowy interior that make it irresistibly tasty. Though the authentic method is oven-dependent, there are plenty of simple ways to replicate naan at home without a tandoor, making it approachable for any kitchen enthusiast eager to add a bit of Indian flair to their bread repertoire.

What sets naan apart from many other flatbreads is its leavening. Unlike unleavened breads such as chapati or roti, naan dough usually contains yeast or sometimes baking powder, which allows it to grow soft and fluffy during cooking. Yogurt and milk are often mixed into the dough, contributing to naan's tender crumb and slight tang. These dairy ingredients also impart richness without making the bread heavy. This balance between softness, flavor, and a hint of chewiness has made naan a staple companion to dishes like butter chicken, saag paneer, and countless other curries and kebabs.

For home bakers, one of the joys of making naan is how adaptable it is. The basic dough requires just a handful of ingredients—flour, yeast, yogurt, water, salt, and a touch of sugar and oil. Each ingredient plays a role in shaping the final texture. Flour forms the structure; yogurt adds moisture and tang; yeast brings the rise, while sugar helps activate the yeast and contributes a subtle sweetness. You don't need specialized equipment to prepare naan, either. While a grill pan, cast-iron skillet, or a very hot oven can help mimic the tandoor's heat, making naan on a stovetop is perfectly doable and delivers delightful results.

Many recipes recommend an initial proofing period for the dough, allowing the yeast to work its magic and create those airy pockets in the final bread. Once the dough is ready, it's divided into small balls, then rolled out into teardrop or oval shapes. The shaping stage is forgiving—naans are rustic by nature and don't need to be perfectly round. The key to achieving that classic naan texture often lies in cooking it quickly over high heat. This method encourages blistering and browning on the outside, sealing in moisture and flavor.

Adding toppings before or after cooking opens up delicious possibilities. Traditional naan might be brushed with melted butter or ghee soon after coming off the heat, sometimes sprinkled with fresh minced garlic, chopped cilantro, or nigella seeds. Garlic naan is particularly popular and adds an aromatic touch that complements nearly any savory dish. Other variations incorporate stuffed fillings, such as spiced mashed potatoes or paneer, making the bread a snack or light meal on its own.

Understanding the science behind naan dough helps home bakers replicate traditional flavors while tailoring the bread to their kitchen tools and taste preferences. For example, using warm milk instead of water deepens the softness, while a longer fermentation can develop complexity in flavor but requires more planning. Some enthusiasts swear by letting the dough rest overnight in the refrigerator to improve texture, similar to slow-fermented artisan loaves, but without complexity or fuss. This flexibility lets beginner bakers experiment and find what works best for their palate and schedule.

Naan's global popularity has inspired countless variations, ranging from whole wheat naan to gluten-free versions using alternative flours like chickpea or millet. This adaptability shows the bread's place not only in traditional Indian settings but as a vibrant, evolving staple. Even for those new to bread making, mastering naan is a rewarding step—it combines basic dough techniques with an instantly gratifying result, perfect for pairing with favorite dips, spreads, and mains.

For the home baker, naan offers a great opportunity to sharpen several bread-baking fundamentals: mixing a slightly sticky dough, allowing proper fermentation, gentle rolling, and mastering quick stovetop cooking to achieve that delightful blistered finish. Once comfortable with these, variations become easy to try. Infusing the dough with herbs, spices, or even seeds adds both flavor and texture, while stuffed naans provide a canvas for culinary creativity.

Besides being delicious, making naan at home connects you to a world of cultural heritage. It's a bread that's been passed down through generations, adapting across regions and families, yet always carrying the essence of warmth and communal dining. Preparing naan from scratch can evoke the feeling of traditional Indian meal times—shared platters, vibrant flavors, and the joy of tearing off warm bread to scoop up curries.

When pairing naan with other dishes, consider its soft and slightly chewy texture as a conduit for saucy or spiced foods. It's also fantastic simply on its own; warm from the pan with a dab of butter, it becomes a snack worth savoring. Whether you serve naan at a family dinner or a casual weeknight meal, the freshness of homemade bread elevates the experience far beyond store-bought alternatives.

In sum, Indian naan bread is an inviting project for anyone looking to expand their bread baking horizons with something that's flavorful, relatively simple, and endlessly versatile. As you explore this recipe, keep in mind that perfecting naan is about balancing the characteristics of the dough, allowing adequate proofing, and cooking at the right temperature. The reward is an authentic piece of Indian culinary tradition right from your own stovetop.

This section aims to inspire home bakers not only to try naan but to embrace the joy of making bread with cultural significance—bread that complements diverse dishes and brings the warmth of Indian cuisine into your kitchen. As you continue your bread baking journey, naan offers a beautiful example of how simple ingredients and straightforward techniques can produce extraordinary results.

GREEK PITA BREAD

Greek pita bread stands out as one of the most versatile and beloved staples in Mediterranean cooking. Unlike many thick and hearty loaves you might be used to baking, pita is known for its light, pocketed structure that's perfect for stuffing with all kinds of delicious fillings—from tender grilled meats to fresh vegetables and tangy tzatziki sauce. It's a type of flatbread that's soft yet sturdy enough to hold every bite without falling apart, making it an ideal choice for home bakers aiming to add a touch of the Mediterranean to their bread repertoire.

What makes Greek pita bread unique is its characteristic pocket. This happens when the dough puffs up during baking, creating a hollow center. Achieving this puff at home might seem tricky at first, but with a few simple tricks and attention to dough temperature and oven heat, you can consistently get that perfect pocket. Traditionally, pita is baked at very high temperatures, which cause steam to form rapidly inside the dough, pushing it outward and forming the signature split. Home ovens can get close enough to this heat to recreate the effect with the right method.

Pita dough itself is fairly straightforward. You'll find it typically uses just basic ingredients—flour, yeast, water, salt, and sometimes a little olive oil to add softness and flavor. The beauty of pita is in its simplicity: no need for fat-laden doughs or lengthy fermentation processes. This makes it a great project for bakers who want something impressive without too many steps. Plus, it's quick to come together; the entire process from mixing to baking usually fits easily into a couple of hours.

One important tip involves the type of flour you choose. While all-purpose flour will do just fine, using bread flour with higher protein content usually helps develop the gluten network necessary for that stretchy, chewy texture and the eventual puff. If you're working with whole wheat or other whole grain flours, be ready for a denser pita, but still very flavorful. Balancing hydration—the amount of water relative to flour—is key; too little, and the bread won't puff properly, too much, and the dough becomes sticky and hard to handle.

Getting your dough to the right consistency is all about feeling rather than just following exact measurements. It should be soft and slightly tacky but still workable, something you can easily knead just enough to develop structure without exhausting yourself. Rest periods after kneading allow the gluten to relax, making shaping much easier and ensuring the pocket forms during baking. Many bakers find letting the dough rise twice—once before shaping and a short proof after—helps improve flavor and texture.

Once your dough has risen, dividing it into small balls is the next step. These will be rolled out individually into thin circles, usually about 1/4-inch thick or even slightly thinner. Uniform thickness and shape help to achieve even baking and proper puffing. Dust your work surface and rolling pin with flour to prevent sticking, but don't overdo it—you don't want dry spots in your dough. Roll confidently, applying steady pressure but avoiding tearing the dough, which would prevent pocket formation.

Baking pita requires a hot oven, ideally preheated to at least 500°F. If your oven can't reach that high, crank it to the maximum it can safely handle. A baking stone or steel placed in the oven during preheating works wonders, mimicking the intense, direct heat pita traditionally experiences in a stone or wood-fired oven. This intense heat is exactly what causes the dough to inflate quickly, trapping steam inside and creating the signature pocket. If you don't have a baking stone, a heavy baking sheet placed upside down will work as a substitute.

When placing your rolled pitas on the hot surface, give them space to puff freely and avoid overcrowding. Baking time is short—usually just 2 to 3 minutes per batch. You'll want to watch closely for the surface to balloon up and develop light golden spots, a sign the interior steam is doing its job. Flip them briefly if you want lightly browned spots on both sides, then transfer immediately to a clean towel to keep them soft and warm. Steaming the fresh pitas in a towel after baking keeps the exterior from drying out and helps maintain that pliable texture perfect for sandwiching.

One fascinating aspect of homemade pita is how wonderfully fresh it tastes compared to store-bought versions. Unlike many commercial pitas that can feel dry or overly soft with added preservatives, homemade pita bursts with a light, slightly chewy texture and a subtle nutty flavor from the flour itself. Fresh pita almost melts when you bite into it, especially when paired with Mediterranean flavors like garlic, lemon, and olive oil.

Homemade pita is incredibly versatile in the kitchen, too. From creating quick sandwiches or wraps to cutting them into triangles for dipping in hummus or baba ganoush, they provide a perfect vehicle for many dishes. Leftover pita can be toasted and served as chips, or lightly grilled and drizzled with herbs and olive oil for a simple appetizer. Because they bake up so quickly, you can whip up a batch even when you want something fresh and homemade but kitchen time is limited.

Alongside understanding the technique, mastering the balance of hydration and the temperature of your ingredients will make a big difference in your results. For instance, slightly warm water wakes the yeast gently without killing it, encouraging a steady rise. Too hot, and you'll risk deactivating the yeast, while too cold might slow fermentation time considerably. Your yeast choice—be it active dry or instant yeast—also makes a minor difference in how the dough behaves, but both work well for pita with minor adjustments to proofing times.

Greek pita bread also invites creativity beyond the traditional plain version. Once you get comfortable with the basics, you might try adding herbs like oregano or thyme into the dough, giving your pita a vibrant lift that enhances any sandwich or dip it accompanies. Some bakers dust the tops lightly with sesame seeds before baking for added crunch and a subtle nutty flavor. These small tweaks personalize pita to your taste and increase the fun of baking.

Because pita dough is relatively forgiving and quick to make, it's a wonderful introduction to bread baking for beginners looking to branch out from softer sandwich breads or classic loaves. Its straightforward ingredients list means no exotic flours or complex equipment are necessary, making it accessible to almost any home baker. Plus, pita offers immediate gratification—fresh bread in under an hour of active time, which goes a long way in keeping motivation high.

One area often overlooked is the shaping and rolling technique, which can dramatically influence the final result. Some bakers prefer to gently stretch the dough balls by hand to maintain more air bubbles and elasticity, while others use a rolling pin to create a perfectly flat circle. The key is to achieve an even thickness so the pita puffs uniformly in the oven rather than forming thin, crisp spots or thick, doughy areas that never rise.

When it comes to serving, traditional Greek pita shines in Mediterranean breakfasts and dinners alike. It pairs famously with gyro, souvlaki, or falafel, but also complements simple spreads of olives, feta cheese, and fresh vegetables. Because the pita pocket is so adaptable, it encourages experimentation with kid-friendly fillings like grilled chicken and cheese or vibrant mixtures of roasted veggies and hummus, making it a family-friendly option too.

Greek pita bread brings a slice of Mediterranean culture to your kitchen without demanding complex ingredients or steps. Its straightforward preparation, quick baking time, and delicious, fresh results make it a standout recipe for anyone eager to expand their bread-making skills beyond the usual loaf. By mastering this humble flatbread, you'll add versatility to your baking toolbox and open the door to countless fresh, flavorful meals that showcase homemade bread at its best.

MOROCCAN KHOBZ BREAD

Moroccan Khobz bread is a staple in Moroccan households and an integral part of their culinary culture. This round, flat loaf is much more than just a side dish; it represents tradition, community, and the art of simple, rustic baking. Unlike many everyday breads that rely on elaborate ingredients or techniques, Khobz comes together with basic pantry staples, making it an accessible and rewarding project for home bakers looking to explore international bread traditions.

The beauty of Khobz lies in its distinctive crust and airy crumb, achieved without the need for fancy equipment or complicated processes. It's typically baked on a griddle or in a heavy-bottomed pan, which imparts a tender yet chewy crust on the outside while keeping the inside soft and slightly open in texture. This bread is often used for scooping up tagines, dips, or salads, so it's soft enough to tear easily but substantial enough to hold up to hearty Moroccan dishes.

What's truly inspiring about Khobz is its versatility. The basic dough is made from white or semolina flour, water, salt, and yeast. Some versions incorporate a little olive oil for subtle flavor and moisture. The dough is easier to handle than many traditional artisan breads and requires only a brief resting period before shaping, which makes it a great choice for beginners. It's also forgiving—if you miss the perfect kneading technique or timing, the outcome is still delicious and satisfying.

One of the defining characteristic techniques when baking Khobz is its shaping. Traditionally, the dough is formed into a round disk, roughly six to eight inches in diameter, with a gently flattened top. Before baking, the surface is often scored or marked with a crisscross or other simple pattern. This not only looks visually appealing but helps the bread cook evenly and adds a bit of texture to the crust. Beyond the aesthetics, this scoring becomes a handy guide for tearing the bread when serving—portions break apart neatly along the scored lines.

Making Khobz also introduces home bakers to semolina flour, a common ingredient in Moroccan bread-making. Semolina lends a unique, slightly gritty texture and beautiful golden hue to the crust, enhancing both flavor and appearance. If you can't find semolina easily, all-purpose flour can stand in, but using semolina will give you that authentic taste and texture experience. Experimenting with flour blends is encouraged if you're looking to tweak the crumb or crust to your preference.

The fermentation stage of Khobz is straightforward but can feel magical. After mixing, the dough is left to rise just enough to double, usually within one to two hours depending on the room temperature. This rise time doesn't demand the long, slow fermentation typical of sourdoughs or multi-stage breads, making Khobz a quicker baking option without sacrificing flavor. During this rest, the yeast works to create tiny air bubbles in the dough that give the bread its tender, porous crumb.

Once shaped, Khobz is placed into a hot, dry skillet or onto a baking stone if using an oven. If using a stovetop, cooking the bread directly on a cast iron or heavy pan really captures the traditional method and results in a wonderful crust. You'll want to cook it over medium heat to allow the outside to brown without burning while the inside cooks through. It's fairly quick and requires a watchful eye, but you'll get a deeply flavorful crust that pairs perfectly with Moroccan meals or just a good smear of butter and honey.

Throughout Morocco, variations of Khobz can depend on region, personal family recipes, and available ingredients. Some bakers add a pinch of sugar to help activate the yeast, while others might include spices like anise or fennel seeds for aromatic notes. Around festive times and special occasions, richer versions of Khobz appear, sometimes sweetened or enriched with olive oil for a silkier texture. These differences highlight the bread's adaptability, allowing bakers to use the same foundational recipe as a base for creative tweaks.

If you're stepping into Moroccan baking for the first time, making Khobz is an excellent introduction to working with simple dough techniques and enjoying bread as an everyday art. Because it doesn't need kneading machines, proofing baskets, or long fermentation, Khobz emphasizes the pleasure of making bread feel accessible. It encourages a connection with tradition while giving you control over ingredients, freshness, and flavors.

The communal aspect of Moroccan bread also comes through when baking Khobz. Traditionally, families gather around meals where everyone tears pieces from the same large loaf, sharing not just food but time and conversation. This spirit can be replicated in your home kitchen, where baking Khobz becomes more than mixing ingredients. It's about creating moments of connection around simple, wholesome food.

From a practical standpoint, Khobz's round, flat shape makes it versatile for sandwiches, dips, or as a scoop for tagines and stews. Its slightly chewy texture contrasts nicely with tender, hearty Moroccan dishes, making it a perfect complement without overpowering. Plus, it stores well for a day or two—wrapped in a clean kitchen towel to keep crust tenderness. If you want a fresh loaf, it reheats beautifully in a warm skillet or oven, reviving its soft crumb and crispy crust.

Getting started with Khobz at home involves just a few simple steps: mixing your flour, water, salt, and yeast; allowing the dough to rise; shaping into a disk; scoring the top; and baking or pan-cooking until golden. Because of its simplicity, this bread is an excellent stepping stone before attempting more challenging international breads with longer fermentations or extensive shaping requirements.

Incorporating Khobz into your baking repertoire allows you to diversify your bread-making experience with a bread that's rich in history yet straightforward enough to bake on a weeknight. It's a wonderful way to explore both flavor and technique from Moroccan culinary traditions without becoming overwhelmed. Once you have it down, you can play with add-ins, different flours, or even turn your kitchen into a mini Moroccan bakery.

Ultimately, Moroccan Khobz bread is an invitation to savor bread not just as a carbohydrate but as a cultural experience. The process connects you to centuries-old baking methods and a community that values bread as the cornerstone of every meal. For the home baker eager to expand their skills and recipe collection, Khobz offers a delicious, rewarding, and authentic taste of Moroccan bread traditions with every warm, tear-apart bite.

Turkish Simit Bread

If you've ever wandered through the bustling streets of Istanbul, you might have noticed vendors selling a particular kind of circular bread that's both crunchy and chewy, often sprinkled with sesame seeds. This is Turkish Simit, one of Turkey's most beloved traditional breads. Simple in its ingredients yet rich in flavor and texture, simit is more than just bread; it's a cultural staple, enjoyed at breakfast tables, street corners, and cafés alike.

Simit's charm lies in its unmistakable ring shape and the distinctive way it's prepared. The dough, usually made from basic ingredients like flour, yeast, water, salt, and a bit of sugar, undergoes a brief rise before the shaping stage. What really sets simit apart, though, is the dipping process: the shaped dough rings are dipped into a thick mixture of water and molasses or grape syrup, then generously coated with toasted sesame seeds. This dipping step gives simit its signature glossy, slightly sweet, and deeply nutty crust.

The clever use of molasses or pekmez creates a beautiful contrast between the tender interior and the crisp, caramelized exterior. The sesame seeds not only add crunch but also a fragrant nuttiness that complements the bread perfectly. This is a bread that works wonderfully on its own but shines as an accompaniment to a breakfast spread featuring cheeses, olives, tomatoes, and strong Turkish tea.

For the home baker, simit offers a satisfying project that's not too complicated but delivers impressive results. The dough is straightforward—no fancy flours or hard-to-find ingredients are needed, just simple pantry staples. While the process involves a step to dip the dough rings before baking, it's quite manageable, especially once you get into the rhythm of shaping and dipping batches.

One of the joys of baking Turkish simit at home is capturing that authentic aroma that fills the kitchen—the deep roasted sesame, the hint of sweetness from the molasses, and the warm yeastiness from the bread itself. Simit bakes quickly, developing a crunchy crust that contrasts beautifully with the soft, airy crumb inside.

Besides being delicious, simit also has a fascinating history that reflects its place in Turkish culture. It dates back centuries, often referred to as 'the circular bread of the Ottoman Empire.' Street vendors, known as "simit sellers," have long roamed the cities with their trays or carts piled high with these rings, calling out to passersby. This bread wasn't just a snack—it was sustenance for workers, students, or anyone needing a quick, portable meal. Baking simit at home connects you to this rich tradition while allowing you to tweak the recipe to your liking.

When making simit, pay attention to the shaping stage—the rings should be neither too thick nor too thin, about an inch or so wide, to achieve the ideal balance of crustiness and soft interior. After you dip the dough in the molasses-water mixture, be sure to coat it with plenty of sesame seeds while they're still sticky. Some bakers like to toast their sesames beforehand for extra flavor; it's a small step that adds depth and aroma.

One useful tip is to let the dough rise just enough to become puffy but not overly airy. Because simit is meant to be crisp outside and tender inside, handling the dough gently helps preserve its structure. The baking process itself favors a hot oven, typically around 450°F (230°C), which helps the molasses caramelize beautifully and the crust to crackle with every bite.

As a home baker, experimenting with simit also opens doors to variations. While traditional simit sticks to the molasses and sesame combo, some bakers introduce additions like nigella seeds or even poppy seeds. There are also versions that incorporate whole wheat flour for a heartier loaf or use a touch of olive oil in the dough for softness. These tweaks allow you to personalize the bread while staying true to its core characteristics.

Pairing simit with other dishes is part of the experience. At home, try serving simit with cream cheese or a drizzle of honey for a simple breakfast. It's also fantastic alongside hearty soups or salad plates, where its crunchy texture adds a satisfying element. Because simit holds up well without getting soggy quickly, it's excellent for sandwiches too—think slices of fresh tomato, cucumbers, or even deli meats tucked inside the ring.

For beginners, simit may seem a bit different from standard loaves due to its dipping step, but once you master it, you'll find it's both rewarding and fun to bake. The dough doesn't require intensive kneading or long fermentation times, making it a great choice for those who want delicious homemade bread without endless waiting. The ingredients are affordable and accessible, so you won't need to hunt for specialty flours or enzymes.

If you want to explore a bit deeper, you could even try baking simit alongside traditional accompaniments like Turkish white cheese or beyaz peynir, freshly sliced cucumbers, and boiled eggs, recreating an authentic Turkish breakfast experience at home. It's a chance not just to bake but to celebrate flavors and rituals from another corner of the world.

Ultimately, baking Turkish simit bread reminds us how much joy simple ingredients and straightforward techniques can bring. This bread carries centuries of history yet fits seamlessly into modern kitchens and meal plans. Whether you're shaping the dough rings, dipping them in molasses, or sprinkling sesame seeds, you're participating in a time-honored tradition. And the final reward—a warm piece of crispy, chewy simit straight from your oven—is well worth every step.

Irish Soda Bread

Irish soda bread holds a special place in the world of international bread traditions. Unlike many other breads that rely on yeast for rising, soda bread is leavened with baking soda and buttermilk. This quick-acting combination allows the bread to rise without any fermentation or kneading, making it incredibly approachable for beginner bakers. Its simplicity and speed make it an ideal loaf for home cooks who want a fresh bread with minimal fuss. Plus, its rich earthy flavor and dense, tender crumb make it a comforting staple.

Historically, Irish soda bread was born out of necessity. In rural Ireland, yeast was expensive and often unavailable, so households turned to baking soda—a cheap and reliable leavening agent. Adding buttermilk, a common leftover byproduct of butter making, not only activated the soda but also gave the bread a subtle tang and moist texture. This method created a filling and wholesome loaf that could be made with whatever flour was on hand, typically soft wheat or barley. The tradition has endured because soda bread is versatile, forgiving, and delicious.

One of the most appealing aspects of Irish soda bread is how quick it comes together. The dough usually requires just four main ingredients: flour, baking soda, salt, and buttermilk. Many families also add a bit of sugar or butter to enrich the flavor. Some variations incorporate seeds, currents, or raisins to offer a touch of sweetness, but the classic loaf remains plain and hearty. Because there's no yeast to proof, the entire process—from mixing to baking—can be done within an hour, perfect for when you need homemade bread on short notice.

When preparing an Irish soda bread, the key lies in handling the dough gently. Unlike yeast doughs where kneading develops gluten, soda bread dough should be mixed just enough to bring ingredients together. Overworking the dough can make the bread tough, so folding it lightly with a spoon or your hands produces the best crumb. After shaping the dough into a round loaf, it's traditional to cut a deep cross on the top before baking. This not only helps the heat penetrate evenly, ensuring thorough cooking, but it also holds symbolic meaning—some say the cross wards off bad luck or invites blessings.

The crust of Irish soda bread forms a lovely, crisp exterior that contrasts with the soft, crumbly interior. It's often golden-brown and robust enough to stand up to hearty stews or thick spreads. It's amazing how such a humble loaf pairs so well with almost anything—be it sharp cheese, salted butter, or smoky bacon. Because the bread doesn't keep as long as yeast breads due to its lack of preservatives, it's best enjoyed fresh on the day it's baked, which encourages bakers to make it often.

One of the reasons soda bread fits beautifully into a beginner's bread-baking journey is the minimal equipment and ingredients needed. There's no need for a mixer or complex ovens—just a bowl, a spoon, and a hot oven. Even the shape can be flexible: classic rounds work wonderfully, but a free-form oval or small individual rolls are great alternatives. This adaptability makes soda bread ideal for experimenting and customizing once you're comfortable with the basic formula.

From a nutritional standpoint, soda bread made with whole wheat or a blend of flours can provide a nice boost of fiber and nutrients. Using whole grain flour adds complexity to the flavor and a nuttier bite, balancing the bread's natural tang. For those who want a more indulgent version, adding a spoonful of honey or some butter integrates sweetness and moisture without complicating the process. On the flip side, keeping it plain keeps the bread perfect for savory accompaniments and traditional meals.

In Ireland, soda bread is often served alongside classic dishes like Irish stew, corned beef, or simple soups. Because it doesn't rely on yeast, it fits into the rhythm of everyday cooking rather than special occasions alone. Baking this bread can be a moment of quiet satisfaction: watching the dough rise as the oven transforms it into a golden loaf ready to break open and share. For many, that shared experience—gathering around warm bread at the table—is the heart of the tradition.

For home bakers, mastering Irish soda bread helps build confidence in working with quick breads and manipulating basic ingredients. It introduces key concepts like acid-base reactions in baking, hydration of flour, and minimal dough handling—all important building blocks for exploring more complex breads. Plus, it's forgiving enough to recover from small mistakes, so it's a great canvas for testing your understanding of bread chemistry without frustration.

Beyond its practicality, soda bread carries a story that connects bakers to a rich cultural heritage. Each loaf represents a slice of Irish history, weaving together threads of survival, ingenuity, and comfort. Baking Irish soda bread at home lets you bring a piece of that tradition into your kitchen, celebrating not just the bread itself but the enduring spirit of a community that cherished simple, wholesome food.

In this book, you'll find recipes that explain how to make Irish soda bread from scratch with clear, step-by-step instructions. Tips on ingredient substitutions and creative flavor additions will encourage you to put your own spin on this classic loaf. Whether you want a traditional version or a modern twist with seeds and herbs, soda bread is ready to welcome your touch.

Even if you've never baked bread before, Irish soda bread offers a gentle introduction—combining ease, speed, and wonderful taste in a loaf you'll want to bake again and again. As you experiment, you'll see how minimal ingredients can create something so satisfying. This bread invites you to embrace the joy of baking without getting overwhelmed, making it an approachable first step toward broader bread-baking adventures.

Most importantly, when you pull a warm loaf of Irish soda bread from your oven, you're not just making food—you're crafting a moment. The aroma fills the room, the crust crackles as you slice, and the first bite delivers comforting flavors that you can share with family and friends. That simple pleasure is why Irish soda bread has endured for centuries, and why it continues to earn its place in kitchens worldwide.

SCANDINAVIAN RYE BREAD

When it comes to hearty, flavorful breads, Scandinavian rye bread stands out as a beloved staple with deep roots in the cuisines of Denmark, Sweden, Norway, and Finland. This bread isn't just a side dish — it's an essential part of daily life, revered for its dense texture, slightly sour tang, and complex flavor profile. For home bakers eager to add something substantial and authentic to their bread repertoire, Scandinavian rye bread provides an excellent challenge, blending traditional methods with approachable techniques.

At the heart of Scandinavian rye bread is rye flour, which gives this bread its distinctive dark color and earthy taste. Unlike wheat, rye has less gluten, which means the dough will often be denser and stickier, resulting in a loaf that's firmer and more flavorful than typical wheat breads. The natural acidity comes from sourdough fermentation, an age-old method that not only develops those signature tangy notes but also greatly improves the bread's shelf life. Even if you're new to sourdough, don't be intimidated—starting with a simple rye sourdough starter can be a rewarding experience, adding an authentic flavor that sets this bread apart.

Traditional Scandinavian rye bread often combines both light and dark rye flours. This blend balances out flavors and moisture, creating a loaf that's rich yet moist without being too heavy. The texture ranges from slightly crumbly to chewy, depending on the recipe and fermentation time. Caraway seeds are frequently added, imparting a warm, aromatic undertone that complements the dense rye perfectly. While optional, they're a classic touch that elevate the bread's character and make it instantly recognizable.

One of the most interesting aspects of Scandinavian rye bread is how it fits into everyday meals. It's typically sliced thin and served with butter, cheese, cold cuts, or smoked fish like salmon. Its robust flavor stands up well to strong toppings, making it an ideal base for open-faced sandwiches or "smørrebrød," a traditional Danish lunch option known for its beautiful, layered ingredients. Incorporating rye bread into your own kitchen routine introduces a new element of flavor and nutrition that pairs well with both simple and elaborate meals.

Baking Scandinavian rye bread at home requires emphasis on fermentation and patience. Because rye dough behaves differently than wheat dough, it's not ideal for quick-rise methods. Many traditional recipes call for slow, cool fermentation, sometimes fermenting overnight or even longer. This slow process allows the rye starches to break down properly, filtering out harsh flavors while deepening the sourness. It also strengthens the dough's structure, letting you achieve that dense yet tender crumb without extreme effort.

Although rye dough can seem intimidating at first due to its stickiness and lower elasticity, working with it becomes much easier once you understand the crucial steps. Unlike wheat dough, kneading rye excessively is usually discouraged because it breaks down the delicate fiber network, leading to gummy crumbs. Instead, gentle folding and stretching — along with a long rise — promote the right loaf texture. Using a mixture of rye and bread flour, rather than pure rye flour, often makes the dough easier to handle for beginners while maintaining rye's characteristic flavor.

For those looking to explore Scandinavian rye bread in their own kitchens, here are a few practical tips. First, pay close attention to hydration. Rye flour absorbs a lot of water, so expect the dough to be quite sticky and dense. Don't be tempted to add too much extra flour in an attempt to make the dough easier to handle; that often results in a dry, crumbly bread. Embrace the sticky texture and remember that careful handling is key. Second, use a good sourdough starter tailored for rye or a rye preferment. This starter is your main flavor driver, responsible for the bread's tang and helping preserve freshness. You can build or refresh your starter a day or two ahead of baking for best results.

Another factor to consider is the baking vessel. Rye bread benefits from baking in a Dutch oven or a heavy lidded pot, which creates steam and preserves moisture in the oven. This environment helps form a crackly crust while keeping the crumb tender inside. Without steam, rye loaf crusts tend to be overly hard or dry. If you don't have a Dutch oven, placing a pan of water in the oven during baking can help simulate the necessary humidity.

Historically, Scandinavian rye breads carried cultural significance beyond everyday nutrition. In Nordic countries, rye was a crop that thrived in cooler climates where wheat struggled, so it became a dietary staple for centuries. Families often passed down recipes with slight variations—some included molasses or malt syrup to add sweetness, others embraced a denser, more sour loaf. This bread was also prized for its longevity; well-made loaves kept for days or even weeks without spoiling, which was crucial during long winters.

In modern kitchens, Scandinavian rye bread is surprisingly versatile. While it excels as a breakfast or lunch bread, it can also be repurposed creatively. Toasting transforms it into a crunchy platform for rich butters, nut butters, or preserves. You can cube leftover rye bread for savory stuffing or layer it in bread puddings enhanced with spices like cardamom or cinnamon. Many bakers also experiment with rye blends for artisan-style loaves that fuse Nordic traditions with contemporary baking trends.

If you're curious about variations, several types of rye breads come from Scandinavia. Dark, dense "rugbrød" from Denmark is particularly famous—this version often contains whole rye kernels or seeds as well, adding extra texture. Swedish "rågbröd" can range from lighter and softer to richly sour and robust. Finnish rye breads sometimes feature a touch of sweetness and less acidity, which makes them approachable for those new to rye. Regardless of style, the common denominator is a deliberate fermentation process that respects rye's unique qualities.

Mastering Scandinavian rye bread can feel like unlocking a door to a whole new baking world. It demands patience and attention but rewards home bakers with loaves that are nourishing, flavorful, and deeply satisfying. The sense of tradition baked into each slice connects you with centuries of Nordic baking heritage while offering practical health benefits, thanks to rye's high fiber and nutrient content.

For beginners, starting with a mixed rye and wheat flour dough, a reliable sourdough starter, and a slow, overnight fermentation curve usually works best. As you gain confidence, experimenting with purer rye flours, different seed additions, or even incorporating molasses can deepen your understanding of this bread's immense potential. Baking Scandinavian rye bread isn't just about making bread; it's about celebrating a resilient and timeless tradition, right in your own kitchen.

Mexican Bolillo Rolls

When diving into the world of international breads, Mexican bolillo rolls offer a fascinating glimpse into a cherished staple of Mexican baking. Bolillos, often described as the country's version of a French roll, carry their own distinct character shaped by local tastes and traditions. These small, crusty rolls are a bread essential in Mexican kitchens, serving as the base for sandwiches, accompanying meals, or just enjoyed fresh with butter or beans. Their presence on street corners and in bakeries showcases their cultural importance as much as their culinary allure.

At a glance, bolillos seem simple — a crusty outer shell envelops a soft, airy crumb. But achieving the perfect balance between a crisp crust and a tender interior is a skill worth mastering. The crust needs enough crunch to contrast the soft middle without being so hard that it detracts from the eating experience. Home bakers often find bolillos rewarding because, although they benefit from careful handling, the overall process is straightforward and highly approachable.

The dough itself is traditionally made from basic ingredients: white wheat flour, water, salt, sugar, and yeast. Because Mexican cuisine favors fresh and flavorful bread but without unnecessary fuss, the recipe usually omits enrichments like fats or dairy, though regional tweaks might add a touch of lard or butter for softness. The simplicity of the ingredients means the quality of the flour and water, combined with proper fermentation, makes all the difference. A moderately hydrated dough, whipped up to elastic perfection, lays the foundation for the roll's distinctive texture.

One characteristic step in making bolillos involves shaping. The dough balls are rolled out into an oval shape before baking. This shaping technique creates the signature look: an elongated roll with tapered ends and a deep slash lengthwise down the center. This single score is not just decorative—it allows the roll to expand properly in the oven, forming that iconic "split" along the top, which enhances the crunchiness of the crust and showcases the beautiful interior crumb.

Baking temperature and steam are crucial for mastering bolillos at home. The oven is usually heated quite high, often between 425 to 475 degrees Fahrenheit, to develop a well-browned, crackling crust quickly. Steam during the first few minutes of baking is essential—it prevents the crust from setting too early, allowing the dough to expand fully and encouraging that gorgeous shine bolillos are known for. Simple methods to create steam include placing a pan of water in the oven or misting the dough before closing the door. This step requires attention but pays off with a bakery-quality finish.

Consistency is key when baking bolillos. Home bakers often find that a few tries help them really dial in the perfect bake time and moisture level. For example, an oven rack positioned in the center or slightly lower might deliver the best heat distribution to brown the bottoms evenly without burning, and adjusting the baking time between 20 to 25 minutes usually produces the ideal crumb. Watching and learning from each batch encourages confidence and offers insight into how the dough responds to environmental factors like humidity and altitude.

Because these rolls are so versatile, they appear all across Mexican eating occasions. They are the star of the "torta," a traditional Mexican sandwich filled with everything from carnitas to fried eggs to avocado and refried beans. The bolillo's crust holds up well against moist or rich fillings, preventing sogginess that can ruin a sandwich in softer bread. At the same time, the soft interior adds a pleasant chew that balances textures perfectly.

Beyond the torta, bolillos function as a sturdy accompaniment to soups, stews, or salsas. In fact, the act of tearing pieces off a warm bolillo to soak up a broth or scoop refried beans is almost ritualistic in many Mexican households. That hands-on way of eating bread makes baking bolillos at home all the more satisfying — it connects you directly to the comforting everyday experiences of Mexican cuisine.

For beginner bakers, the good news is that bolillo dough is forgiving enough to experiment with. It's a yeast dough that can be mixed by hand or with a stand mixer, and the shaping is simple enough to learn quickly. Even though bolillos might look like an artisan bread, they don't demand hours of intensive kneading or complicated techniques. The key is patience during the rising times and paying attention to the dough's feel and elasticity rather than relying strictly on the clock.

Another useful tip when making bolillos is the use of a baking stone or steel, if available. These tools mimic the intense, even heat of traditional brick ovens, resulting in a superior crust and better oven spring. If a stone isn't accessible, a heavy baking sheet turned upside down and preheated in the oven serves as a good substitute. Ensuring your oven is fully preheated before introducing the dough helps replicate the effect of a hot bakery oven, triggering that crucial oven spring where the rolls puff up beautifully.

While it's tempting to rush through the process, enjoying the sensory cues along the way enhances both results and enthusiasm. Feeling the dough stretch smoothly, smelling the yeasty aroma as it rises, and watching the crust golden to perfection builds confidence and connection to the craft. Each batch of bolillos reinforces not just technique but also an appreciation for bread's central role in daily life and celebration.

Mexican bolillo rolls showcase how straightforward ingredients, paired with thoughtful technique, can create something truly special. They invite home bakers to explore the rhythm and patience of bread making without overwhelming complexity. Serving warm bolillos fresh from the oven evokes a sense of tradition and comfort that few other breads match. They remind us that sometimes the simplest bread can bring the greatest joy.

If you're new to making international breads or looking to expand your repertoire with authentic yet manageable recipes, bolillos are a delightful project. Their everyday presence in Mexican kitchens, combined with their flexible use and delightful texture, guarantees you'll want to make them again and again. Use them to build sandwiches, dip in flavorful sauces, or simply enjoy with butter and coffee—the possibilities are wonderfully endless.

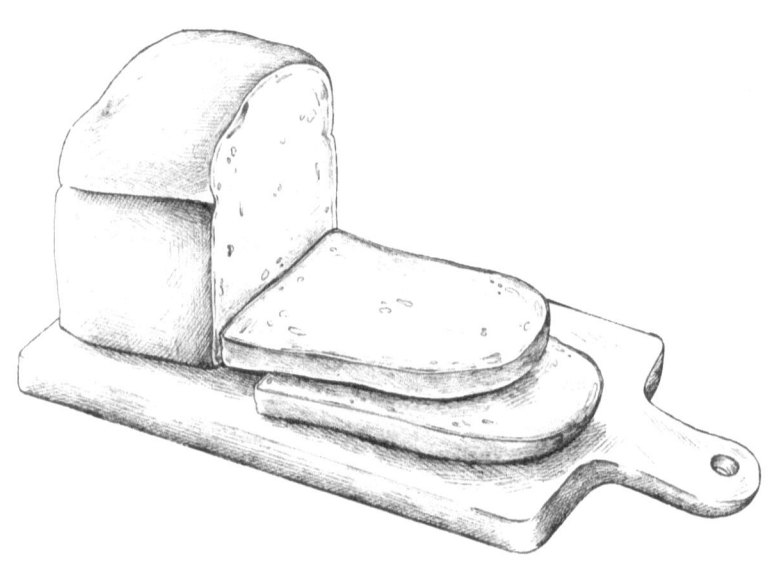

Chapter 6
SWEET AND ENRICHED BREAD RECIPES

For those who love their bread with a touch of sweetness and a richer, more indulgent texture, this chapter offers a delightful collection of recipes that go beyond the basics. These breads often combine ingredients like butter, eggs, sugar, and sometimes even cream, transforming simple dough into tender, flavorful loaves perfect for breakfast, snacks, or dessert. Whether you're drawn to the classic buttery brioche, the swirled decadence of chocolate babka, or the comforting warmth of pumpkin spice bread, these recipes provide straightforward steps and helpful tips to achieve that perfect golden crust and soft crumb. You'll find options suited for various occasions, from festive panettone to everyday banana nut bread, all designed to bring that special homemade charm to your kitchen without overwhelming your schedule. This chapter celebrates the joy of enriched breads that you can feel proud to share with family and friends.

Classic Brioche Bread

Brioche bread stands out among sweet and enriched breads for its incredible tenderness and subtly rich flavor. This French classic combines a high butter and egg content, which melts into the dough, creating a soft, buttery crumb that practically melts in your mouth. It may seem intimidating at first, but with a bit of patience and attention to detail, making classic brioche at home can be a truly rewarding baking experience.

The beauty of brioche is in its balance—rich but not heavy, slightly sweet yet perfectly suited for savory applications too. Its golden crust and tender interior come from ingredients working in harmony: eggs lend flavor and moisture, butter delivers richness, while the yeast ensures a light, airy structure. Unlike lean breads where water and flour dominate, brioche feels more like baking with a pastry dough, so expect a longer mixing and rising time to develop the dough's strength without overworking it.

When starting brioche dough, temperature is key. The eggs and butter should be at room temperature to blend smoothly. Cold butter can result in a lumpy mixture and uneven crumb, while too-warm ingredients risk overproofing early on. Once mixed, the dough will feel sticky and soft, often requiring more gentle kneading or a stand mixer fitted with a dough hook. Proper gluten development is essential here—it helps trap the air produced by yeast and supports that signature fluffy texture.

One of the secrets to successful brioche is in the rising stages. Because of its richness, the dough takes longer to rise than typical bread. Don't rush it; letting the dough proof slowly in a warm but not hot environment allows the yeast to work steadily. This slow rise results in a light crumb filled with the delicate air pockets that brioche is known for. Often, the dough will be refrigerated between rises, which deepens the flavor and makes handling easier when shaping.

The shaping process itself offers plenty of room for creativity. Brioche can take various forms—from the classic round loaf with a small "nub" on top known as a "tete," to braided loaves or individual buns. Regardless of shape, brushing the finished dough with an egg wash before baking gives the crust a beautiful glossy sheen and helps it brown evenly. That shiny, golden crust contrasts perfectly with the soft, buttery inside, creating a stunning loaf both in look and taste.

Baking brioche demands attention to temperature and timing. Because of the high fat and sugar content, it tends to brown faster than other breads, so watching closely during baking is important. Too high a temperature risks a crust that's too dark while leaving the inside undercooked. The ideal bake will produce a loaf with a rich aroma, an inviting golden surface, and a slightly springy feel when pressed gently.

Storage and serving also play a key role in enjoying your brioche. Freshly baked brioche tastes best the same day—warm, tender, and aromatic—but because it's so rich, it's less prone to drying out quickly. To keep it fresh, store it wrapped tightly at room temperature for up to two days. Brioche also freezes well, so you can slice and freeze extra loaves for toast or decadent sandwiches down the line.

Brioche is incredibly versatile. It shines simply toasted with a touch of jam or honey, yet it also serves as the perfect base for more elaborate treats like French toast or bread pudding. Its buttery richness makes it an excellent companion for both sweet spreads and savory fillings like ham and cheese. No matter how you choose to enjoy it, home-baked brioche elevates meals with its tender crumb and buttery flavor.

Though the process may feel challenging at first, classic brioche is a wonderful way to deepen your baking skills. Working with enriched dough teaches control over fermentation, dough handling, and shaping—all foundational techniques that will serve you well across many types of bread. Once you master the basics, you can experiment by adding nuts, dried fruits, or turning brioche dough into decadent pastries or rolls.

For those who want a straightforward brioche recipe, focus on the basics: high-quality butter, fresh yeast, and good flour. Accuracy in measuring and patience during rises are more important than speed. If your kitchen feels cool, consider using your oven's proofing setting or placing the dough near a warm (not hot) spot. Always remember that enriched doughs like brioche respond well to gentle care and can be forgiving when handled thoughtfully.

By embracing the process, you'll find this rich bread rewarding to make and share. Its tender crumb and rich flavor deliver a true crowd-pleaser, whether served at breakfast, as a sandwich base, or alongside a hearty stew. Once you bring brioche into your baking repertoire, it opens up a world of sweet and savory possibilities, making it a staple worth returning to again and again.

CHOCOLATE BABKA BREAD

Chocolate babka bread is one of those special treats that feels both indulgent and comforting at the same time. Originating from Eastern European Jewish cuisine, babka has become adored worldwide for its rich layers of dough and glossy, chocolate-filled swirls. If you're familiar with the idea of enriched breads from earlier in this chapter, babka takes that concept to a dreamy next level. It combines a soft, buttery dough with the decadent sweetness of chocolate, creating a loaf that's as beautiful to look at as it is to eat.

What really sets chocolate babka apart is its distinctive appearance—the twisted, layered effect comes from rolling and folding the dough with a generous chocolate filling before baking. This gives every slice a unique pattern of chocolate ribbons that's almost too pretty to eat, yet you'll find yourself reaching for more anyway. Its glossy finish, often achieved with an egg wash or simple syrup glazing, adds to its irresistible charm. Baking a babka at home may sound intimidating, but with a little patience and care, it's well within reach, even for those who've only just started baking bread.

The dough in a chocolate babka is what you might call "enriched," meaning it contains butter, eggs, sugar, and milk, which all contribute to its tender crumb and slight sweetness. It's similar to brioche dough but a bit less rich, striking a great balance between fluffiness and structure. This base dough makes the bread soft and pillowy, perfect for soaking up the luscious chocolate inside without becoming overly heavy. Because of the butter and eggs, the dough needs a good amount of kneading and some time to rest and rise, but each of these steps helps build the bread's texture and flavor.

Filling the babka is where you can let your creativity shine. The traditional filling is made with bittersweet or semisweet chocolate, sometimes combined with cocoa powder for added depth. Some bakers mix butter and powdered sugar into the chocolate to create a smooth, spreadable paste. You can also add finely chopped nuts like walnuts or pecans for a crunchy contrast, or even a hint of cinnamon or espresso powder to intensify the flavors. The filling should be generously spread onto the dough so every bite delivers a chocolatey punch.

Once filled, the dough is rolled up tightly and then cut lengthwise to expose the layers of dough and chocolate. This is one of the most satisfying parts of making babka: twisting those two halves together to create a beautiful, swirling pattern. There's an almost meditative quality to the shaping process as you see the chocolate ribbons emerge. How tightly you twist the dough will affect the final shape and crumb, but don't worry too much—some imperfections only add to the homemade charm.

Baking babka requires some patience, as the enriched dough benefits from a slow, steady rise. This helps develop flavor and ensures that delicate crumb structure. It's best to keep the dough somewhere warm but not too hot—a draft-free spot around 75°F is perfect. During baking, the loaf will puff up and turn a deep golden brown, and it's important to watch closely to prevent the chocolate from burning. Because the filling contains sugar and fat, it can caramelize quickly, so keeping the oven temperature moderate is key.

One of the reasons chocolate babka is such a popular choice for home bakers is its versatility. While the classic version features chocolate, the same technique works wonderfully with other fillings like cinnamon sugar, Nutella, or even fruit preserves. It's a wonderful canvas to experiment with flavors that suit your taste or special occasion. Plus, babka stores well—wrapped well, it can last several days at room temperature and tastes fantastic when gently reheated.

Serving chocolate babka is an experience in itself. The rich, buttery layers combined with that luscious chocolate filling make it perfect for breakfast or an afternoon treat with a cup of coffee or tea. Because of its decadent nature, a thin slice is often enough to satisfy sweet cravings. However, it's equally welcome as a dessert, especially when paired with a scoop of vanilla ice cream or a drizzle of whipped cream. It's the kind of bread that brings people together, inviting sharing and conversation.

Baking your own chocolate babka also offers a rewarding sense of accomplishment. Watch as simple ingredients transform into a loaf overflowing with flavor and visual appeal. The process reinforces important bread-making skills—kneading enriched dough, rolling and filling, shaping, and understanding proofing times—all while keeping things approachable for someone just discovering bread baking. Even if your first attempt doesn't look exactly like those glossy baker's shop versions, it will taste fantastic, and each loaf teaches valuable lessons for the next.

In this recipe book, the babka recipe is designed to be practical and straightforward, so you don't get overwhelmed by too many steps or complicated techniques. You'll learn how to mix and knead the dough properly, how to prepare a smooth chocolate filling that spreads easily, and tips for shaping the loaf so your swirls really pop. There's also guidance on timing your rises and baking to ensure a tender interior and beautiful crust. Whether you want to bake for a holiday, a weekend brunch, or just to treat yourself, this chocolate babka is a showstopper that's surprisingly simple to pull off.

Remember, one of the joys of bread baking lies in experimentation. While this recipe offers a classic chocolate take, feel free to add your own twist, whether it's a handful of chocolate chips, a swirl of peanut butter, or a splash of orange zest in the filling. As you gain confidence, you might find yourself tweaking the dough for different textures or trying new shaping methods. Chocolate babka provides a delicious foundation for this exploration.

Finally, a small but important note on ingredient quality: because this bread is all about the chocolate, it's worth investing in good-quality chocolate that melts smoothly and tastes rich. The difference is noticeable in the end product and well worth the small extra cost. The same goes for using fresh butter, active yeast, and fresh eggs, all of which contribute to that irresistible texture and flavor.

Chocolate babka bread is more than a recipe; it's a baking tradition filled with warmth and indulgence. Its rich dough, glossy chocolate swirls, and tender crumb offer an unforgettable sensory experience that many home bakers cherish. With some patience and simple tools, you can bring this special bread into your own kitchen, impress family and friends, and enjoy the satisfaction of creating something truly delicious from scratch.

STICKY CINNAMON ROLLS

Cinnamon rolls hold a special place in the hearts of many home bakers, combining the warmth of spices with the softness of enriched dough. Sticky cinnamon rolls, in particular, elevate this classic treat by adding a rich, gooey topping that clings lovingly to each swirl. These rolls are perfect for those mornings when you want a cozy, indulgent start to your day, bursting with the comforting flavors of cinnamon, butter, and sugar, all embraced by a tender, fluffy bread base.

Making sticky cinnamon rolls from scratch might seem intimidating at first, but with the right approach, they're surprisingly straightforward. It all begins with a soft, enriched yeast dough—a key characteristic that sets these rolls apart from more rustic breads. This dough is enriched with ingredients like butter, sugar, eggs, and milk, which not only add flavor but create that melt-in-your-mouth texture you crave. The warmth and moisture from these enrichments help the dough stay tender as it rises, giving you rolls that are soft and airy rather than dense.

One important tip is to allow the dough to rise until it almost doubles in size. This can take anywhere from one to two hours, depending on your kitchen temperature. Don't rush this step; it's critical to developing the right crumb structure. A well-risen dough results in delicate layers and those iconic, spiral swirls you want to see in every piece. After the first rise, gently roll out the dough into a rectangle, keeping its surface lightly floured to avoid sticking but not so much that the dough dries out.

The magic of sticky cinnamon rolls truly comes from their filling and glaze. The filling is a simple but flavorful blend of softened butter, brown sugar, and cinnamon. Brown sugar works wonderfully here because it melts into a luscious caramel as the rolls bake. For an added touch, some recipes call for a pinch of salt or even a dash of nutmeg to deepen the flavor profile. When spreading the filling, don't skimp—generous layers ensure each bite is bursting with warmth and sweetness.

Once the dough is spread with the cinnamon sugar mixture, rolling it up into a tight log is the next step. The tightness of this roll affects the overall texture and appearance of the final cinnamon rolls. If the roll is too loose, the centers risk being a bit flat or underfilled; too tight and the layers might become compressed and dense. Finding the right balance means rolling just enough to maintain distinct spirals but keeping the dough airy.

Cutting the roll into even pieces sets the stage for that classic cinnamon roll shape. Using a sharp knife or a piece of unwaxed dental floss works well to slice through without squashing the dough. Each piece is then placed snugly in a baking dish, allowing the rolls to rise again. This second rise is crucial because it's when the dough relaxes and puffs up, bringing back its softness and preparing for that perfectly tender bake.

The sticky element comes from the rich glaze applied before or after baking—or sometimes both. A common method is to prepare a caramel-like sauce with butter, brown sugar, and cream or milk. This sauce is poured into the bottom of the baking pan before placing the rolls on top. As the rolls bake, the mixture bubbles up, soaking into the bottoms and sides, creating a luscious sticky layer. When inverted right after baking, this layer becomes a delicious topping that clings to every spiral with a shiny, irresistible glaze.

Another popular approach is to drizzle or spread a cream cheese frosting over the warm rolls just before serving. The tanginess of cream cheese balances the caramel sweetness beautifully, adding a fresh dimension that makes sticky cinnamon rolls a decadent treat. If cream cheese isn't your thing, simply dusting the rolls with powdered sugar or a simple vanilla glaze can highlight the buttery cinnamon flavors without overpowering them.

The best sticky cinnamon rolls often call for a bit of patience, especially with dough that needs time to rest and rise. It might feel like a wait, but the results speak for themselves—soft, flavorful layers with a gooey, sticky finish that melts in your mouth. A warm kitchen filled with the scent of cinnamon and caramelizing sugar is also a fantastic bonus, making these rolls perfect for weekends, special occasions, or even an indulgent breakfast any day of the week.

It's also worth noting that sticky cinnamon rolls are incredibly forgiving. Slight variations in temperature or ingredient proportions rarely ruin the final product. The enriched dough can adjust easily to imperfect measurements, and the sweetness of the filling and glaze lends itself to small tweaks based on personal taste. For instance, those who prefer less sugary rolls can reduce the sugar in the filling or opt for a lighter glaze.

If you're looking to get creative, sticky cinnamon rolls offer plenty of room for customization. Adding chopped nuts like pecans or walnuts to the filling introduces a pleasant crunch, while incorporating diced apples or raisins gives the rolls a fruity twist. Some bakers enjoy experimenting with spices beyond cinnamon—cloves, allspice, or cardamom all bring new warmth to the classic recipe. The key is balancing enough spice to complement without overpowering the buttery dough.

When it comes to baking tools, a simple non-stick or well-greased round baking pan works perfectly. The snug fit of the rolls encourages them to rise upwards and press against each other, resulting in soft sides that almost pull apart with ease. For an extra-special presentation, you can sprinkle a handful of coarse sugar or cinnamon on top before baking, adding crunch and visual appeal.

Finally, storing and reheating sticky cinnamon rolls is easy and worthwhile. These rolls keep well at room temperature for a day or two if covered loosely with plastic wrap or foil. For longer storage, they freeze beautifully—just wrap them tightly in plastic wrap, then foil to protect against freezer burn. To reheat, a few seconds in the microwave or a warming oven bring back their fresh-baked softness, as though they just came out of the oven.

Sticky cinnamon rolls invite bakers into a world where baking meets comfort food in the most delightful way. Their rich, tender dough wrapped around sweet, warmly spiced filling and topped with that luscious sticky glaze make them a recipe worth mastering early in your bread baking journey. Whether for weekend brunch, holiday mornings, or an anytime treat, these rolls combine simple ingredients with thoughtful technique to create moments of home-baked joy.

Monkey Bread Loaf

Monkey Bread Loaf is the perfect sweet and sticky treat that transforms the simple act of bread baking into a fun, interactive experience. This pull-apart bread is beloved for its gooey caramel coating and soft, fluffy interior. If you've been searching for a recipe that's as visually impressive as it is delicious, monkey bread fits the bill. It's a crowd-pleaser for breakfast, brunch, or even dessert, and its nature invites sharing and hands-on eating, making it ideal for family gatherings or cozy weekend mornings.

Unlike traditional loaves, monkey bread isn't baked as one solid piece. Instead, it's made from small pieces of dough rolled in cinnamon sugar and then layered in a pan with a gooey butter sauce or caramel. As it bakes, the dough pieces meld together, soaking up the sweet sauce and creating a magnificent tangle of tender bites that pull apart effortlessly. That delightful combination of crisp edges and melt-in-your-mouth centers is what sets monkey bread apart from any other sweet bread.

Preparing monkey bread might seem intimidating at first, but the process is surprisingly straightforward and satisfying. It's very forgiving for beginners too—you don't need any advanced shaping or intricate techniques. You'll start by preparing a slightly enriched dough, one that's soft and supple, enriched with butter, sugar, and eggs to achieve that tender crumb. This dough can be roughly made by hand or with a mixer, which means you can comfortably attempt it even if you've only recently started baking bread.

One of the greatest joys of making monkey bread is how customizable it can be. The classic version relies on cinnamon and brown sugar, but you might want to experiment with adding chopped nuts, mini chocolate chips, or even bits of dried fruit to the layers. Some bakers love incorporating a touch of vanilla or even a pinch of nutmeg in the dough or coating to elevate the flavor complexity. These small touches let you tailor monkey bread to your own taste and occasion, allowing creativity to take the spotlight.

The magic of monkey bread comes to life during baking. As the dough rises in the warm oven, the butter and sugar melt together into a luscious syrup that caramelizes around each piece. This process forms crisp, golden pockets of sweetness, contrasting with the soft, pillowy bread beneath. You'll want to be careful with timing here—too little baking and the dough stays undercooked inside, too much and the sugary coating can harden or burn. Following precise oven temperatures and baking times ensures that perfect balance.

Once your monkey bread loaf is out of the oven, it needs some cooling time before you dig in. That cooling phase lets the caramel set just enough to hold the loaf's shape without becoming overly sticky or spread out. When cooled, the loaf lifts out of the pan in a stunning dome-shaped cluster of sweet rolls that pull apart like magic. It's practically irresistible, but it's best served slightly warm for the ideal combination of soft dough and melted caramel. A light dusting of powdered sugar or a drizzle of glaze on top adds an elegant finish for presentation, especially if you're serving guests.

While monkey bread is naturally sweet and rich, you can manage its sweetness by adjusting the amount of sugar or swapping out some ingredients. For instance, using coconut sugar or maple syrup in the coating imparts a more complex flavor and less refined sweetness. Another approach is to pair the bread with slightly tart accompaniments like fresh berries or yogurt to balance its richness. These small tweaks allow you to enjoy monkey bread as a special treat without feeling too indulgent.

This pull-apart loaf also provides a wonderful canvas if you're interested in layering flavors. Many bakers choose to experiment with drizzles after baking—cream cheese glaze is a popular choice, offering a tangy creaminess that complements the sweet bread perfectly. Honey or caramel sauce can be added as well for an extra shine and flavor boost. You might also try folding in spices like cardamom or cloves in the dough for a warm, aromatic twist that shines especially well during cool weather baking.

In terms of presentation and serving, monkey bread shines in its simplicity. It's traditionally baked in a bundt pan or similar round pan that lets the individual pieces stack up beautifully, creating a striking centerpiece straight from the oven. Bringing this dish to the table offers more than just flavor—it invites interaction, sharing, and a little bit of fun. Everyone gets to pull apart their own bite-sized piece, which makes it especially great for kids or casual gatherings where formal slicing isn't as convenient.

Storing monkey bread is quite simple too. Since the dough is enriched and moist, the loaf tends to stay soft for a day or two at room temperature when covered with plastic wrap or stored in an airtight container. If you want to keep it longer, refrigeration is an option, though you might prefer to reheat individual pieces to bring back that fresh-baked softness and gooey texture. Reheating can be done gently in the microwave or in a low-temperature oven with a light cover to prevent drying out.

Because monkey bread is such a fun entry point into enriched bread baking, it's a wonderful recipe for those expanding their home baking repertoire. It builds confidence with yeast dough while delivering immediate, impressive results. Plus, its forgiving nature means you can experiment freely without much risk of failure. By mastering this loaf, you'll get a feel for handling enriched dough, working with layers, and understanding how sugar and butter can transform simple bread into something special.

Monkey bread loaf is also a great way to introduce friends and family to the joys of homemade bread. Its approachable, hands-on nature makes it perfect for baking sessions with kids or beginner enthusiasts, encouraging participation and curiosity about the baking process. The reward—tearing apart warm, sweet breads dripping with caramel—is motivation enough to try again and again.

For home bakers aiming to expand their sweet bread skills, monkey bread offers a welcome break from the usual sliced loaves or rolls. It's a reminder that bread can be playful and indulgent, capturing the comforting memories of cinnamon rolls while showcasing the basics of yeast bread in a unique form. Whether made for weekend breakfasts, holiday treats, or as a conversation-starting centerpiece, monkey bread loaf transforms everyday ingredients into a luscious, shareable delight.

In summary, monkey bread loaf deserves a spot in your baking arsenal. It's easy enough to make on a busy day, versatile enough to suit different flavor preferences, and charming enough to impress any crowd. With a bit of patience, basic ingredients, and a willingness to pull apart and enjoy, you'll discover why this classic sweet bread continues to be cherished by bakers around the world. So, grab your mixing bowl and prepare for a hands-on bread adventure that's equal parts delicious and delightful.

LEMON POPPY SEED LOAF

Adding a bright twist to the world of sweet breads, the Lemon Poppy Seed Loaf is a refreshing and vibrant option everyone should have on their baking roster. It perfectly blends the tangy zing of fresh lemon with the subtly crunchy poppy seeds, creating a loaf that's as delightful to eat as it is to smell while baking. This bread strikes an ideal balance between sweet and tart, making it a wonderful choice for breakfast, an afternoon snack, or even a light dessert alongside a cup of tea or coffee.

What makes a lemon poppy seed loaf especially appealing for home bakers, particularly beginners, is its straightforward preparation and forgiving nature. Unlike some enriched breads that rely heavily on kneading or precise timing, this loaf welcomes a gentler, more relaxed approach. You can prepare the batter with basic mixing tools, no fancy equipment needed, and the result will still be impressive. Plus, the ingredients are mostly common pantry staples – flour, sugar, eggs, butter, fresh lemons, and poppy seeds – making it convenient to whip up any time you want a citrusy treat without a trip to the store.

The texture of the loaf is another highlight. It manages to be soft and tender inside, with a slightly crisp but not tough crust. This delicate crumb structure is achieved partly through the use of enriched ingredients like butter and eggs, which give the bread a rich mouthfeel without being heavy. The poppy seeds introduce subtle little bursts of texture, adding interest without overwhelming the palate. The loaf also keeps well for several days if stored properly, allowing the citrus flavors to mellow and deepen, which many find even more enjoyable with time.

Starting your lemon poppy seed loaf is all about understanding the method of combining wet and dry ingredients without overmixing. Overworking the batter can lead to a dense, tough texture, so it pays to fold ingredients gently until just combined. Freshly squeezed lemon juice and grated zest are essential here—don't settle for bottled lemon juice if you want the fullest flavor. The zest imparts a fragrant brightness that complements the lemon juice's acidity, rounding out the loaf's citrus profile beautifully.

The batter itself has a consistency closer to a thick cake batter rather than traditional bread dough, which makes this loaf more like a quick bread in technique but still satisfying as a bread choice. This difference means it doesn't need rising times or kneading but rather bakes directly in a loaf pan. Depending on your oven and loaf pan size, expect about 50 to 60 minutes of baking time, occasionally checking for doneness by inserting a toothpick in the center. If it comes out clean or with just a few moist crumbs, your loaf is ready.

One of the most enjoyable parts of making this loaf is the aroma that fills your kitchen. The scent of fresh lemon mingled with warm vanilla and buttery notes creates an inviting atmosphere even before the bread is out of the oven. That sensory reward alone often inspires bakers to repeat this recipe time and again. It's the kind of aroma that makes a moment feel special and cozy, perfect for relaxed weekend mornings or casual get-togethers.

While the classic lemon poppy seed loaf keeps things simple and bright, there's room to personalize the recipe to your taste. Some bakers like to add a light glaze made of powdered sugar and lemon juice on top, which enhances the lemon flavor and adds a shiny finish. Others may fold in a handful of blueberries or even a dash of almond extract to introduce more complexity. These variations allow bakers to experiment without complicating the basic framework of the recipe, maintaining ease and accessibility.

When it comes to ingredient choices, quality matters, especially in a recipe with relatively few components. Use fresh eggs at room temperature to help the batter emulsify properly and achieve the best rise. Opt for unsalted butter, which gives you better control over the loaf's salt content, allowing the lemon brightness to shine through without interference. High-quality poppy seeds will offer a nuttier flavor and a more noticeable crunch; given their small size, even subtle differences can be detected in the final loaf.

From a practical standpoint, the lemon poppy seed loaf is a fantastic make-ahead bread. It freezes well once fully cooled, wrapped tightly to prevent freezer burn. When you want to enjoy it, simply thaw it at room temperature. This makes it a go-to option for bakers who want easy, flavorful bread on hand for quick breakfast or snack needs. Because it keeps so well, you can also slice and serve parts of the loaf over several days without worrying about it drying out quickly.

For home bakers just stepping into the world of sweet and enriched breads, this loaf teaches excellent foundational skills. You practice mixing techniques without kneading, understanding how citrus interacts with sweet batters, and how baking times and temperatures affect results. By mastering this recipe early on, you build confidence that carries over to more complex recipes down the line. The lemon poppy seed loaf distills these lessons into one delightful, approachable recipe.

Beyond the basics, there's something inspiring about making a loaf that feels both classic and contemporary. The lemon poppy seed flavor combo has risen in popularity precisely because it's fresh, light, and universally appealing. It suggests care and creativity, all while being incredibly simple to pull off. This loaf invites bakers to enjoy the sensory pleasures of baking—the smells, the tactile mixing, the golden crust—without requiring the expertise that artisanal breads might demand.

In a broader sense, enriched sweet breads like this one open doors to the endless possibilities in bread baking. Exploring recipes that highlight fruits, nuts, seeds, and spices encourages experimentation and helps build a versatile skill set. The lemon poppy seed loaf fits neatly as a dependable favorite. It's both approachable enough for beginners and interesting enough to keep more experienced bakers engaged. Every slice offers a little celebration of fresh ingredients transformed by a simple, loving process.

Whether you're aiming to expand your repertoire beyond basic sandwich loaves or seeking a reliable recipe for homemade gifts and gatherings, this lemon poppy seed loaf is an excellent choice. It pairs wonderfully with a variety of spreads—from clotted cream and honey to mascarpone and marmalade—offering different ways to enjoy each bite. As you work with this loaf, it becomes easier to appreciate how subtle variations in mixing time, lemon zest quantity, or baking environment can shape the final product, sharpening your senses as a baker.

In conclusion, the lemon poppy seed loaf is much more than just a sweet bread—it's a testament to how simple ingredients and straightforward techniques can come together to create something truly special. It stands out in any bread basket with its cheerful flavor and inviting texture. By making this loaf a regular part of your baking routine, you not only nourish yourself and those around you but also deepen your understanding of how enriched bread doughs respond to hands-on, home baking. This loaf promises satisfaction in every slice, inspiring bakers to continue exploring the vivid world of sweet and enriched breads.

Pumpkin Spice Bread

When the air cools and leaves begin to turn shades of amber and gold, few things capture the essence of the season quite like pumpkin spice bread. This loaf is more than just a treat; it's a warm invitation to savor autumn's flavors right from your oven. The aroma that fills your kitchen while it bakes is often enough to spark a cozy, nostalgic feeling, reminding many of chilly mornings and leisurely weekends wrapped in a blanket. For anyone new to bread baking, pumpkin spice bread offers a delicious way to explore enriched doughs that rely on a blend of warm spices and moist, tender crumb.

The beauty of this bread lies in its balance between spice and sweetness. Ground cinnamon, nutmeg, ginger, and cloves work together to build a flavor profile that's both comforting and vibrant. These spices resonate perfectly against the subtle pumpkin puree that keeps the loaf moist while lending a naturally sweet depth. Unlike some breads that require intense kneading or complex shaping, pumpkin spice bread offers a forgiving dough that's straightforward to mix and shape, making it perfect for home bakers eager to try something seasonal yet simple.

What sets pumpkin spice bread apart from many quick breads is that it uses yeast as a leavening agent rather than baking powder or soda. This means you get that signature bread texture—soft inside with a slightly chewy crust—that quick breads simply can't replicate. While the process takes a bit longer because of the rising times, the result is a loaf with a complex, developed flavor that you can't rush. Plus, working with yeast helps you build foundational bread-making skills without the intimidation of more elaborate artisan techniques.

Starting with the ingredients, fresh pumpkin puree is key. Whether you cook and mash your own pumpkin or buy quality canned puree, it's essential to avoid pumpkin pie filling, which contains added sugars and spices that will throw off the balance. The puree not only adds moisture but also a subtle earthiness that complements the warm spices. Brown sugar or molasses can be incorporated to enhance that deep sweetness, but be mindful to adjust amounts if you prefer a sweeter loaf or want to dial back the sugar for a less rich version.

Flour choice also plays a crucial role here. All-purpose flour is typically the go-to for achieving the soft crumb, but for added texture and nutrition, a portion of whole wheat or spelt flour can be introduced. Keep in mind that whole grain flours may absorb more liquid, so slight tweaks to the liquid ratios might be necessary. When mixing the dough, it's important to combine wet and dry ingredients thoroughly but avoid overmixing, which can toughen the bread. You want to see a cohesive dough that feels tacky but not overly sticky.

After the dough has come together, it needs to rise until doubled in size. This stage is crucial because it develops the bread's structure and flavor. Depending on ambient room temperature, this could take one to two hours. While waiting, enjoy the fragrant hint of pumpkin spice floating around your kitchen. Once the dough has risen, gently punch it down to release any large gas bubbles, shape it into a loaf or place it in a simple bread pan, and allow it to proof again. The second rise is shorter but equally important for that light, airy texture.

Baking pumpkin spice bread is a rewarding experience especially as you peek through the oven window to watch it develop a deep golden crust. Once baked, the loaf needs to cool completely before slicing to prevent a gummy interior. The wait can be the hardest part, but this cooling period lets the crumb set fully and the flavors mellow perfectly. When sliced, you'll find a tender, moist crumb flecked with warm spices and balanced sweetness—ideal for breakfast or an afternoon snack paired with coffee or tea.

One of the great joys of this bread is its versatility. You can enjoy it plain or dress it up with a simple cream cheese glaze, a drizzle of maple syrup, or a schmear of butter. Some bakers enjoy adding chopped nuts like walnuts or pecans for a pleasant crunch, while others swirl in a ribbon of brown sugar cinnamon mixture just before baking to create pockets of sweet, caramelized goodness. These small tweaks make the bread your own without complicating the process.

For those who like to plan ahead, pumpkin spice bread also freezes well. Slice it and wrap individual portions so you can thaw just as much as needed for a quick treat. This makes it practical for busy days when you want something homemade but don't have time to bake from scratch. Reheating gently in a toaster or microwave revives its softness and releases those inviting spices once again.

This bread presents a wonderful gateway into more elaborate sweet and enriched recipes. It demonstrates how simple ingredients can transform into something special with a bit of time and care. Mastering this pumpkin spice loaf not only introduces you to yeast dough techniques but also builds confidence in balancing flavor and texture—important skills that you'll carry forward to other enriched breads in this collection.

While the spice blend mentioned is traditional, don't hesitate to experiment with your favorites. Cardamom or allspice can add new dimensions for those who enjoy exploring different flavor profiles. The pumpkin base is quite forgiving, allowing you to get creative without fear of failure. Try adjusting spices or adding dried fruit for a festive twist, keeping in mind the moisture content so the bread bakes evenly.

Because this recipe doesn't rely on complex techniques, it's perfect for beginner bakers looking to expand beyond basic white or whole wheat loaves. It teaches patience through rising times and offers a tactile experience mixing dough rich with wet ingredients and spices. The end product is not just bread—it's a seasonal statement, a fresh-baked embrace that fills your home with comfort and joy.

In summary, pumpkin spice bread captures the warmth of fall with every slice. It's a rewarding project that yields a soft, flavorful loaf perfect for breakfasts, brunches, or a lovely snack. Baking this bread encourages experimentation with yeasted dough in an approachable way, enriching your baking repertoire with delicious skills that bring lasting satisfaction. Whether you stick to the classic formula or personalize the spices and add-ins, pumpkin spice bread is a must-bake for anyone ready to deepen their baking confidence while celebrating the flavors of the season.

Banana Nut Bread

Banana nut bread holds a special place in the world of sweet and enriched breads. It's that warm, comforting loaf that feels like a hug in bread form, perfect for breakfast, afternoon snack, or even dessert. For home bakers, it's an excellent recipe to master because it combines simplicity with delicious results, requiring minimal kneading yet offering rich flavor and moist crumb. Overripe bananas, which might otherwise go to waste, act as the star ingredient here, naturally sweetening the bread and keeping it moist. Adding nuts provides a satisfying crunch that pairs beautifully with the tender crumb.

One great thing about banana nut bread is how forgiving it is, making it accessible to beginner bakers. You don't need precise techniques or special equipment to achieve success. The mixing process is straightforward: typically, you just combine your wet ingredients—including mashed bananas and oil or butter—with your dry ingredients like flour, baking soda, and salt, then fold in your nuts before popping the loaf into the oven. This ease makes it a favorite starter recipe for anyone looking to transition from simple yeast breads to something a bit more indulgent.

Texture plays a key role in great banana nut bread. The goal is that perfect balance between moistness and structure. Too dry, and it feels crumbly; too wet, and it's dense or underbaked. The bananas themselves do a lot of work here—they add natural moisture and flavor, so the quality and ripeness of your bananas matter more than you might think. The freckled, overly soft bananas provide the best sweetness and aroma, ensuring your bread comes out tender and flavorful every time.

Nuts are almost non-negotiable in classic banana nut bread. Walnuts are the traditional choice, lending a slightly bitter, earthy note that complements the sweet banana beautifully. Pecans are a tasty alternative if you prefer something a bit sweeter and softer. Toasting the nuts lightly before folding them in can intensify their flavor and add a crisp crunch that contrasts nicely with the bread's softness. Just be mindful of the quantity—too many nuts can overwhelm the loaf and make it difficult to slice cleanly.

While the basic banana nut bread recipe is straightforward, there are plenty of ways to customize it. Some bakers like to add a pinch of cinnamon or nutmeg for warmth and a hint of spice. Others may fold in chocolate chips or dried fruit for extra bursts of flavor and texture. A splash of vanilla extract or a tablespoon of yogurt can also enrich the batter, contributing to a softer crumb and enhanced flavor nuances. These tweaks can make the loaf feel more special or tailored to your personal taste without complicating the process.

Another advantage of banana nut bread is its wonderful aroma. As it bakes, your kitchen fills with the sweet scent of ripe bananas mingling with toasted nuts and vanilla. This makes the baking experience sensory and rewarding, even before taking the bread out of the oven. The golden-brown crust that forms offers a slight crispness, contrasting with the tender center and making each bite deeply satisfying.

When it comes to choosing the right pan, a standard 9-by-5-inch loaf pan usually works perfectly for banana nut bread. This size ensures the loaf bakes evenly and rises well. Using a metal pan tends to produce a slightly crisper crust, while glass or ceramic can slow baking time slightly but gives a beautiful even color to the loaf. Whichever you use, greasing and flouring the pan or lining it with parchment paper helps prevent sticking and keeps the loaf intact when you remove it.

Baking time is another important consideration. Generally, banana nut bread takes around 50 to 60 minutes at about 350°F. However, ovens vary, so check for doneness by inserting a toothpick or skewer into the center. If it comes out clean or with just a few moist crumbs attached, the bread is ready. Underbaking leaves a gummy texture, while overbaking dries it out. Allow the loaf to cool in the pan for around 10 minutes before transferring it to a wire rack to cool completely. This resting time lets the bread set up and makes slicing easier.

Storage is fairly simple with banana nut bread. It keeps well at room temperature, wrapped tightly in plastic wrap or stored in an airtight container for up to four days. For longer storage, it freezes beautifully. Cut the loaf into slices, then wrap them individually before freezing to enjoy fresh bread anytime. When ready to eat, simply thaw at room temperature or warm slices gently in the microwave or toaster oven.

One thing to keep in mind is that banana nut bread's natural sweetness and moisture content mean it doesn't need additional syrup or frosting, though some enjoy a light glaze or a smear of butter or cream cheese for extra indulgence. The bread also pairs wonderfully with coffee, tea, or a glass of cold milk, making it a versatile treat throughout the day.

For those who want to experiment beyond the traditional, swapping out nuts or adding seeds can introduce new flavors and textures. Some bakers gently fold in shredded coconut or grains like flaxseed for an added nutritional boost, making it feel a bit more wholesome without sacrificing the loaf's characteristic tenderness. It's these small personal touches that make banana nut bread such a beloved staple; it can be as classic or as creative as you like.

In sum, banana nut bread perfectly encapsulates the charm of sweet and enriched breads. It's an easy, approachable recipe with room for personalization, making it an essential chapter in any home baker's repertoire. Baking this loaf consistently will build your confidence in combining flavors, monitoring dough texture, and timing your bakes precisely—skills that will serve you well as you explore more advanced bread recipes.

By keeping things simple and focusing on quality ingredients—ripe bananas, fresh nuts, good flour—you can bake a loaf that delights your senses and brings a sense of accomplishment. The next slice you share with family or friends will be more than just bread; it will be a connection made in the warmth of your kitchen, reminding you why homemade bread is worth every moment invested.

BLUEBERRY BREAKFAST LOAF

When it comes to sweet and enriched breads, nothing quite captures the cozy, comforting spirit of morning like a Blueberry Breakfast Loaf. This loaf isn't just a treat for your taste buds; it's a warm invitation to start your day on a bright and flavorful note. Packed with juicy blueberries and wrapped in a tender, lightly sweetened dough, it strikes the perfect balance between indulgence and nourishment. For home bakers who are still getting comfortable with bread-making, this recipe offers a wonderful opportunity to try something a little different without feeling overwhelmed.

This loaf shines because it blends the familiarity of a classic bread texture with the fresh burst of fruit. Blueberries add both moisture and a tangy sweetness that feels just right with a hint of cinnamon or lemon zest, if you choose to include that extra lift. Unlike the more complex bread recipes that demand precise control over fermentation and shaping, the Blueberry Breakfast Loaf is forgiving. Its slightly enriched dough—meaning mixed with eggs, milk, and a bit of butter—helps keep the crumb soft and fluffy, ensuring that even if your kneading isn't perfect the first time, you'll still end up with a delicious result.

One of the joys of this loaf is its versatility. It works wonderfully fresh out of the oven, with the blueberries warm and bursting. But the flavor and texture actually develop beautifully after a day or two, making it a fantastic baked-ahead choice for busy mornings. Toast it lightly and spread some butter or cream cheese for a breakfast that feels special but takes minimal morning effort. You can even slice it thin to serve alongside coffee or tea during a casual brunch or family gathering.

Baking the Blueberry Breakfast Loaf also gives you a chance to practice timing and temperature control in a straightforward way. Most enriched doughs, including this one, benefit from gentle rises at room temperature, which help develop flavor without risking overproofing or collapse. Because the loaf isn't overly sticky, shaping it into a simple loaf shape or placing it in a well-greased pan is easy for beginners. Before baking, a light brush of egg wash can offer a gentle sheen and enhance the golden crust, making your homemade bread look as good as it tastes.

Adding fresh blueberries directly to the dough might seem tricky, but with a few simple tips, you'll avoid sinking fruit or uneven distribution. Tossing the berries in a small amount of flour before folding them into the dough helps prevent them from bleeding too much juice into the batter before baking. This little extra step keeps your loaf looking inviting—a beautiful swirl of deep purple pockets—and prevents overly soggy areas in the crumb. You can experiment with wild blueberries, which tend to be smaller and more flavorful, or regular cultivated ones depending on what you have available and your personal taste.

This recipe also opens the door to delicious variations. For example, a sprinkle of coarse sugar or chopped nuts on top before baking introduces a welcome crunch and textural contrast. Incorporating a dash of lemon zest or a splash of vanilla extract can heighten the loaf's aromatic appeal and deepen its flavor profile. Many bakers find that blending these subtle hints transforms the Blueberry Breakfast Loaf into a beautifully layered experience, advanced enough to impress guests but still accessible for any home-baking skill level.

Practically speaking, this loaf fits nicely into the daily routine because its ingredients are pantry staples for many home cooks. Flour, sugar, eggs, milk, and butter form the backbone, while a pinch of salt and a teaspoon of yeast bring the structure and rise. You don't need any fancy equipment, and a standard mixing bowl and loaf pan will get the job done beautifully. If you've worked through the beginner no-knead recipes earlier in this book, you likely already have a good handle on how to judge dough consistency and rising progress, skills that will enhance your confidence here.

Thinking about the baking process, timing is key but flexible. The loaf usually bakes for about 35 to 45 minutes at moderate oven heat, allowing the inside to cook through without drying out. A toothpick test is your best friend: inserted in the center, it should come out clean or with just a few moist crumbs once the bread is ready. If you see batter on the toothpick, the loaf just needs a bit more time. Once cooled, the loaf slices easily without crumbling apart, offering a satisfying, slightly dense crumb that's typical of enriched breads.

Enjoying this loaf fresh is a daily pleasure, but it also freezes well, making it an excellent candidate for batch baking. Simply slice and store pieces in an airtight container or freezer bag, then thaw them by leaving at room temperature or warming gently in a toaster or oven. Having homemade blueberry bread ready on hand means you can nourish yourself or your loved ones with something wholesome and homemade, even on rushed mornings.

Perhaps what makes this Blueberry Breakfast Loaf most special is its accessibility paired with comforting flavors. It's ideal for beginner bakers looking to step beyond plain breads and explore gentle enrichment and fruit inclusions. At the same time, it rewards more experienced bakers with its potential for creative flair and seasonal twists. Blueberries are naturally bursting with summer freshness, but frozen berries work beautifully year-round, which means you can bake this loaf whenever you want to brighten a breakfast table or enjoy a sweet snack with the family.

In conclusion, the Blueberry Breakfast Loaf offers a delightful mix of ease and elegance. It's a bread that invites you to embrace home baking as a daily pleasure, not a chore. The recipe encourages experimentation while guaranteeing satisfying results, making each baking session feel like a reliable success. Whether you slice it warm, toast it crisp, or enjoy it plain, it delivers on the bread's promise: fresh, homemade goodness that nourishes the body and soul, one slice at a time.

HOLIDAY PANETTONE

When it comes to sweet and enriched breads that elevate your baking to festive heights, holiday panettone holds a special place. This Italian classic, originally from Milan, is more than just a bread—it's an experience. The tall, dome-shaped loaf bursts with tender crumb, studded with dried fruits and citrus zest that bring warmth to any holiday table. Making panettone at home may seem ambitious at first, but it's an incredibly rewarding project that fills your kitchen with enticing aromas and offers a soft, buttery treat perfect for sharing.

Unlike everyday breads, holiday panettone relies on a lengthy proofing process that helps develop its unique airy texture. The dough is enriched with eggs, butter, and sugar, providing a soft, delicate crumb that melts in your mouth. Achieving the signature lightness comes down to patience and proper folding techniques during fermentation. As the dough rises slowly, it builds strength and structure, which allows it to expand without collapsing. It's a bit like nurturing a living entity; the rewarding smells and anticipation only build as the hours pass.

A key to a successful panettone is the combination and preparation of dried fruits. Traditionally, raisins and candied orange peel or citron are soaked beforehand, often in rum or water, to plump them up and intensify their flavors. This soaking not only keeps the fruits juicy but also helps distribute their sweetness throughout the loaf evenly. The contrast between the slightly tart citrus peels and the sweet custardy dough gives panettone its distinctive festive flair. While the classic recipe is beloved worldwide, feel free to experiment by adding chopped nuts, dried cherries, or even chocolate chips for your own twist.

One of the most valuable tips for home bakers is to avoid rushing the dough or taking shortcuts. The beauty of panettone lies in its slow build, so giving it ample time to ferment ensures a tender texture and deep flavor development. You might find yourself three or four proofing sessions in before the loaf is ready to bake, but this gradual process is what sets panettone apart from simpler sweet breads. It's definitely worth the wait—you end up with a loaf so airy and flavorful it feels like a true holiday gift.

If you're decorating or serving panettone, there are a few traditional touches that elevate its presentation. Typically, it's baked in tall, cylindrical paper molds that help maintain its height and iconic shape during baking. These molds also prevent the delicate dough from spreading too wide and dense. Once baked and cooled, dusting your panettone with a light sprinkle of powdered sugar adds a beautiful snowy effect that fits perfectly with winter celebrations. Some bakers like to drizzle a thin glaze or coat the top with a sugar and almond crust for added texture and visual appeal.

The versatility of holiday panettone makes it an excellent choice for festive breakfasts and brunches. Slices toasted lightly and spread with butter or ricotta cheese showcase its tender crumb beautifully. You can also use day-old panettone in recipes like bread pudding, French toast, or even trifle—turning leftovers into new delicious treats. This kind of bread serves as a centerpiece both for holiday gatherings and cozy family mornings, wrapping everyone in sweeter seasonal memories.

Don't worry if baking panettone for the first time feels intimidating. Start by carefully measuring your ingredients and maintain a warm, draft-free environment for proofing. Using a stand mixer with a dough hook will make kneading easier, but mixing and folding by hand can be just as effective if you're willing to put in the effort. Also, pay close attention to the dough's texture—it should be soft, slightly sticky, and stretchy, not dry or crumbly. Don't hesitate to give your dough additional time to rise if it's not quite there yet; slow fermentation leads to better flavor and structure.

Once you've tried making panettone, you'll appreciate how its rich yet subtle flavors differ from the usual sweet breads. The buttery dough has a mild vanilla note complemented by the bursts of fruity sweetness throughout. While it's traditionally enjoyed around Christmas, panettone is wonderful whenever you want to feel a little festive or enjoy something truly special. Sharing homemade panettone, whether as a gift or a centerpiece, offers a personal touch that's hard to beat.

In terms of shelf life, panettone keeps well at room temperature when stored in an airtight container or wrapped in plastic wrap. Its moisture-rich crumb will stay fresh for several days, though it will gradually become firmer over time. To revive slightly stale panettone, warming slices briefly in the oven or toaster restores softness and aroma, making it almost as delightful as fresh from the oven. This longevity means you can bake your holiday loaf ahead of time without sacrificing quality or taste.

For those looking to make panettone without commercial yeast, natural leavening can be used, but it requires even more patience and care for a good rise. Whether you opt for traditional yeast or sourdough starter, the principles remain the same—balanced ingredients, proper fermentation, and gentle handling. Don't be discouraged if your first panettone doesn't come out perfectly tall or fluffy. Like any baking skill, it improves with practice and attention to detail. The journey itself is part of the seasonal joy.

When serving panettone, pairing it with complementary drinks enhances the experience. Hot beverages like a rich cocoa, spiced chai, or classic espresso contrast beautifully with the bread's light sweetness. For celebrations, a glass of sparkling wine or even a modest sweet dessert wine can elevate the loaf to a festive treat suitable for toasts and holiday cheer. These combinations make each bite not just tasty but an occasion.

Lastly, making holiday panettone at home gives you creative freedom. You can adjust sweetness, experiment with different dried fruits, or infuse the dough with spices such as cinnamon, cardamom, or nutmeg to suit your taste. Some bakers like to add citrus zest right into the dough for extra brightness or brush the loaf with melted butter after baking for a shiny finish. While the recipe is deceptively simple, these personal touches transform panettone into your own signature bread—perfect for gifting or keeping.

In summary, holiday panettone stands out as a crowning jewel in the world of sweet and enriched breads. It invites bakers—especially home cooks eager to try something special—to slow down, engage with the dough, and celebrate through the craft of baking. The result is a bread with a tender crumb, a touch of sweetness, and a festive spirit that warms hearts in more ways than one. With the right techniques and a bit of patience, your holiday panettone can become a favorite tradition that brings joy year after year.

Apple Fritter Bread

When it comes to sweet and enriched breads, few recipes capture the warmth and comfort of homemade baking like Apple Fritter Bread. This loaf combines tender, spiced dough with pockets of soft, caramelized apple pieces, mimicking the delicious flavors of a classic apple fritter pastry. Baking this bread brings cozy autumn mornings to mind, full of inviting cinnamon aromas that fill the kitchen and promise satisfying bites.

The beauty of Apple Fritter Bread is in its balance. It isn't as dense or rich as a traditional brioche, but it's still incredibly tender thanks to the enriching ingredients in the dough. Butter, eggs, and a little sugar create a soft crumb that complements the fruit without overwhelming it. And don't worry—this recipe is beginner-friendly. The steps may seem involved, but with a bit of patience, you will find the process straightforward and rewarding.

This bread is especially delightful because it folds together tender apple chunks coated in warm spices like cinnamon and nutmeg, then sprinkles in a cinnamon-sugar swirl that melts into the dough as it bakes. The result is a moist loaf with contrast between the sweet apples and the lightly crisped sugary crust. You'll want to slice it slightly thick to truly appreciate the gooey pockets of apple through each bite. Whether served warmed with butter or enjoyed just as it is, this bread makes an inviting breakfast or afternoon snack.

Let's talk about the dough. It's enriched but not overly sweet, allowing the apples and spices to stand out. The flour and yeast combination creates a good rise, giving the bread a light and fluffy texture. To get that perfect lift, be sure to proof your yeast properly, and allow the dough to rise in a warm draft-free spot. If you're working in cooler climates, an oven with just the light on can provide a great environment. A well-proofed dough will feel puffy and soft to the touch.

Preparing the apples is another important step. Using firm, tart apples such as Granny Smith adds a bright counterpoint to the sweetness and spice. Dice the apples into small pieces so they distribute evenly throughout the loaf and release just the right amount of juice during baking. Toss them with the cinnamon and sugar mixture to coat every morsel—this ensures they caramelize beautifully and infuse the bread with flavor.

Once the dough has risen, rolling it out to layer in the apples and cinnamon sugar swirl is where the magic happens. Spread the apple mixture over the dough and then carefully roll it up tight like a jelly roll. This rolling technique creates layers that make each slice a swirl of spiced apple goodness. Pinch the seams well to avoid the filling escaping during baking, which can cause a sticky mess in your oven.

Baking Apple Fritter Bread requires patience, but the aroma wafting from your oven will make every minute worthwhile. You want to bake the loaf until it's a deep golden brown and sounds hollow when tapped on the bottom. The sugars caramelize and form a slightly crisp crust that contrasts perfectly with the soft inside. Once out of the oven, a quick brush of butter over the warm loaf adds extra richness and sheen.

This bread also lends itself well to variations. Add chopped nuts like pecans or walnuts into the apple filling to introduce a pleasing crunch. For extra decadence, drizzle a simple glaze made from powdered sugar and milk after the loaf cools. The glaze adds just the right touch of sweetness and makes the bread look bakery-worthy. You might even consider a splash of maple syrup or vanilla extract in the dough or filling to deepen the flavor profile.

Serving Apple Fritter Bread is versatile. Slices toasted lightly with butter make a comforting start to the day, while a thick slice paired with cream cheese or a smear of fruit preserves elevates this humble bread to a special treat. It's an excellent choice to bring to brunches or weekend family gatherings when you want to impress without fuss.

For home bakers looking to expand their repertoire beyond basic loaves, Apple Fritter Bread offers a satisfying project with delicious results. The dough handling skills are accessible for beginners, and the outcome is a stunning, flavorful loaf that tastes far more complicated than the effort it requires. Plus, this bread freezes well—wrap slices tightly in plastic wrap and pop them in the freezer to enjoy later. Thaw and toast or warm in the oven for a quick homemade indulgence anytime.

One tip to keep in mind is not to overload the dough with too many apples or too much sugar, as that can affect the loaf's rise and texture. Keep the apple pieces evenly sized, and distribute the cinnamon sugar filling sparingly but thoroughly for the ideal balance. Resist the temptation to rush the rising times; letting the dough properly develop ensures that soft crumb you'll love.

Apple Fritter Bread also offers a pleasant way to incorporate seasonal fruit into your baking without the need for pies or crisps. The bread format maintains softness and moisture while giving you that nostalgic apple fritter flavor experience. It's a wonderful alternative on cold mornings or as a snack with your favorite cup of coffee or tea.

In summary, this bread brings together warmly spiced apples, tender enriched dough, and a delightful cinnamon swirl to create a loaf that's rich in flavor and comforting in texture. With a bit of attention to detail and time for proofing, even novice bakers will find the process enjoyable and rewarding. The resulting bread feels like a special occasion, yet it's easy enough to make any time you're craving something homemade, sweet, and satisfying.

So whether you're growing confident in your bread-making skills or simply want a new recipe to try, Apple Fritter Bread offers a delicious and approachable sweet bread option. It's a perfect way to bring the spirit of home baking into your kitchen, one slice at a time.

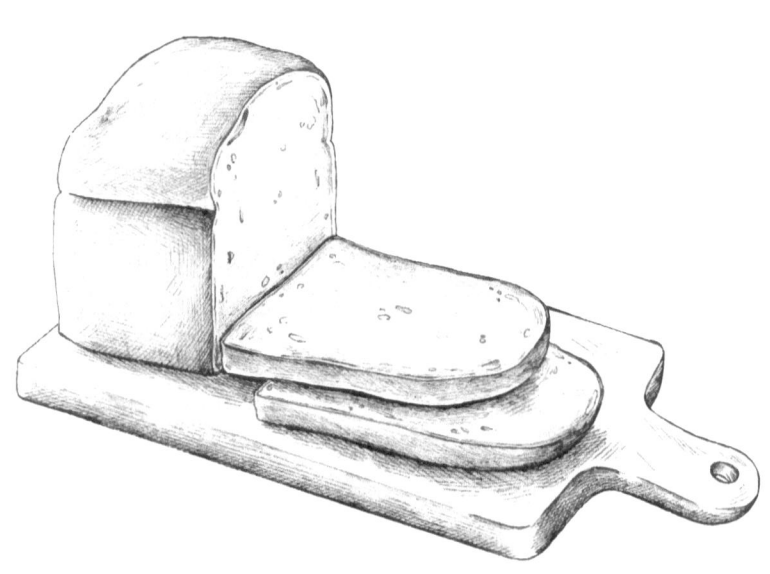

Chapter 7
SPECIALTY AND FUN HOMEMADE BAKES

Stepping beyond the basics, this chapter invites you to explore breads that bring both joy and creativity to your kitchen, making baking not just a routine but an experience. From the delightful crust of soft pretzels to the impressive shapes of braided challah and stuffed bread rings, these recipes offer playful twists on traditional favorites. Whether you're shaping a spiral swirl loaf or crafting mini bread loaves perfect for gifting, each bake promises a satisfying blend of flavor and fun. With easy-to-follow instructions designed for home bakers of all skill levels, you'll find yourself confident in trying out herb-infused tear and share breads or even homemade bagels that rival your favorite bakery. It's about turning fresh ingredients into beautiful, delicious creations that bring warmth and excitement to every meal.

BREAD BOWLS FOR SOUP

One of the most comforting ways to serve soup is nestled inside a warm, crusty bread bowl. Bread bowls are not only visually impressive but also add a delicious, edible element to your meal that enhances the overall eating experience. They're perfect for casual dinners or special occasions, offering a rustic feel that's far more satisfying than a simple bowl.

Making bread bowls at home might sound a bit ambitious, but with some basic bread baking techniques introduced earlier in this book, you'll find it pretty straightforward. The key is to bake a loaf that's round, sturdy, and thick enough to hold liquid without becoming soggy too fast. Typically, these bowls are modeled on sourdough or artisan white loaves that develop a firm crust and chewy crumb. If you've already tackled beginner loaves or rustic skillet bread, you're well on your way to handling bread bowls confidently.

When choosing your dough recipe, focus on those that yield a thick, chewy crust rather than soft sandwich bread. A crusty exterior resists moisture, helping the bowl maintain its shape as you enjoy your soup. You can use classic no-knead dough or any of the more flavor-packed yeast breads from previous chapters. It's a good idea to avoid extremely soft or fluffy doughs because they'll leak more easily. Remember, texture matters just as much as flavor when it comes to bread bowls.

Shaping the bread bowl takes a bit of practice but is mostly about rounding your dough into a tight, round ball before the final rise. Avoid letting the dough spread too wide or flatten; you want good height and a domed shape. Once baked, let the loaf cool completely before hollowing it out to ensure it holds up without tearing.

Hollowing out is where you get to customize your bread bowl. Using a serrated knife, simply slice off the top like a lid, then gently scoop out the inside, leaving about an inch-thick wall all around. This wall thickness is essential to prevent soup leaks while giving you plenty of bread to tuck into after your meal. Don't toss the removed bread! Cut it into cubes for dipping into your soup or toasting as croutons. Nothing goes to waste.

One reason bread bowls have become so beloved is the way the bread soaks up flavorful soup juices as you eat. This pairing is especially fantastic with thicker soups or chowders—think creamy clam chowder, hearty chili, or loaded baked potato soup. The bread's crust shields it from immediate sogginess, but the inside still absorbs the rich broth, delivering a dynamic eating experience with contrasting textures and tastes on each spoonful.

For home bakers, experimenting with different dough flavors for bread bowls is fun and rewarding. You can infuse them with herbs, garlic, or even cheese incorporated into the dough for an extra flavor kick. Imagine a garlic-rosemary bread bowl filled with tomato bisque, or a cheddar-flecked bowl holding a creamy broccoli-cheddar soup. These variations turn a simple meal into something memorable without adding too much complexity to your baking.

Warming your bread bowls before serving can enhance the experience too. A few minutes in the oven—just enough to heat without drying out—revitalizes the crust and warms the bread's interior, making it all the more inviting and soft inside. This little extra step lifts your homemade soup dinner from good to great.

Portion size is another consideration when baking bread bowls. A personal-sized bowl about the size of a small round loaf works well as a hearty single serving. If you're serving a crowd or want larger options, you can create oversized bread bowls but keep in mind these will take longer to bake through and might need adjustments in timing and temperature. On the flip side, mini bread bowls are charming for appetizers or party dips, offering bite-sized fun that guests love.

You might be wondering about the best soups to serve in bread bowls. Thick, creamy, or chunky soups stand out as top choices because they aren't too watery and pair perfectly with the dense bread walls. Tomato soup, loaded potato soup, creamy mushroom, and chili are classic favorites. Avoid thin brothy soups here since they tend to make the bowl soggy too quickly. If you feel inspired, you can even create your own signature soup to pair with your bread bowl creation.

Cleaning up after bread bowls is a dream—well, almost. The greatest mess you'll have to handle is crumbs, which are easy to sweep or wipe away with a damp cloth. Unlike traditional bowls, there's no washing involved after you eat, plus zero dishes. That's a big win when you want a cozy meal with minimal fuss.

For beginners, bread bowls represent a fun, hands-on project that combines fundamental bread baking skills with creativity. They help develop your shaping, proofing, and baking timing while satisfying your craving for something a little different. It's a smart recipe to add to your repertoire partly because it stretches your baking muscles in a fun and rewarding way.

Once you've mastered the basics, don't hesitate to start experimenting. Try adding seeds on top before baking for extra crunch, or brush the crust with an egg wash for a glossy appearance. Some bakers even like to sprinkle coarse sea salt or parmesan cheese onto their bowls just before baking to amp up the flavor and texture. These small tweaks let you personalize your bread bowls and keep the baking process exciting.

In summary, bread bowls for soup tie together homemade bread baking with an inviting way to serve warm meals. They showcase the versatility of bread and how it can elevate a simple dish. From careful dough selection through shaping, baking, and serving, this technique enriches your kitchen skills while making soup time an event. Once you experience that first dip into your own freshly baked bread bowl, you'll understand why it's such a beloved comfort food classic.

Enjoy experimenting with bread bowls as part of your home baking adventure—they're a fantastic way to impress family and friends with something both delightful and practical. And as you become more confident with your breads, these charming edible vessels will undoubtedly become a go-to for cozy meals any time of year.

STUFFED BREAD RINGS

Stuffed bread rings are one of those delightful creations that bring both visual appeal and rich flavor to the table. They're essentially breads shaped into a circular form, filled generously with ingredients ranging from savory meats and cheeses to vegetables and herbs. This style of bread baking invites creativity and allows you to experiment with flavors, textures, and colors, making every loaf feel like a centerpiece rather than just a side. For home bakers who have tackled some basic loaves and want to try something a bit more impressive without going overboard, these bread rings can be a perfect next step.

Crafting a stuffed bread ring involves combining the fundamental techniques of dough making with a clever assembly process. The dough itself should be soft yet sturdy enough to hold the fillings without breaking, so recipes often recommend enriched doughs similar to those used for dinner rolls or sandwich bread. These doughs bring just enough softness and elasticity to create that satisfying chew but also maintain structure after baking. Once your dough is ready and rested, rolling it out and layering in your chosen fillings is the next exciting part.

One of the joys of making stuffed bread rings is the endless variety of fillings you can incorporate. Classic combinations often include melted cheeses that bind everything together, cured meats like pepperoni or ham, and fresh or roasted vegetables such as spinach, mushrooms, or roasted peppers. Herbs, spices, and even a drizzle of olive oil or marinara can elevate the flavor profile dramatically. Whether you prefer Italian-inspired flavors, something with more of a cheesy, gooey center, or a lighter vegetable-focused option, stuffing the dough offers an endless canvas.

When assembling the ring, the key is to keep the fillings well-distributed so that every slice presents a layered bite of dough and stuffing. After rolling the dough flat and evenly spreading your chosen fillings, you roll it up like a jelly roll. From here, you shape the long cylinder into a ring, pinching the ends together carefully. Some bakers choose to score or cut slits in the dough before shaping it into a ring, which creates beautiful exposed layers once baked. These not only look stunning but also help steam escape during baking, preventing sogginess inside.

Baking stuffed bread rings requires a moderate temperature to ensure even cooking. Too hot, and the exterior may brown too quickly while the inside filling stays cold; too low, and you risk a pale, undercooked crust. Most recipes suggest a bake at around 350°F to 375°F (175°C to 190°C), giving the dough time to rise and cook thoroughly while melting the fillings inside. Placing the ring on a parchment-lined baking sheet or a pizza stone can help maintain even heat and make cleanup easier.

In terms of presentation, stuffed bread rings are almost always a crowd-pleaser. Their circular shape allows for easy slicing into wedges, perfect for sharing at gatherings or family dinners. The exposed swirls from the cut dough and fillings create a visually inviting pattern that hints at the delicious flavor inside. Plus, because these loaves are quite portable, they're fantastic for potlucks, picnics, or as an impressive appetizer for parties.

While stuffed bread rings can seem more advanced than your basic loaf, they're surprisingly accessible. Most home cooks with experience mastering simple yeast doughs can successfully make these with a bit of care and attention to timing. The skill of rolling, filling, shaping, and baking becomes quite rewarding once you see the beautiful results. Plus, experimenting with different stuffing combinations turns baking into a fun, creative project rather than a routine task.

To keep things manageable, it's smart to start with familiar fillings and gradually build toward more adventurous blends. Classic mozzarella and pepperoni with Italian seasoning offer a reliably delicious combination for beginners. Once comfortable, you can add caramelized onions, roasted garlic, or olives to elevate the flavor. For vegetarians or those wanting lighter options, consider a mix of sautéed spinach, feta cheese, and sun-dried tomatoes. All of these variations can be tailored to your family's tastes, making these stuffed rings versatile and adaptable crowd-pleasers.

There's also something inherently satisfying about the tactile process of shaping the dough into a ring. It becomes a hands-on learning experience, where you can see firsthand how dough behavior changes depending on hydration, flour types, and kneading. The folding and shaping steps encourage observation and adjustment, helping refine your bread baking instincts. This practical knowledge is invaluable for any home baker looking to gain confidence beyond simple loaves and rolls.

For those worried about the fillings leaking out or weighing down the dough too much, proper sealing is important. When pinching the ends of the ring, make sure the dough edges are pressed firmly together and any tears are gently patched. This prevents filling from oozing out during baking and keeps the ring intact. Some bakers lightly brush the dough with an egg wash or water before sealing to help the dough stick better. However, avoid overfilling – a balanced approach will help the dough rise and bake evenly without collapsing.

The aroma of stuffed bread rings as they bake is another compelling reason to include them in your recipe repertoire. The scent of warm bread mingled with herbs, melted cheese, and spices fills the kitchen and invites anticipation well before the timer goes off. This sensory appeal adds an extra layer of joy to homemade bread baking and often sparks memorable moments around the table.

If you're inspired to take your bread baking a little further, stuffed bread rings offer a meaningful way to combine technique and flavor exploration. They serve beautifully as appetizer bread, party fare, or even as part of a casual dinner served alongside a fresh salad or soup. With relatively simple ingredients and straightforward steps, you can create something that feels both special and homemade with relative ease.

Finally, stuffed bread rings also lend themselves well to customizing for dietary preferences or restrictions. Using gluten-free flour blends or alternative cheese options can make this recipe more inclusive. As you grow more comfortable, try swapping ingredients while maintaining the basic dough and assembly structure, so you maintain the integrity of the bread ring form. This flexibility helps make the recipe truly yours, inspiring repeated enjoyment and sharing.

In summary, stuffed bread rings represent a wonderful crossroads between baking skill and indulgent flavor. They allow novice bakers to move beyond plain breads, offering a chance to play with fillings and shapes that wow visually and delight the palate. Whether made for weeknight dinners or festive occasions, these breads bring warmth, flavor, and a beautiful handcrafted touch to your homemade baking collection.

Herb-Infused Tear and Share Bread

Tear and share bread brings a delightful twist to homemade loaves, turning an ordinary bread experience into a communal event. This style of bread is all about soft, pull-apart pieces infused with fresh herbs and often enriched with butter or olive oil. It's an inviting centerpiece for gatherings, simple family dinners, or even an impressive addition to a holiday table. Once you get the hang of it, this bread is not only easy to make but also incredibly rewarding. Imagine the aroma of fragrant herbs mingling with warm bread filling your kitchen as you bake — it's a sensory pleasure hard to beat.

What sets tear and share bread apart is its unique structure. Rather than forming one large loaf, the dough is shaped into many small balls or rolls packed closely together in a pan. When baked, these pieces stick side by side but remain soft and easy to pull apart. Infusing the dough with herbs like rosemary, thyme, or sage ensures that every bite bursts with flavor. Plus, it's a fantastic way to experiment with fresh and dried herbs or even add garlic for an extra punch. The finishing touch—brushing the bread with melted herb butter—takes it over the top, creating a golden, flavorful crust that's just begging to be pulled apart with your fingers.

Beginning bakers often hesitate with more complex bread recipes, but tear and share bread is surprisingly forgiving. The dough generally follows a straightforward yeast bread formula, making it approachable for those new to yeast or bread baking. Using simple kitchen tools and basic ingredients, you can create a loaf that looks impressive yet relies on the comfort of familiar techniques. The dough's softness means you don't need heavy kneading, and this type of bread tolerates slight variations in proving times. Plus, the visual appeal of a cluster of golden, herb-speckled rolls is worth the effort no matter how experienced you are in the kitchen.

When choosing herbs for your tear and share bread, fresh is always best if you have them on hand. Rosemary pairs beautifully with olive oil and garlic, offering a piney, aromatic profile. Thyme offers subtle earthiness that works well mixed with parmesan or cheddar, while basil can swirl in for a slightly sweeter, peppery pop. Another great option is oregano, especially if you want a Mediterranean flair. Combining several herbs can create a complex flavor profile, but be careful not to overwhelm the dough with too many strong flavors. Keep the balance subtle enough to enhance the bread without masking the natural richness.

Preparation begins with mixing a soft yeast dough, enriched with just a bit of butter or oil, flour, salt, sugar, and water or milk. Once the base is ready, gently incorporate finely chopped herbs into the dough or brush them on later during shaping. The kneading process doesn't require heavy work; just enough to develop some gluten so the dough is elastic and smooth. Allowing the dough to rest and rise is crucial, offering those tiny yeast bubbles time to expand and set the stage for a light, tender crumb. Timing will depend on your room temperature, typically between one and two hours for the first rise.

After the initial rise, divide the dough into small, uniform balls—about the size of golf balls is a good rule of thumb. Place these close together in a greased baking pan or cast iron skillet so they'll bake up joined but easily pulled apart. Before the final rising stage, brush the tops with herb-infused butter for that extra boost of flavor and moisture.

This step locks in aroma and gives the bread a shiny, inviting finish. Once shaped and brushed, the dough needs a second rise, which just takes 30 to 45 minutes for that nice puffiness, making sure the rolls aren't too tight or overcrowded in the pan.

Baking tear and share bread should be done at a moderate temperature, usually around 350°F (175°C). It takes roughly 25 to 30 minutes to develop a golden crust while keeping the interior soft and pillowy. You'll know it's done when the tops are beautifully browned and a toothpick inserted near the center comes out clean, or the bread's internal temperature reaches about 190°F (88°C). If the tops start browning too quickly, a loose tent of foil can prevent burning while allowing the bread to finish cooking. Let the bread cool just enough to hold but still warm to the touch—too hot and it crumbles, too cold and it loses that fresh-out-of-the-oven softness.

The magic of herb-infused tear and share bread lies in its interactive nature. It invites guests or loved ones to gather around, dipping pieces in olive oil, rich butter, or even a tangy balsamic reduction. It's perfect alongside soups and stews, or paired with a cheese platter for a simple snack. Because it's pull-apart, portion control is effortless, and people can take just as much as they want without the need for slicing. This makes it especially practical in casual settings where conversation and sharing food go hand in hand. Plus, it tastes just as wonderful warm out of the oven as it does hours later, making it ideal for make-ahead events.

For those wanting to customize the recipe, try mixing in different cheeses between the dough balls before baking. Sharp cheddar, mozzarella, or even creamy goat cheese complement the herbs wonderfully. You can also experiment with toppings like flaky sea salt, sesame seeds, or finely grated parmesan sprinkled on top before baking for an extra layer of flavor and texture. Adding roasted garlic cloves between the rolls gives a subtle sweetness that's irresistible. Don't hesitate to get creative—this bread adapts well to a variety of additions, allowing you to tailor it to your own taste preferences.

One of the best parts about making tear and share bread is how it builds confidence in the kitchen. Watching a simple dough transform into a gorgeous, aromatic loaf reinforces just how satisfying homemade bread can be. No need to stress over perfect shaping — this is all about softness and flavor coming together in a relaxed, fuss-free way. The method encourages learning from each bake and adjusting herbs or baking times to suit your style. Whether it's a casual weeknight dinner or centerpiece for a celebration, herb-infused tear and share bread has a charming way of elevating the everyday to something special.

This bread also stores well. Leftover rolls keep nicely in an airtight container at room temperature for a couple of days, or they freeze beautifully for longer storage. To revive frozen portions, simply warm them in a low oven covered with foil to refresh that inviting softness. This makes tear and share a smart choice for batch baking, planning ahead for busy weeks, or packing for picnics where fresh bread is a treat. Its simplicity and versatility make it a staple recipe every home baker should have in their collection.

In the end, herb-infused tear and share bread is so much more than just a loaf. It's comfort made edible — soft, fragrant, and begging to be pulled apart piece by piece. As you explore this recipe, don't hesitate to make it your own, adjusting herbs, adding cheeses, or experimenting with toppings. The joy is in sharing not only the bread but also the moments created around breaking it together. This approachable and delicious recipe will expand your bread-baking repertoire, offering a hands-on project that rewards you with glowing smiles and empty plates.

Spiral Swirl Loaves

Spiral swirl loaves offer a stunning visual treat that's just as enjoyable to bake as they are to eat. This style of bread often becomes the centerpiece of any meal or gathering because their beautiful spiraled pattern hints at the flavors packed inside. Whether you're a beginner or looking to add a bit of excitement to your baking routine, these loaves strike a wonderful balance between impressive presentation and approachable technique.

The secret behind a perfect spiral swirl loaf lies in the layering and rolling technique, which creates those signature concentric rings once the loaf is sliced. Unlike simpler breads, spiral loaves invite the baker to think about how ingredients can be folded and combined to create both texture and flavor in every bite. Don't let the process intimidate you. With a little patience and practice, you'll find that these breads become a rewarding project.

Typically, the dough for spiral swirl loaves mirrors that of a basic yeast bread—flour, water, yeast, salt, and sometimes a touch of sugar or fat to enrich the crumb. What sets these loaves apart is the inclusion of flavorful layers or fillings rolled into the dough before baking. Popular choices often include cinnamon and sugar for a sweet treat or herbs, cheese, and spices for a savory twist. Spreading a thin layer of butter or oil on the dough before sprinkling on fillings helps ensure the spirals stay distinct and moist.

One of the lovely things about spiral swirl loaves is their versatility. You can start with simple combinations like cinnamon and sugar or garlic and herb blends, then graduate to more adventurous fillings such as sun-dried tomatoes with basil, or even caramelized onions paired with sharp cheddar. For home bakers, this flexibility means you're not only crafting beautiful bread but also tailoring your loaf to match your mood, meal, or occasion.

Getting the rolling step right is key. Once your dough has risen, you gently roll it out into a rectangle and spread your chosen filling evenly. Starting from one edge, you then roll the dough tightly but without squeezing out the air, creating a log of dough that will reveal the swirl after baking. The dough log is tamed into the chosen loaf shape, whether that's a classic round spiral or a longer loaf form, before it gets the final proof.

During the second rise, the loaf puffs up, and the layers become tender, setting the stage for that striking interior pattern. When baking, the crust develops a golden, sometimes slightly caramelized exterior that contrasts with the soft, flavorful swirl inside. This contrast elevates the eating experience—there's a crunch or chew that complements the soft crumb and rich fillings.

For those new to bread baking, the spiral swirl loaf is a fantastic way to practice dough handling and shaping. The steps involved teach control over dough elasticity and the importance of even spreading of fillings. Plus, because the process uses familiar dough recipes you might already know, it feels like a natural next step after mastering basic loaves. Once you get comfortable, you can experiment with timing and textures by trying whole wheat or multigrain bases for added nutrition.

Besides their aesthetic appeal, spiral swirl loaves also make excellent sandwich bread or accompaniment for dips, soups, and salads. Imagine slicing into a rosemary and garlic loaf to serve alongside a steaming bowl of tomato bisque or a pesto chicken salad sandwich crafted from a freshly baked cheddar swirl. The possibilities stretch wide and can inspire creativity both in baking and meal planning.

To make your experience smoother, here are a few practical tips. Always let the dough rest sufficiently after rolling up to avoid spring-back—that's when the dough tries to unroll and lose the swirl shape. Keeping your fillings dry or well-drained is another key; moisture-heavy ingredients can make the dough soggy and harder to manage. Finally, pay attention to oven temperature and baking time because you want that perfect balance between a crust that browns beautifully and crumb that stays moist and tender.

Another important point to remember is the benefit of using quality ingredients. Whether it's the butter in your swirl, freshly ground spices, or herbs picked right from your kitchen garden, these small details shine through in the final product. The difference between mediocre and memorable often comes from the care you put into your ingredient choices and preparation.

Spiral swirl loaves also make fantastic gifts. There's something deeply satisfying about sharing a loaf that looks as good as it tastes. Wrapping your loaf in parchment or a simple cloth adds that homemade charm. Friend or family recipients almost always appreciate the effort and creativity behind these hand-crafted breads more than any store-bought equivalent.

For bakers with an eye on presentation, glazing the loaf with an egg wash or melted butter before baking can add a glossy surface that catches the light and highlights the textures of the crust. Sometimes a sprinkle of coarse salt, sesame seeds, or even a handful of toasted nuts can finish your loaf with an extra layer of flavor and crunch. Experimenting with these finishing touches is part of the fun and offers another way to customize your loaf's character.

In summary, spiral swirl loaves are much more than just pretty bread. They invite you to explore filling combinations and dough techniques that deepen your understanding of bread baking while offering delicious results. Whether you keep it simple for weekday dinners or elevate the flavors for weekend brunches, these loaves reward both effort and creativity in equal measure. Taking on spiral swirl loaves is a wonderful way to grow your skills and confidence, producing bread that feels truly special every time you slice it open.

Savory Pizza Bread

One of the most satisfying and flavorful variations you can bake at home is savory pizza bread. It's a fantastic way to combine the best elements of pizza—melty cheese, tangy tomato sauce, and fragrant herbs—with the comforting texture of freshly baked bread. Unlike a traditional pizza, this bread brings everything together in one delicious loaf or pull-apart style, making it perfect for casual dinners, snacking, or even taking to a party as a crowd-pleaser. The best part? It's surprisingly simple to make, even if you're new to bread baking.

At its core, savory pizza bread starts with a basic bread dough that's soft and tender but sturdy enough to hold all the tasty fillings. A well-balanced dough often includes just a few staple ingredients: flour, water, yeast, a pinch of salt, and a touch of olive oil. These ingredients work together to create a lovely crumb that's chewy but light, which allows the bold flavors of the pizza toppings to really shine through without feeling heavy.

Preparing the dough is straightforward—you'll mix, knead, and let it rise until it doubles in size. This rising phase is crucial because it develops the gluten structure and ensures the bread will have a great texture. Don't rush this step; giving your dough the time it needs to ferment results in better flavor and a lighter crumb. Once risen, you can get creative with shaping and filling your loaf.

The beauty of savory pizza bread lies in its versatility. Traditional pizza flavors like tomato sauce, mozzarella cheese, fresh basil, and pepperoni can be layered inside the dough or incorporated as toppings. But you're not limited to these classics. Think sliced olives, roasted red peppers, caramelized onions, or even crumbles of spicy sausage. Each addition adds complexity and texture, turning your loaf into a multi-dimensional taste experience.

One common method for assembling the bread is to roll the dough flat and spread a thin layer of seasoned tomato sauce across the surface. This helps keep the bread moist and infuses it with acidity that balances the richness of the cheese and oil. After that, you sprinkle your choice of cheeses—mozzarella, provolone, or even a sharp Parmesan work beautifully—and scatter your toppings evenly. Then, the dough is rolled up like a jelly roll, pinched to seal, and baked until golden brown with a crispy crust.

Another popular approach is to make pull-apart pizza bread. This style involves cutting the dough into pieces—sometimes squares, sometimes triangles—and layering them with sauce, cheese, and toppings in a loaf pan. Once baked, the bread can be pulled apart with fingers, making it fun and shareable. It's perfect for serving at family gatherings or casual get-togethers, where people can take as much or as little as they want.

Timing and baking temperature play a big role in achieving the perfect pizza bread. Often, a moderate oven temperature around 375°F works best. It allows the bread to bake through evenly while melting the cheese and caramelizing the edges of the toppings without burning them. Keeping an eye on your bread in the last few minutes helps you decide when it's perfectly done. The top should be golden with some toasty spots, and the interior soft and fragrant.

One helpful tip when working with savory breads is to resist overloading the dough with too many toppings. Too moist or heavy a filling can make the bread dense or soggy in the center. It's tempting to pile on all your favorite pizza ingredients, but moderation keeps the texture balanced and the loaf easy to slice or pull apart without falling apart.

There's also a lot of room for seasoning in savory pizza bread. Incorporating Italian herbs like oregano, basil, thyme, or crushed red pepper flakes either in the dough or the sauce adds that authentic pizzeria touch. Fresh garlic or garlic powder can enhance the aroma as well. Don't forget to brush the crust with olive oil or melted butter before baking to give it a beautiful shine and extra flavor.

For beginners, the idea of combining bread baking with all these fillings might seem intimidating, but the process is actually very manageable. Start by perfecting the basic dough in earlier chapters, then have fun experimenting with toppings that suit your taste. Making mistakes along the way—like uneven baking or too-thick fillings—just teaches you more about how to balance moisture and heat for the best results next time.

Savory pizza bread also offers great opportunities for customization based on what you have in your kitchen. Leftover vegetables, bits of cured meats, or different cheese blends can all find a home inside this loaf. It's a fantastic way to reduce food waste while making something everyone will enjoy. Plus, because it's so filling, even a small piece goes a long way, making it budget-friendly too.

When serving your pizza bread, warm slices paired with a side salad, a bowl of soup, or even just a cold beer can make a comforting meal. Leftovers reheat nicely in the oven or toaster oven, allowing the crust to regain its crispiness and the cheese to soften again. If you're thinking of adding a homemade marinara or dipping sauce, that's an extra layer of flavor that can elevate the bread even more.

With every loaf you bake, you'll gain confidence and skill. Soon, you can start adjusting the dough hydration, trying whole wheat or multigrain flours, or incorporating sourdough starter for extra depth. But at its heart, savory pizza bread is about bringing joy to your kitchen through simple techniques and delicious ingredients. It's proof that you don't need to order takeout to enjoy the flavors of pizza.

Baking this at home means you know exactly what's going into your food, and that always tastes better.

In the end, savory pizza bread is more than just a recipe—it's an invitation to experiment, share, and savor every bite of homemade goodness. Whether you keep it classic or turn it into a creative canvas of toppings, this bread will become a favorite in your baking repertoire. It's a fun, approachable way to expand your skills and impress family and friends with something both comforting and exciting.

So, when you're ready for something a bit different from the usual loaves, give savory pizza bread a try. It's where the worlds of bread baking and pizza-making collide, making every slice a tasty, aromatic slice of handcrafted delight.

Braided Challah Bread

There's something undeniably magical about braided challah bread. Its glossy, golden crust and intricate braids make it not only a feast for the taste buds but also for the eyes. This bread, steeped in tradition, brings a sense of warmth and celebration to any kitchen, perfect for home bakers wanting to step up their bread game with something a little special yet entirely approachable.

Challah is a rich, slightly sweet yeast bread that's soft and tender on the inside with a beautiful sheen on the crust, thanks to an egg wash applied before baking. Traditionally associated with Jewish culture and Shabbat dinners, today it's enjoyed by many who appreciate its delicate flavor and tender crumb. Its braided shape isn't just for looks—it symbolizes unity and connection. For anyone learning to braid dough for the first time, challah offers a practical introduction to this skill, plus there's a lot of room for creativity with different braid sizes and styles.

Making challah from scratch might seem intimidating at first, but it's truly a rewarding experience. The process starts with preparing a slightly enriched dough, where eggs, a bit of sugar, oil, and yeast combine to create a base that's soft yet resilient enough for braiding. The dough's elasticity is key; it needs to stretch without tearing during the braiding process. When you mix and knead challah dough just right, it becomes almost buttery in texture, a wonderful contrast to leaner breads like baguettes or ciabatta that you might be more familiar with.

One of the great advantages of braided challah is how versatile it is. While the traditional flavor profile leans slightly sweet, it can be easily adapted by adding ingredients such as raisins, honey, or even herbs for a unique spin. Its tender crumb also makes it ideal for a variety of uses beyond simply slicing. It's equally delicious toasted with butter or transformed into French toast or bread pudding—the possibilities are delightful and abundant.

When it comes to braiding, there's no need to feel overwhelmed. The simplest challah uses three strands, which is perfect for beginners. Lay the strands side by side, pinch them together at one end, and then weave them over and under in a neat pattern before sealing the other end. A few light practice runs with strips of paper can help before you start working with the dough. If you're feeling adventurous, you can explore four, five, or even six-strand braids, and the finished loaf will look as impressive as it tastes.

Timing and temperature play vital roles in getting challah right. Like many yeast breads, challah dough benefits from a slow rise, which builds flavor. Allow the dough to double in size during the first proof, then gently shape and braid it before its final rise. Your kitchen's warmth can drastically impact this step—a cool environment may require longer proofing times. Of course, the best sign that your dough is ready comes from experience: it should feel airy and bounce back slowly when pressed.

The egg wash is another crucial detail that gives challah that iconic shiny, golden crust. Just before baking, brush the loaf generously with beaten egg—sometimes with a pinch of salt or a splash of water to thin it slightly. Some bakers sprinkle poppy or sesame seeds on top at this stage for a textural element and subtle nuttiness. Just remember, skipping this step will make your challah look a bit duller and less enticing.

Baking challah requires attention but isn't complicated. The bread typically bakes at a moderate temperature—usually around 350°F (175°C)—for 25 to 30 minutes. You'll know it's ready when the crust deepens to a rich amber color, and tapping the bottom of the loaf produces a hollow sound. If you can, let the bread cool completely on a wire rack to set the crumb. Cutting it too soon might cause the texture to seem gummy rather than fluffy.

For bakers mindful of ingredients, challah is surprisingly straightforward without requiring elaborate components. The basic pantry staples—flour, yeast, eggs, sugar, water, and vegetable oil—come together to create a complex, layered flavor. Using high-quality bread flour can improve the structure, but all-purpose flour also works well. There's room to experiment with whole wheat or spelt for a heartier, more rustic version, though this may affect the loaf's softness and rise.

In terms of storage, challah can last a few days wrapped in foil or stored in an airtight container at room temperature. Because it's a slightly enriched bread, it tends to dry out faster than lean loaves, so for longer storage, freezing is a great option. Slice it before freezing, so you can thaw individual pieces as needed—perfect for quick breakfasts or snacks.

Whether you're baking challah to celebrate a holiday, as a centerpiece for a family meal, or simply for the pure joy of bread making, its braided beauty and tender crumb will never disappoint. Once you master the basic technique, this bread becomes a canvas for personal touches and creative adaptations. Adding spices like cinnamon or cardamom, swirling in fillings of chocolate or nuts, or shaping it into smaller rolls opens new doors to trying your own signature spin on this time-honored classic.

Braided challah bread isn't just a recipe—it's a joyful ritual that links patience, skill, and tradition in every loaf. It shows how simple ingredients, when treated with care and a bit of practice, can transform into something truly special. For any home baker seeking to build confidence and hands-on experience with enriched doughs and decorative shaping, challah offers a fulfilling and delicious challenge.

So, the next time you're ready to graduate from simpler loaves and want to impress in the kitchen, pull out your mixing bowl, roll up your sleeves, and give braided challah a try. From the glossy gold finish to the soft, pillowy slices inside, it's a bread that brings more than just flavor to the table—it brings joy and pride in your baking journey.

BAGELS MADE EASY

Bagels have an undeniable charm that goes beyond just being a breakfast staple. Their dense, chewy texture combined with a glossy, golden crust creates a bite that's both satisfying and comforting. For many home bakers, bagels may seem intimidating, with their unique boiling step and dough consistency. But in reality, making bagels at home is much simpler than you might think. This section breaks down the process into straightforward steps so you can enjoy fresh, homemade bagels without stress.

The foundation of a good bagel starts with the dough. Unlike softer sandwich breads or fluffy rolls, bagel dough is stiffer and less hydrated, which helps develop that signature chewy crumb. When you mix your ingredients—typically flour, water, yeast, salt, and sometimes a bit of sugar or malt syrup—you want the dough to be firm yet pliable. This firmness gives the bagel strength and helps it hold shape during boiling and baking. Don't worry if your dough feels denser than you're used to; that's exactly what makes a great bagel.

One of the defining moments in bagel baking is the boiling. It may sound unusual to boil bread dough, but this step is essential. After shaping your rolls into rings, boiling them briefly sets the crust and creates that shiny exterior many people associate with bagels fresh from a bakery. The boiling water can be plain or slightly sweetened with honey or malt syrup, which adds a bit of flavor and encourages browning during baking. This quick dip also gives bagels their firm, chewy crust while keeping the inside tender.

When boiling, timing is everything. Usually, bagels are boiled for about 30 to 60 seconds on each side. Boil too short, and the crust won't develop properly; boil too long, and your bagels might become too dense or even soggy. Using a slotted spoon or skimmer, gently lower each bagel into the simmering water to prevent them from breaking apart. Once done, remove them carefully and transfer to a baking tray. They are then ready for baking, which crisps up the exterior into that glorious golden finish.

Speaking of baking, the oven environment can influence the perfect bagel crust. While traditional bagels are baked on stone surfaces in commercial ovens, you can achieve excellent results using your home oven. A preheated baking stone or heavy-duty baking sheet works wonders. Some bakers like to spray a little water onto the oven floor or use a pan of hot water to create steam, which helps produce a shiny crust.

Once boiled and placed on your prepared baking surface, the bagels bake relatively quickly—usually 15 to 20 minutes—until they're crisp and golden brown. Keep an eye on them toward the end. Every oven behaves a little differently, and you want that ideal balance where the crust is firm without burning and the middle is cooked through. Once they're out of the oven, allow them to cool on a rack; bagels continue to set as they cool, and this resting period improves their texture.

One major joy of making bagels at home is the chance to customize toppings. Classic bagels might include sesame seeds, poppy seeds, or coarse salt. Some prefer everything bagels, loaded with combinations like dried onion, garlic, and seeds. To apply toppings, simply brush the boiled bagels with an egg wash or a bit of water, then sprinkle the toppings generously before baking. This simple step adds texture, flavor, and visual appeal. You can also experiment with less traditional options like cheese, herbs, or even crushed nuts.

Don't shy away from mixing your bagel dough with add-ins, either. Incorporating ingredients like cinnamon and raisins, dried blueberries, or even chopped jalapenos can transform a standard recipe into something uniquely yours. When adding extra ingredients, fold them gently into your dough during the initial mixing stage to avoid overworking the dough and compromising the bagel's structure.

Another great tip for ease and success is letting the shaped bagels rest a bit before boiling. This short proofing period helps the dough relax, making the boiling process gentler on the rings so they don't lose their shape. Around 10 to 20 minutes of resting at room temperature is usually enough. If you're tight on time, you can even prepare bagels ahead, refrigerate or freeze them after shaping, and boil and bake whenever you want fresh bagels. This flexibility makes homemade bagels a weekend treat or even a spontaneous indulgence.

For bakers just starting, it's helpful to remember that bagels don't require complicated tools. A sturdy mixing bowl, a large pot for boiling, a slotted spoon, and a baking sheet or stone are the major essentials. You won't need specialized equipment to achieve bakery-quality results. Mixing the dough by hand or with a stand mixer both work well, depending on your preference and available gear. The rewarding smell of baking bagels and the pride in slicing into a fresh, warm batch are well worth the effort.

Feeling a bit anxious about the boiling step? Keep in mind that it's a quick, forgiving process. Even if your first few bagels aren't perfect rings, they'll still taste delicious. The bagel's dough and texture are the stars, and minor shape imperfections won't take away from the experience. As you practice, you'll gain confidence in shaping and boiling, eventually nailing that classic round form with a perfect, smooth crust.

Beyond the traditional flavors and methods, home bakers can make bagels their own culinary canvas. Bagels go beyond breakfast; they pair beautifully with savory spreads, smoked fish, cream cheese variations, or even used as unique sandwich bases. Their dense texture holds up well with hearty fillings, making them versatile for all kinds of meals. Homemade bagels offer not just flavor, but also control over ingredients, letting you tailor the healthfulness or indulgence to your liking.

Incorporating bagel baking into your bread repertoire opens new doors. With a bit of practice, you'll find that the process is highly enjoyable and less daunting than it first appears. This recipe book aims to encourage you to try new techniques without fear of failure. Bagels are the perfect project for when you want a rewarding baking challenge that's well within reach.

Remember, the joy of bread baking is in both the journey and the result. Homemade bagels deliver sensory satisfaction from the moment you mix your flour and yeast through the final bite of a warm, chewy slice. With just a few key steps and thoughtful tips, you can master this classic bread style and bring a beloved bakery item right into your kitchen consistently.

So next time you're in the mood for that iconic bagel experience, don't reach for store-bought—try your hand at making bagels at home. The process is straightforward, the ingredients simple, and the taste? Absolutely unbeatable.

Soft Pretzels

Soft pretzels hold a special place in the world of homemade bread baking. Their inviting golden crust, chewy interior, and unique salty bite make them a favorite snack for many. Crafting these delightful twists at home might seem intimidating at first, but with a straightforward approach, anyone can master them. This section will guide you through the essentials of making soft pretzels in your own kitchen, offering practical tips and inspiration to add variety to your baking repertoire.

The charm of soft pretzels starts with their distinctive shaping. Traditional pretzels are recognizable by their beautiful twisted loops, creating a form that's as much a work of art as it is delicious. While shaping may look tricky, it quickly becomes second nature once you get the hang of it. In fact, working with soft, pliable dough makes shaping a satisfying and tactile part of the process, especially compared to other bread forms. It's a creative moment where you can enjoy the feel of the dough and the anticipation of how it will bake up into those classic pretzel shapes. For beginners, rolling the dough into ropes and forming the loops follows an easy pattern with just a bit of practice.

One key step that sets soft pretzels apart from other bread is the boiling bath before baking. This quick dip in a baking soda solution is what gives pretzels their unique crust texture and that marvelous deep brown color. The alkaline bath interacts with the dough's surface, creating a flavorful crust with a slight sheen. While it might seem unusual to boil dough, this technique is what transforms the pretzel. It also helps establish the distinctive chewy bite that soft pretzel lovers crave. Don't skip this step, since it's a hallmark of authentic pretzel making and critical to getting the results you expect.

The dough itself for soft pretzels is fairly straightforward, yet subtle adjustments can elevate your baking. Typically, a combination of all-purpose flour, warm water, yeast, salt, and a touch of sugar forms the base. This recipe offers enough structure for shaping while remaining tender inside. Adding a bit of butter or oil enriches the dough and contributes to softness. Keeping your ingredients simple and fresh makes a big difference in the final flavor. Also, because pretzels are often enjoyed warm and fresh, baking something with a reasonable rise time works best to avoid long waits or overly dense results.

Once you master the basic pretzel dough and shaping, the variations start to open up. Sprinkling coarse kosher salt on top right after boiling and before baking is classic and truly essential for that salty contrast. But there's room to get creative here too. Many bakers like to experiment with toppings such as sesame seeds, poppy seeds, or even grated cheese to vary the taste and texture. For a hint of sweetness, try brushing the pretzels with melted butter and honey after baking, creating a delicious contrast to the salty crust. This way, one basic dough recipe can spawn dozens of personalized treats, each perfect for different moods or occasions.

Baking soft pretzels also introduces you to excellent techniques that build confidence in bread baking. Controlling oven temperature and timing is especially important with pretzels, since overbaking risks drying them out, while underbaking leaves the dough gummy. Watching the transformation from pale dough ropes to deeply caramelized golden pretzels teaches the value of precise baking. This skill easily carries over to other bread shapes and recipes in your collection. Plus, the instant reward of pulling piping hot pretzels from your oven is a wonderful motivator to keep baking regularly.

Soft pretzels suit a wide range of occasions and can be enjoyed in various ways. They're fantastic party snacks, perfect for game day or casual gatherings. Kids love them with mustard or cheese dip, while adults can pair them with craft beer or hearty soups. You might even slice and use them as the base for sandwiches or sliders, bringing a fun twist to lunchtime. The versatility is part of their appeal—soft pretzels are equally at home as a simple snack or as a star component of a more ambitious spread. You're likely to find that once you start baking your own, store-bought options won't quite compare anymore.

For those new to yeast breads, soft pretzels offer approachable steps that build confidence. The dough isn't heavy or difficult to handle, and the shaping moves are almost like playing with dough on a fun, creative level. It's also an excellent way to learn about proofing yeast and the importance of letting dough rest and rise. Watching the dough expand from a handful of ingredients to a plump, glossy form ready for boiling and baking brings a sense of achievement. And because pretzels bake relatively quickly, the full process stays engaging without dragging on for hours.

Even with all these benefits, a few tricks make all the difference in getting soft pretzels just right. Using fresh active yeast ensures steady rise and light texture. The baking soda bath needs to be just warm enough to avoid shocking the dough but hot enough to trigger that unique crust effect. If coarse salt seems too aggressive, mixing salt with a little water before sprinkling can help it stick without overwhelming a bite. Also, spacing pretzels properly on the baking sheet guarantees even baking, avoiding sticky clumps or uneven browning. These tips prevent common pitfalls and boost success with every batch.

When it comes to storing and enjoying your homemade soft pretzels, timing matters. They're best eaten fresh and warm, right out of the oven, when their crust shines and interior remains tender. Leftover pretzels can be wrapped in foil and briefly reheated to regain some of that softness. Unlike some breads that improve with age, soft pretzels start to lose their texture within a day. That said, freezing them before baking is a handy option; simply thaw and bake as usual when you want a quick treat. This flexibility ensures you can enjoy your homemade creations without worrying about last-minute baking.

Once comfortable with soft pretzels, there's even room to explore regional variations and cultural twists. From German beer garden favorites to American-style cinnamon sugar versions, pretzels offer a broad canvas for flavor exploration. Each variation teaches you something new about dough handling, flavor balancing, or baking techniques. Over time, these experiments deepen appreciation for bread artisanship and inspire new ideas across your baking journey.

To sum up, soft pretzels combine straightforward ingredients with rewarding technique, making them an excellent entry into specialty bread baking. Their fun shape and unique cooking process encourage hands-on learning, while their warm, salty goodness delights family and guests alike. Whether you're experimenting with toppings, perfecting your twist, or simply enjoying a warm pretzel fresh from the oven, this recipe offers something delicious and satisfying for bakers of all experience levels. Soft pretzels are the perfect blend of fun and function in the world of homemade bread.

CRUSTY BREADSTICKS

Crusty breadsticks are the perfect addition to any meal, whether served alongside a fresh salad, dipped into marinara, or enjoyed as a simple snack. Their delightfully crunchy exterior paired with a tender, chewy interior makes them irresistibly satisfying. If you've ever been intimidated by breadsticks, don't worry—making them at home is far easier than you might think. This section will guide you through crafting classic crusty breadsticks that impress every time, using straightforward techniques and accessible ingredients.

One of the best things about homemade crusty breadsticks is how customizable they are. While the traditional recipe leans toward a simple, lightly salted dough, you can easily experiment with herbs, garlic, or cheese to add flair. However, the foundation stays the same: a well-developed gluten structure that yields that coveted chewiness, and a baking environment that encourages a deep golden crust with satisfying crunch. Learning to balance these factors will boost your confidence in bread baking and broaden your kitchen repertoire.

Starting with the dough, you'll want basic bread flour, water, yeast, salt, and a touch of olive oil. Bread flour is important here because its higher protein content helps create a better structure, leading to a crispier bite and chewier crumb. Don't let the simple ingredient list fool you—each has a job that affects the final texture and flavor. Yeast leavens the dough, salt controls fermentation and enhances flavor, and olive oil lends just the right amount of tenderness without sacrificing the crust's crunch.

Hydration, or the ratio of water to flour, plays a key role in texture. For crusty breadsticks, you're aiming for a dough that's elastic but not too sticky—comfortably pliable enough to handle without great fuss. A moderate hydration level allows for good oven spring and crust development without the dough collapsing or becoming too dense. Once mixed, the dough should be allowed to rise until doubled in size. This first rise is where the yeast works its magic, developing flavors and creating those tiny gas bubbles that give breadstick interiors their characteristic lightness.

After the initial rise, shaping the breadsticks is straightforward yet so important. The trick is to roll the dough into fairly long, thin strips, ensuring they're even in thickness so they bake uniformly. This step is part art, part feel—if you're new to shaping breadsticks, it might take a couple of tries to get the hang of consistent sizing. Applying gentle, even pressure with your hands prevents tearing and helps stretch the gluten network just enough. Trust your instincts here, and remember, a little variation in size can add a rustic feel that's charming and authentic.

Once shaped, a second rise allows the dough to relax and puff slightly before baking. This final proof ensures the breadsticks stay light inside and achieve optimal volume. During this stage, you can lightly brush them with olive oil or simply sprinkle some flaky sea salt on top for added texture and flavor punch. Aromatics like fresh rosemary, garlic powder, or even grated Parmesan cheese elevate their taste remarkably without complicating the process. If you're feeling adventurous, try twisting the breadsticks gently before baking to create an eye-catching spiral pattern that crisps up beautifully in the oven.

Baking crusty breadsticks requires a hot oven, ideally around 425°F (220°C). The intense heat is critical for forming that golden-brown crust that crackles delightfully as you bite into it. Many bakers swear by placing a small pan of water in the oven during baking to create steam, which enhances crustiness. This technique mimics professional bread ovens and helps keep the crust from hardening too quickly, allowing the interior to finish cooking without drying out. If you don't have a way to add steam, don't worry—the breadsticks will still bake up nicely with a crisp exterior, especially if you brush them with a little olive oil beforehand.

If the baking time is too short, the breadsticks might come out pale and doughy. Too long, and they risk burning or becoming overly hard. A typical baking time ranges from 12 to 15 minutes, but keep an eye on them, especially the first few times you try the recipe. You're aiming for a deep golden color with slightly darker spots on the edges. Letting the breadsticks cool completely on a rack helps the crust set and maintain its crunch. Resist the temptation to wrap or seal them while still warm; trapping moisture will soften the crust, which you want to avoid.

Serving crusty breadsticks straight from the oven is rewarding, but they also store well for several days when wrapped loosely in parchment paper or a paper bag to preserve their crunch. You can always refresh them with a quick reheat in a hot oven for a few minutes to bring back their crispness. This makes breadsticks a handy make-ahead option for busy weeknights or unexpected guests. Plus, they freeze beautifully if you want to prep a batch in advance— simply thaw and crisp up in the oven as needed.

Don't overlook breadsticks as a canvas for creativity. While traditional plain crusty breadsticks have timeless appeal, sprinkling them with different toppings really boosts their fun factor. Smoked sea salt offers a subtle depth, freshly cracked black pepper adds a sharp kick, and a dusting of coarse cornmeal on the baking sheet lends a rustic crunch to the base. Chopped fresh herbs like thyme, oregano, or basil can be pressed into the dough before baking, releasing fragrant oils and bright notes into every bite. Think of breadsticks as both a complement to meals and a snack in their own right—versatile, flavorful, and endlessly adaptable.

For home bakers still building confidence, this recipe balances approachability with rewarding results. No complicated techniques or rare ingredients, just solid breadmaking fundamentals: good flour, proper fermentation, thoughtful shaping, and baking heat that coax out the signature crunch. With a few bakes under your belt, you'll quickly find yourself reaching for dough to whip up a batch whenever you want that satisfying crunch paired with soft, airy bread inside. Crusty breadsticks can elevate a simple dinner or become the star of a casual gathering—either way, making them from scratch is an accomplishment worth savoring.

Finally, remember that practice improves both your feel for the dough and your timing while baking. Don't be discouraged if your first loaf isn't perfect. Each attempt teaches you more about how your oven behaves and how small tweaks can dramatically change texture and freshness. As you get more comfortable, start experimenting with flavors and shapes. There's something special about sharing a basket of warm, homemade crusty breadsticks with friends or family. It not only fills the table with aroma and warmth but also gives you a deeper connection to the art of breadmaking itself.

Embrace the process, enjoy the results, and keep baking—your journey to crusty breadstick mastery is just a few loaves away.

Mini Bread Loaves for Gifts

Mini bread loaves aren't just charming—they're the perfect homemade gift that shows you care without demanding too much time or effort. These petite loaves offer a personal touch, ideal for sharing with friends, neighbors, or coworkers during holidays, birthdays, or just because. Their smaller size makes them easy to package and distribute, plus they give a delightful variety when you want to gift an assortment of flavors. If you've ever wanted to wow someone with the warmth of fresh-baked bread but felt intimidated by large loaves, mini bread loaves provide a perfect middle ground. They're approachable, manageable, and just as delicious.

One of the nicest things about baking mini loaves is how flexible the recipes can be. Almost any standard loaf recipe from your repertoire can be scaled down to the smaller pans, and you'll find the baking times shorten considerably, too. That means less time waiting around and more time enjoying the smells of fresh bread filling your kitchen. Mini loaves often have a tender crumb and delightful crust-to-crumb ratio that can feel especially cozy and comforting to your gift recipients. Plus, because they're smaller, you can experiment with different flavors in one baking session—imagine wrapping up a bundle with a cinnamon swirl, a honey oat, and a rustic whole wheat.

Packaging mini bread loaves to give as gifts is where your creativity can really shine. Whether you choose simple parchment paper tied with twine, festive cellophane bags, or small reusable cloth bags, the presentation becomes part of the gift experience. Adding small handwritten tags with baking notes or suggested pairings—like a favorite jam or cheese—makes the gift feel personalized and thoughtful. You can even include a tiny jar of homemade butter or a flavored olive oil dip on the side for a complete bread gift package that's both practical and indulgent.

When baking mini loaves, pan choice is key. Most standard mini loaf pans produce loaves about 5 by 3 inches, which is a perfect handheld size. They're also small enough to bake multiple mini loaves at once, meaning you can fill your oven with several different flavors or batches quickly. For the beginner baker, these pans are less intimidating than large brioche or artisan loaves and they allow for more consistent results. Because mini loaves cook faster, keep a close eye in the last few minutes to avoid overbaking. The toothpick test works well—if it comes out clean, the loaf is ready to cool and wrap.

Mini loaves are fantastic for seasonal gifts. For the holidays, you might bake cinnamon swirl or spiced pumpkin loaves, filled with warming spices that instantly evoke cozy gatherings. Springtime gifts could highlight lighter flavors like lemon poppy seed or blueberry breakfast loaves. And during autumn, something like a walnut-raisin or honey oat miniature loaf can feel just right, matching the tastes and textures of the season. Offering a variety of flavors packed in small loaves allows you to share a taste of the season while showcasing your baking skills.

The size also lends itself well to dietary accommodations. If you have loved ones with specific preferences, bake small batches of gluten-free, whole grain, or vegan mini loaves without tying yourself to an entire large loaf recipe. This way, you can still spread joy through homemade bread that's accessible and considerate of dietary needs. And for anyone nervous about the bread turning out just right, the smaller loaf is less daunting, which builds confidence and encourages further experimentation. Mini bread loaves bridge the gap between baking for yourself and baking as an act of giving.

Another advantage of mini loaves is they're easy to freeze and store. Gift recipients can enjoy freshly baked bread now or keep it in the freezer for convenience later. This can be thoughtful for those with a busy lifestyle, giving them the option to savor your gift over time without rushing. For you, it means you don't have to bake every batch right before gifting, making holiday or event preparation less stressful. Wrap mini loaves tightly in plastic wrap before freezing, then thaw at room temperature or warm briefly in the oven when ready to eat.

For a beginner baker really looking to make memorable gifts, mini bread loaves invite playful creativity with add-ins and toppings, too. Swirled cinnamon, chopped nuts, dried fruits, seeds, or herbs bring texture and interest to these small loaves without overwhelming the baking process. Glazes or simple powdered sugar dustings serve as finishing touches that elevate the appearance without complexity. Remember, beautiful gifts don't have to be complicated; they just need that bit of thoughtful detail that shows intention.

In terms of technique, mini bread loaves are forgiving because their reduced size means less chance of uneven baking, and the surface area ratio often creates an appealing chewy crust. This makes them ideal for those who want solid practice mastering dough handling and shaping without the stress of large, finicky loaves. Plus, if you mess up one mini loaf, it's much less of a setback than losing an entire big loaf. This small-scale baking encourages a growth mindset, helping you gain confidence step by step.

Often, gifting bread is about more than just the bread itself—it's about sharing a sensory moment. The scent of yeast and baking bread opens doors of connection, nostalgia, and comfort. Presenting mini loaves in a thoughtful way taps into that emotional thread, giving people a reason to slow down and savor something truly homemade amid busy schedules. Bread, after all, is one of the oldest and most universal forms of hospitality. Mini loaves carry that spirit wrapped up in a convenient package that's easy to give and delightful to receive.

Finally, mini bread loaves can also be a way to introduce friends and family to new flavors or styles of bread they may not usually try. A sampler of mini loaves lets gift recipients taste-test different recipes without committing to a whole large loaf. This can spark curiosity and appreciation for your baking efforts and inspire others to start baking bread themselves. It's a wonderful way to share your passion and grow a community around the joy of homemade bread.

In short, mini bread loaves hold a special place in the world of homemade baking gifts. They combine practicality with charm, effort with generosity. Whether you're turning out a batch for holiday giving or just a thoughtful surprise, these little loaves build bridges through flavor, warmth, and the simple magic of fresh bread straight from your oven. With minimal fuss and maximum heart, they're sure to brighten tables and lift spirits all year round.

Conclusion

The journey through the art and craft of bread baking has been as rich and rewarding as the loaves you've learned to create. From the simplicity of no-knead breads to the complexity of sourdough mastery, this collection was designed to guide you every step of the way—whether you're just starting out or looking to expand your baking horizons. Baking bread at home isn't just about putting ingredients together; it's about discovering a rhythm, a connection to time-tested traditions, and the joy that comes from pulling a warm, fragrant loaf from your own oven.

Each recipe brings something unique to the table, from comforting everyday basics to exciting international varieties and indulgent sweet breads. But beyond any single recipe, the key takeaway is that bread baking is accessible. It might seem intimidating at first, but with patience and practice, your confidence will grow, and so will your skills. This book has aimed to demystify techniques and ingredient choices, helping you to embrace the process rather than fear it.

Remember that even the most experienced bakers have faced dough that didn't rise as expected or crusts that turned out crunchier than intended. These are all part of learning. The magic happens in the kitchen when you experiment, adjust based on your environment or tastes, and then enjoy the fruits of your efforts. There's a satisfaction in kneading dough, seeing it transform, and sharing homemade bread that's unmatched by prepackaged loaves.

The versatile nature of bread means it can be a humble daily staple or a centerpiece for special occasions. Whether you're making a quick sandwich loaf for weekday lunches or shaping a beautiful braided challah to celebrate a memorable moment, the power of bread to bring people together remains constant. It nourishes both body and soul in ways that extend beyond the oven. That's why investing time and love into your bread baking is so worthwhile.

This book's recipes have been crafted with real home bakers in mind—balancing ease with variety so you won't feel stuck in a rut. You've seen how simple ingredients like flour, water, salt, and yeast can be transformed with small twists: adding herbs, infusing flavors, incorporating whole grains, or playing with rising times. These tweaks open up a world of possibilities, and once you become comfortable with the basics, you'll find yourself experimenting in your own kitchen.

Developing a baking routine that suits your lifestyle is just as important as mastering the recipes. Many of the breads here can be made ahead or adapted to fit your schedule, so freshness doesn't require a complicated time commitment. Using techniques like overnight fermentation or no-knead methods, you'll discover that homemade bread is attainable, even on busy days. Finding the right balance will keep your baking enjoyable and prevent it from feeling like a chore.

In exploring international bread traditions, you've gained more than recipes—you've gained insight into different cultures and histories expressed through their breads. Baking something like Indian naan or German Bauernbrot is a way to connect with heritage and diversity, expanding what home baking means. These loaves tell stories, and through your hands, you become part of that narrative. It's a special bond that flourishes when you open yourself up to new styles and flavors.

Let's not forget the fun and celebration that enriched and specialty breads bring into the mix. Sweet brioche or sticky cinnamon rolls can brighten a weekend morning, while braided loaves and stuffed rings make memorable gifts and festive table additions. These breads remind us that baking can be an act of kindness and creativity—gifts to share, moments to savor. There's endless pleasure in baking something a little fancier once in a while, and now you have the tools to make those treats approachable and even routine.

One of the greatest advantages of baking your own bread is control—over ingredients, flavor profiles, and texture. For those looking to bake healthier options, whole grains and gluten-free alternatives are included to inspire you. You can craft bread that fits your dietary needs without sacrificing taste or quality. This flexibility is empowering; bread baking becomes not just an art but a way to nurture yourself and your loved ones thoughtfully.

Your baking space will grow with you. Over time, you might find yourself investing in better tools, learning more nuanced techniques, and pushing the limits of your creativity. But none of that happens overnight. Starting simple and building your knowledge incrementally, as this book encourages, is the best way to keep your passion alive. Enjoy the process and celebrate your progress. Every loaf you bake is a step forward—an accomplishment to be proud of.

In summary, this comprehensive guide was created to be your companion in embracing the joy, challenge, and satisfaction of bread baking at home. Whether you return to recipes for comforting standards or experiment with new styles and ingredients, the confidence you've gained will serve you well. Bread has a way of bringing people together and elevating everyday moments, and now you hold the key to creating those experiences in your own kitchen.

So as you close this chapter and look ahead, know that the possibilities are vast. Your journey with bread baking is only just beginning. With practice, patience, and curiosity, each loaf you bake becomes richer in flavor and significance. Keep exploring, learning, and enjoying the simple pleasures of homemade bread—it truly is one of life's sweetest rewards.

Appendix

The journey through bread baking is filled with rewarding experiences, and this appendix is here to support your adventure in the kitchen. It gathers helpful resources, handy tips, and essential info that can make your bread-making smoother and more enjoyable.

Throughout the book, you've encountered a variety of recipes, techniques, and flavors. This section doesn't repeat those details but instead complements them with practical insights that every home baker should have at their fingertips. From ingredient substitutions to troubleshooting common issues, this appendix aims to be your quick-reference guide whenever questions arise.

Measuring ingredients accurately is key. Whether you use cups or grams, understanding how to measure flour, liquids, and yeast correctly can make all the difference in your loaf's texture and rise. This appendix offers advice on proper measuring methods that prevent common pitfalls like dense bread or overly sticky dough.

Temperature control is another vital factor—both for proofing your dough and baking. You'll find notes on ideal room temperatures, how to tell when your dough has properly risen, and tips on creating warm environments for fermentation without special equipment.

Additionally, this section touches on the best way to store your homemade bread and how to keep it fresh longer, whether you plan to enjoy it right away or save it for later. It includes advice on freezing, thawing, and reviving day-old bread to maintain that fresh-baked taste and texture.

Many home bakers wonder about equipment too. Here, you'll get pointers on must-have tools and clever alternatives if you don't have everything listed. From mixing bowls to baking stones, understanding what each tool does will help you bake confidently and efficiently.

Finally, don't forget the importance of patience. Bread baking is as much an art as it is a science, and sometimes a batch won't turn out exactly right the first time. This appendix encourages a spirit of experimentation and persistence, reminding you that every loaf teaches you something new and brings you closer to the perfect bake.

Keep this appendix handy as your quick guide while you experiment with the recipes in this book. It's designed to support your success, turning each bake into a delicious and fulfilling experience.

www.ingramcontent.com/pod-product-compliance
Lightning Source LLC
Chambersburg PA
CBHW030230170426
43201CB00006B/168